MYSTERY

Gideon Haigh is a journalist in Melbourne, Australia, who writes regularly for the *Guardian* and *Wisden Cricket Monthly*. His other books include *The Cricket War* and *The Summer Game* and, most recently, *The Big Ship*, a biography of the legendary Australian Test captain Warwick Armstrong (also published by Aurum).

'Australia's finest cricket writer' – Frank Keating

'Haigh's research, his writing, his subject all combine to make a wonderful book' – Will Buckley, *Observer*

'This is more than just a book about a cricketer. It is a genuine biography, a serious attempt to get to the heart of a more involved mystery than the way its subject bamboozled batsmen' – Simon Rae, *Times Literary Supplement*

'Gideon Haigh pursues his extraordinary subject with a breadth of awareness rare in the sports-biog trade' – Robert Winder, *New Statesman*

'Brilliantly reconstructs this almost forgotten figure… Iverson's career was like no other cricketer, and Gideon Haigh has written a superb book about him' – Stephen Moss, *Guardian*

ALSO BY GIDEON HAIGH

The Battle for BHP
The Cricket War: Kerry Packer's World Series Cricket
The Border Years
One Summer, Every Summer: An Ashes Journal
Australian Cricket Anecdotes
The Summer Game: Australian Test Cricket 1949–71
One of a Kind: The Story of Bankers Trust Australia 1969–1999

THE LIFE AND DEATH OF AN EXTRAORDINARY CRICKETER

MYSTERY SPINNER

GIDEON HAIGH

AURUM PRESS

First published in Great Britain
2000 by Aurum Press Ltd
25 Bedford Avenue, London WC1B 3AT

This paperback edition published 2002

Published by arrangement with Text Publishing Co., Melbourne, Australia

A catalogue record for this book is available from the British Library.

ISBN 1 85410 855 7

10 9 8 7 6 5 4 3 2 1
2006 2005 2004 2003 2002

Designed by Chong Weng-Ho
Set in Janson
Printed by Bookmarque, Croydon, Surrey

In memory of
Julie Elizabeth Tootell
1938–1999

ONE

It is commonly said that nothing in cricket occurs for the first time. Players reset statistical benchmarks, of course, and attain new standards of excellence. But styles and theories of batting, bowling, fielding and captaincy allegedly exist in a cycle of creative reinvention, endlessly echoing those gone before. The former Australian captain Victor Richardson used to tell his grandsons, the brothers Chappell: 'Don't believe that anything is new in cricket. It's all been tried before…If you hang onto a suit long enough it will come back into favour.'

Fifty years ago, however, there appeared a tall, shy, shambling Australian called Jack Iverson to challenge this verity. He bowled like no man before and a mere handful since, clasping the ball snugly between the thumb and a folded middle finger as though giving it a secret handshake. And extending that middle finger while maintaining the fulcrum of the opposable thumb turned cricket physics on its head; from the same grip, with slight alterations of the arm's angle at release, Iverson bowled top spinners and wrong 'uns that looked like leg breaks, leg breaks that resembled off breaks. If slow bowling is the art of deceit, Iverson ranks with the perpetrators of the Zinoviev letter and the Cottingley Fairies.

They called him, allusively, a 'mystery spinner', nicknamed him 'The Freak'. And when he routed England in a Test at Sydney in January 1951, Jack Iverson and his spin-bowling sub-genre of one became the sensations of their time. 'He has skill extraordinary and the demeanour of a thoughtful player,' wrote English journalist John Kay. 'His like come seldom. When they arrive, every effort should be made to keep them on the scene!' But stay, he did not. Within a few years, virtually all that remained of Jack Iverson in cricket's annals were memories, statistics and a few fading photographs of that impossible grip.

It was with those photographs that my own fascination with Jack Iverson began about twenty years ago. Insatiably curious about cricket, I took a photocopied page from Jack Fingleton's *Brown & Company* into my family's backyard and began experimenting on a tennis ball with my own version of the Iverson grip. Even with the softer sphere, it was confounding. The ball would disappear either side of the driveway, spinning like a malfunctioning satellite. Yet I read that Iverson, with a *cricket ball*, kept line and length as an atomic clock keeps time. What manner of talent must this man have been?

Fanning my curiosity, too, was that I had just enrolled at what I knew to be Iverson's old school: Geelong College, *alma mater* also to Lindsay Hassett, Ian Redpath and Paul Sheahan, and an institution unstintingly proud of its sporting sons. Yet Iverson featured nowhere on its honour rolls. It was a paradox I could unravel only by further reading, for there was more to Iverson's singularity than technique.

For most who ascend cricket's heights, recognition is the result of years of toil and aspiration. Not for Jack Iverson. That crowded hour when he was Australia's cynosure of spin was essentially the sum of his cricket life: he was thirty-one when he took the game up in 1946, thirty-five when he played Test cricket, thirty-five when he withdrew from it, thirty-eight when he played his final first-class match.

Comet-like careers themselves are not unusual in Australian cricket: about four in ten of the players in its record books have played no more than five Tests. Usually it is because Test cricket's unique demands stretch them beyond their talent and temperament, or because form deserts them at inopportune moments, or because rivals of similar ability are in abundance. But again, none of these applied to Iverson. For the seven years from his unannounced appearance in sub-district ranks to the end of his first-class career, he was perhaps the world's most destructive bowler, harvesting in all classes of cricket more than 500 wickets at a cost of just over 12 runs each. He headed the bowling averages in Brighton's premiership season of 1947–48, then in Melbourne's of 1948–49. The following season he headed the Sheffield Shield averages and the first-class averages on an undefeated Australian tour of New Zealand. Finally he led the Test averages in a 4–1 Ashes victory in 1950–51.

After a handful of further first-class matches, however, Iverson faded from view, like a line of handwriting where the ink has unexpectedly petered out. The bowler whom Keith Miller and Richie Benaud still believe would have dissolved batsmen on contact in English conditions never went there, preferring to become a suburban estate agent collecting rents and pacing out frontages. He died young, at fifty-eight, in apparently benighted circumstances, and considering himself a 'broken-down old cricketer' whom 'no-one remembered'.

I never met Jack Iverson. I never saw him play. And the raw material from which sporting biography is extruded is quite different to that involved in other life stories. Writers leave behind books. Painters leave behind pictures. Musicians leave behind compositions and recordings. With athletes, the only permanent objectified record comes in the form of scores and statistics: poor clues to the inner life. One might as well judge a writer by tallying their words, a painter by counting their brushstrokes, a musician by aggregating their notes.

As athletes are usually people to whom deeds matter more than words, moreover, it is a rare sportsman who leaves any quantum of correspondence or personal journals. And even where they have, one can search in vain for a sense of the consciousness behind them. Few better examples exist than the diary kept by Victor Trumper on his 1902 tour of England. As an artefact of the journey on which this preternatural talent first became legend, it is incomparably precious. As an aperture to his thoughts, it is next to useless. Study 24 July, the day he scored Test cricket's first century off scratch, before lunch on the first day, and Trumper seems further away than ever: 'Wet wicket. Fourth Test. Won Toss. Made 299. Self 104. RAD [Reg Duff] 50. 1st wicket 135. England five for 70. Tate [Fred Tate] 1st Test.'

In more recent times, of course, there is the boon of testing one's impressions of an athlete against footage. This can convey a powerful sense of the individual's transcendence: one could scarcely write of Ray Lindwall, for instance, without having seen his delectably smooth approach and final bound. But watching sportsmen and women on film or peering at them in a photograph, while descriptively helpful, creates a deceptive intimacy. Watching footage of Graeme Pollock cover driving at the crease, or for that matter of Jackson Pollock painting in his studio, answers only part of the question how, and none of the question why.

Sporting biographers fill this abhorrent vacuum with two principal sources. The first is contemporaneous reportage of their subjects' achievements. Usually abundant in its availability, this is limited in its usefulness. Writing about an innings from press reports is rather like trying to reconstruct a novel from its reviews. The other source is memory. The recollections, anecdotes and impressions of a subject's friends and enemies are the very staff of life. These can come from an observation in the middle or, sometimes even better, away from it. When I think of Sir Donald Bradman, for instance, I think of vignettes like Jack Fingleton's flavoursome description of him at lunch during a big innings: 'He had, in Sydney, the inevitable light batting lunch in the dressing room of rice custard, stewed fruit and milk. Each slow mouthful was an essay in method, in digestion, in cold planning and contemplation of the feast to follow in the middle.'

But what if there had been a cricketer of fame great but fleeting, who throughout his abbreviated career at the top maintained a circumspect distance from his fellows, and whose life otherwise was as far from the limelight as one can retreat to? Researching the life of Jack Iverson, it soon emerged, would involve more than following the route of sporting biography enshrined by convention. It would be about recovering the vestigial traces of a man's life a quarter of a century after his passing. On occasion in this book, in fact, I will explain the processes by which I sought to reconstruct his journey: sometimes with only limited success. For as I set off after this fugitive personality, armed with the handful of books that devoted him more than a few paragraphs, and a bundle of yellowing newspaper clippings, there would be some occasions when his trail seemed to dematerialise completely. At other times, however, he felt almost close enough to touch.

In his sublime memoir of literary biography, *Footsteps*, Richard Holmes described the feelings he experienced during his peregrinations round the various houses in which his subject Percy Shelley had dwelt in Italy: 'I came to suspect that there is something frequently comic about the trailing figure of the biographer: a sort of tramp permanently knocking at the kitchen window and secretly hoping he might be invited in for supper.' In my own far less momentous way, I soon experienced similar sensations. There was so little on record about Jack Iverson, in fact, that I couldn't even locate the right kitchen window. One of my early follies, for instance, thinking Iverson's connection to Geelong far stronger than it proved, was to ring a dress shop there which I remembered being run by a woman called Iverson. Mrs Iverson's bemused shop assistant politely offered a telephone number, and Mrs Iverson with equal politeness told me that she was no relation to someone of whom she'd never heard.

Holmes also wrote delightfully: 'I mark my beginning as a professional biographer from the day when my bank bounced a cheque because it was inadvertently dated 1772.' My own most ludicrous moment, perhaps, was visiting Sydney on the strength of advice that there was an ABC picture of Jack Iverson in the Australian Archives, only to discover that it was a man holding a trumpet, called Jack Iversen: a Queensland band leader from the 1960s.

While grappling for that first handhold, however, I made a small discovery. The property section of the *Age* newspaper of 8 August 1998 reported that Jack Iverson's old Brighton home at 44 Black Street was to be sold, describing him as 'the famous Test bowler with the unique leg-spin grip'. I imagined that the house had changed hands a few times since, was probably now occupied by someone with little idea of its provenance, and it seemed as good a place as any to begin.

Brighton itself is a comfortable and conservative beachside suburb with wide, shady streets commemorating the original generation of settlers in 1841: Dendy, Were, Cole, Blanch, Male, Munro, Carpenter, Boxshall. Local guidebooks glorify the suburb's contributions to Australian culture. Composer Percy Grainger played his first piano at 299 New Street, a house called Binghal. Novelists Henry Handel Richardson,

Marcus Clarke and Martin Boyd all dwelt in the area at various times. Poet Adam Lindsay Gordon shot himself on the foreshore at the end of Park Street in January 1870, the day before his *Bush Ballads and Galloping Rhymes* was published, and his grave in the local cemetery became the subject of an annual pilgrimage by admirers.

Cricket also goes a long way back. Brighton was barely a year old when it hosted its first cricket match, successfully challenging the much larger Melbourne in November 1842. For the next decade, it was among the most powerful clubs in Australia. Many of the great and the good in its first fifty years were involved in the game: merchant and parliamentarian Jonathan Were had a ground on his estate; ubiquitous local politician and future premier Tommy Bent was a 'vigorous roundarm bowler'. A park in Burrows Street, meanwhile, bears the name of the Brighton Cricket Club's most famous son. Captain Robert Grieve was awarded the Victoria Cross after the Battle of Messines in July 1917, when he immobilised a German pillbox by hurling grenades through its narrow firing slit. This image fusing war and sport seemed piquant, as legend had it that Jack Iverson first experimented with his unique style while on active service.

On a balmy afternoon in Brighton with few cars and fewer pedestrians, I still felt light years removed from Jack Iverson. In fact, I was dumbfoundingly close. The middle-aged woman who answered the door of 44 Black Street responded to my explanatory introduction by revealing herself as Jack Iverson's daughter, Mrs Beverley McNamara. I'm not sure who was more surprised.

Mrs McNamara was polite, but manifestly uninterested in

answering any questions. 'You can look it up in books,' she said. 'It's all there if you really want to know.' When I telephoned her a week later, I felt an even more importunate and unwelcome petitioner, and I wasn't altogether surprised when she hung up on me.

I had located a 'kitchen window', but failed to gain admission. It was a salutary introduction to what Holmes called 'the constant paradox of biography' which is that 'everyone would like to be fully understood but few people want their privacy invaded, even by an imagined posterity'. It was a reminder, too, that even as I investigated the dead, I also trespassed on the living. Placed in Mrs McNamara's position, accosted by an intrusive stranger, a glorified tomb robber, I'd probably have responded similarly. Of her suggestion about 'looking up' Jack Iverson in books, I was rather less confident. But I had to start somewhere.

TWO

Iverson is not a common surname in Australia, but Iversen in Germany assuredly is. Jack Iverson's roots are in the old duchies of Schleswig and Holstein, not far from the modern border of Denmark and Germany, about thirty kilometres from Hamburg, and the progress of his forebears was almost as unlikely as his own.

What is today Germany was two centuries ago a jigsaw of 300 ill-fitting regional pieces, part of the disintegrating Holy Roman Empire. The Congress of Vienna in June 1815 rationalised these to a German Confederation of thirty-nine states, but many rough edges remained, not least the duchies: united since the middle ages with the King of Denmark as Duke, even though Holstein was almost wholly German and Schleswig partly so. They became in due course one of Europe's most flammable regions, inspiring British prime minister Benjamin Disraeli to his famous *aperçu* that only three men had ever known the answer to the Schleswig-Holstein Question: one was dead, one was mad and he, Disraeli, had forgotten.

Ludwig Iversen, Jack Iverson's grandfather, was born on 1 July 1825 in the fishing village of Apenrade, the youngest of six children. Little is known of his upbringing, though musical talent appears to have manifested itself early in his life, for he studied violin at the Vienna Conservatoire. Family lore also has it that he saw military service, and carried a musket ball in his shoulder the remainder of his life: if true, the wound was probably sustained during the Three Years' War, which commenced when Danish nationalists sought to annex the duchies in 1848 and were resisted by the local populace with Prussian assistance.

It cannot be said why Ludwig Iversen decided that his future lay in the new antipodean colony of Victoria. But in all likelihood the lure was gold, uncovered in the Pyrenees in July 1851, just a fortnight after Victoria's disaggregation from New South Wales, at Ballarat a month later, and at Bendigo four months after that. The renown of these new and bountiful goldfields swiftly circled the world. The Victorian census of April 1854 enumerated 67,000 souls in the towns of Castlemaine, Sandhurst, Ballarat, Beechworth, Omeo and Heathcote. By March 1857, this had grown to 166,550; and by April 1861, to 228,181.

Ludwig headed for Heathcote, 110 kilometres from Melbourne on the road to Bendigo. Perhaps he knew someone there, for by 1861 there were 27,000 Germans in Australia, 10,000 of them in Victoria with some 6000 on the goldfields.

Whatever the case, culture shock must have been vivid. Heathcote had been a fashionable destination during the rush's first jostling surge. After gold's discovery there in January 1853, its 400 original inhabitants had been overrun by 20,000 ambitious interlopers. At its zenith, the town had boasted seven churches and fifty hotels. Quartz mining had now given it a second lease on life and, to the general environment of extravagance, lawlessness and alcoholic dissipation, a classically-trained violinist from Schleswig-Holstein would have seemed an incongruous addition.

Heathcote was no stranger to grisly murder and violent crime. In March 1861, the case of Henry Cooley, proprietor of a refreshment tent *en route* to the diggings, was briefly talk of the colony. When police questioned him after his wife's mysterious disappearance, Cooley pleaded ignorance. But it was not long before her charred remains were discovered, eliciting from Cooley the admission that he had accidentally slain her with an axe blade while wood-chopping and tried in his grief-stricken dysphoria to incinerate the corpse. So convincing was Cooley's remorse in the dock that jurors were half-inclined to acquit him, but he ultimately went to the gallows.

Five months later, three bushrangers invaded the McIvor Inn, trussed its occupants, and went on an alimentary spree: mutton chops and two dozen duck eggs washed down with six bottles of champagne, a bottle of brandy and copious quantities of ale. Though they melted away after relieving the captives of their valuables, one was identified in a Melbourne music hall three weeks later and also hanged.

Some Germans became renowned on the goldfields:

Fredrick Vern from Hanover was one of Eureka Stockade's principal incendiaries and had a hefty price placed on his head when he slipped from sight after its bloody climax. Others were exceptionally lucky: Bernard Holtermann from Hamburg discovered the world's largest specimen of reef gold—a 286 kilogram whopper called 'Holtermann's Nugget'—and devoted the balance of his years to indulging an enthusiasm for wet-plate photography and fostering a vast pictorial archive. Ludwig Iversen, however, became neither famous nor fortunate. No more details survive of his auriferous achievements than a remark by one of his obituarists: 'He was not favoured by fortune in his mining adventures.'

He did, however, marry. Mary Ann Elizabeth Lipson Carpenter de Pomeroy, a Southampton housemaid, arrived in Melbourne aboard the *Theresa* on 28 October 1863, one of 184 'government immigrants': women constituted only a third of the goldfields' population, and authorities were anxious to redress the imbalance. She found employment with an E. Nicholson of St Kilda, then six months later with a John Perry of Heathcote, and on 20 July 1864 married Ludwig Iversen. Photographs show Ludwig as a somewhat stern figure, gaze sharpened by small spectacles, downward turn of his mouth almost obscured by a luxuriant moustache; Mary Ann bears an altogether softer expression, her head at a bashful tilt, fine features framed by dangling braids.

The couple soon set out for South Australia, purchasing an allotment in Greenock on the periphery of the Barossa Valley where their first son Thomas Louis was born on 28 April 1865. The attractions were obvious: the valley was Australia's largest German settlement, established a quarter of a century earlier by Lutheran refugees round the towns of Klemzig and Hahndorf. Gold fixation leeched, Ludwig set up as a land and commission agent, auctioneer and valuer; the same career that his son Harry and grandson Jack would also follow.

To outsiders, the Barossa of the period was like 'a little corner of Germany wrapped in cotton wool and deposited in Australia'. Certainly, Lutheranism predominated, and there were strong German-language newspapers like *Tanunda Deutsche Zeitung* and *Australische Zeitung*, while the stunning news of Germany's unification in January 1871 with Wilhelm I of Prussia as emperor occasioned a euphoric parade in Tanunda. Within the community, however, many more frictions and fissures existed. Lutheranism was divided by differing degrees of doctrinal dogmatism, the German language was in decline, and the original generations of Protestant dissenters were being diluted by emigrants of more assimilationist tendencies. Ludwig Iversen, in fact, could be regarded as exemplary of this type. His religious beliefs were ecumenical—though he and his wife listed themselves as Anglican on their marriage certificates, their first three children were baptised by Lutheran pastors—and he suffered no pangs about anglicising his name at the time to Louis Iverson. All six of the children Mary Ann bore at Greenock, including two who died in infancy, bore the new spelling of the surname.

Louis Iverson became accepted as an upstanding community figure. Locals entrusted him, for instance, with the management of the Greenock telegraph, which he ran from his residence. His interest in music was rekindled. A community history cites him as 'a dynamic personality' and 'secretary and organiser of many public activities' and accompanist on violin and piano at 'many of the local concerts of the time'. When he left the village after twelve years with wife and four children—his activities as a telegraphist having ceased with the opening of a new post office—he was intent on putting his training in Vienna to good use. Arriving about 1881 in Albury in New South Wales, on the border with Victoria, he promptly posted newspaper advertisements: 'L. IVERSON, PROFESSOR OF MUSIC. Applications received at the Offices of the *Border Post* and *Banner*. PIANOS TUNED.'

It was a late career change—Louis was in his late fifties—but one entered into *con brio*. His reputation was as a talented and diligent instructor; something of a martinet, in fact, noted for rapping errant piano pupils over the knuckles with a ruler when their fingers faltered. He and his teenage daughter Therese gave a number of public recitals. He also fathered two more children. Christina Dorothea, born in June 1882, died in infancy. William Henry, born on 15 January 1885, was Jack Iverson's father.

Harry Iverson's birth certificate makes melancholy reading. In the column reserved for 'previous issue', the notation reads: '2 males living, 2 females living, 2 males dead, 1 female dead'. Losing three children before the age of three must have tried Louis severely, and further tragedy was in store on 19 March 1886 when his wife died. She was forty-two. Official cause of death is 'strangolated herine' (sic), though Harry would tell his own children she had died from the effects of being hit by a swing. Louis was sixty with five children in his care ranging from Thomas Louis, twenty, to Harry, fourteen months. Thomas had been working for four years with Albury merchants T. H. Mate & Co., but the four others depended on the income of a provincial music teacher. It may be, indeed, that the family was in somewhat straitened circumstances. Louis certainly met his wife's death with severe practicality: she was buried the day she died, without a headstone.

The Iversons remained in Albury another couple of years before Louis enjoyed a lucky break. The centenary of British settlement in Australia was to be marked by an ambitious international fair at Melbourne's Royal Exhibition Buildings, built and baptised for a similar event eight years before. The Centennial Exhibition was intended to be even grander and gaudier than this earlier spectacle: illuminated by the modern miracle of electricity, brimming with artefacts of progress from telephones to torpedoes, and featuring a giant scale model constructed entirely from champagne bottles of the incomplete Eiffel Tower. From Louis's perspective, however, the festival's cultural lining was significant. He was one of a host of musicians recruited for what amounted to Australia's first symphony orchestra, under the direction of the world's most celebrated conductor: Englishman Frederic Cowen, who had just succeeded Sir Arthur Sullivan as head of the London Philharmonic Society.

No expense was spared marshalling the Centennial Exhibition Orchestra. Cowen's stipend for six months was a princely £5000, while his orchestra consisted of no fewer than seventy-three musicians: Louis Iverson—who brought Therese, his second daughter Toma and Harry with him while Thomas Louis and Charles remained in Albury—became one of fifteen first violins. Nonetheless, the orchestra fully earned its keep, playing 263 concerts between opening day 1 August 1888 and closing day 31 January 1889, often with the assistance of a choir of 700 voices; 'an astonishing programme,' believed historian Geoffrey Serle, 'which might never have been equalled anywhere'.

Its *piece de resistance* was *The Centennial Cantata*, a grandiose orchestral and choral vision of Australian settlement humming with progressive sentiments ('See the spires of the great city gleam/Is it all but the dream of a dream?'). But of longer-term cultural significance was its introduction to the colony of symphonies by composers such as Schumann, Schubert and Brahms, and the first operas by Wagner heard since a Melbourne production of *Lohengrin* in 1877.

Cowen and his orchestra were judged a success, though Wagner was at first insufficiently euphonious for colonial ears. 'I learned to be a Wagnerite,' commented the novelist and society belle Ada Cambridge, 'after several unsuccessful attempts'. Cowen himself remembered the colonists' enthusiasm with a mixture of humour and patrician condescension:

> After a performance of my oratorio 'Ruth', a friend of mine asked a rich squatter how much he liked the work to which he replied: 'My dear friend, it was simply lovely! It reminded me all the while of weaning time among my sheep; first the old ewe (meaning the contralto) got up and said: "Baa!" Then the old ram (the tenor) got up and answered: "Baa! Baa!" Then all the lambs behind the fences (the choir) cried: "Baa! Baa! Baa!" You tell Cowen to come to my place and I'll show him how musical the sheep are.'

The Exhibition itself, meanwhile, was judged an egregious flop. Having been budgeted to cost £25,000, its expenses mushroomed to £400,000. Having been intended as a showcase of the world's wares and wonders, its otiose flourishes overwhelmed human scale. Melbourne could, however, afford such profligacy. The land boom was at its apogee, Melbourne at its most 'marvellous'. Made rich by gold and populous by immigrants, the city throbbed with the industry of 3000 factories and the inventiveness of many more speculators. The climate of squandermania was embodied around the time of the Centennial Exhibition by the syndicate which offered £300,000 for the partially erected St Paul's Cathedral in order to replace it with an office block. They only narrowly failed.

There seemed something for everyone in this most cosmopolitan of cities: splendid opera, first-rate theatre, fine dining. With Germans now representing the colony's largest non-British minority, Louis could choose from no fewer than three German associations: the German Club, the Turn Verein and the Tivoli. And, having been part of Australia's most distinguished orchestra, he found his services as a teacher in demand. After the Exhibition closed, Louis became chief music instructor at Kew's prestigious Xavier College. He spent four years there, and the respect he enjoyed is reflected in the value of the gift he received on departure—three volumes of the complete works of Mozart, Schubert and Beethoven—and its inscription: 'To Herr Iverson as a token of favours continually and cheerfully rendered. New Year's Day 1893.'

By the time Louis's tenure at Xavier ended, however, Melbourne had changed altogether. The thriftless 1880s had given way to the austere 1890s with the collapse of real estate prices and an attendant banking panic. There were more than 600 bankruptcies, private compositions and arranged liquidations in 1892 alone. Ada Cambridge applauded the purifying effects of the city's swift reversal of fortune: 'A better example of the vulgarising effects of wealth, and of the refining effects of being without it, was never packed in a neater compass.' Others suffered severely: more than 50,000 left the city, including in due course the Iversons. The *Albury Border Post* in November 1896 noted Louis's reopening for business in Olive Street, abetted by Therese and Toma, accepting pupils 'for Piano, Violin, Theory of Music and Cultivation of the Voice'.

Though reunited with all his children after eight years, Louis was not destined to remake his mark in the border town. At about 7pm on 13 January 1897, shortly after finishing a violin lesson with a local pupil, he suffered a stroke. He was found 'in a state of complete unconsciousness' by one of his sons, who summoned a doctor called Andrews, but died forty-eight hours later. The *Albury Daily News and Wodonga Chronicle* proposed overwork as the cause: 'Though advanced in years, Mr Iverson had always devoted himself arduously to his duties as a professor of music and the mental strain was no doubt responsible for the fusion which resulted in his death.'

The passing of its patriarch seems to have had a marked impact on the family Iverson. In a copy of an obituary notice pasted in the music books that had been Louis's parting gift from Xavier, all references to Albury were fastidiously deleted, apparently by their inheritor Toma. Was this a gesture of annoyance at having been dragged back to the provinces after the city's heady sensations? Or did Toma's brothers nurse a sense of grievance about being left behind in the first place? Whatever the case, the children dispersed speedily after their brief reunion. Thomas Louis remained in Albury, marrying in April 1899, as did Therese, persevering as a musical instructor. Charles headed for Sydney, where he married in September 1901, and was joined presently by Toma. Harry, meanwhile, spent time in both households, but in neither was he happy. In his mid-teens, he detached from his family permanently and irrevocably.

For Harry, the trauma of his mother's death in infancy and his father's death a day before his twelfth birthday must have been formative. Perhaps he was the unidentified son who discovered Louis in the aftermath of his stroke; certainly he hardly spoke of his family in later life. We do know that a serious and unbridgeable rift opened between Harry on one hand and Thomas Louis and Therese on the other, but beyond that Harry seldom ventured. His surviving daughter Ruth says: 'My mother would say: "Daddy will tell you if he wishes." But he never did.'

Harry was also coy about his young adulthood. He referred proudly to 'making his own way in the world', but never explained how. Family lore has it that, like his own father, he spent time panning gold around Bendigo. He also commenced a law degree at Melbourne University, though he did not graduate; study would have been expensive for someone of modest means. When Harry first appears on electoral rolls in 1910—having passed the voting age of twenty-one—his residence is listed as East Melbourne's Gipps Street, his occupation 'manager'. But of what, we cannot say. We know only that he trained and practised as an accountant: a popular standby for bright young men of the period unable to afford tertiary fees but prepared to attend night schools or undertake home tuition. Young Harry appears in photographs as a sturdy figure of firm chin and determined mien, smart in dress and straight of spine. He would have impressed those he met as a young man making good. And he seems to have impressed one family in particular.

The Whites were among the most distinguished families in the settlement of Romsey, about sixty-five kilometres from Melbourne, then a pleasant and prosperous rural enclave of almost 4000 to which many wealthy urbanites retreated at weekends. William White had arrived in Australia in October 1854, acquired a splendid property which he called Rochford Hall, and opened the area's first general store. Under the catchy names of The Hall of Commerce, The Universal Provider and finally The Full and Plenty Store, it served the district for eighty years. White became the archetype of a settler cum civic father: keeping the register of births, deaths and marriages, planting the elms still lining Romsey's Main Road, and running the local *Romsey Examiner*.

When he left the district, one son got the store, another the newspaper. The latter, Henry Charles White, became shire secretary in 1909, and continued in the role when Romsey incorporated the neighbouring shires of Lancefield and Springfield. Henry and his wife Emma Sophia ran a severe household: despite her family's circumstances, their daughter

Edith Joyce made do while growing up with used bottles for dolls. But when she met young Harry Iverson around 1911 or 1912, he must have impressed her parents with his prospects and his undeviating attentiveness as a suitor: while courting, he would cycle from East Melbourne to Romsey every Saturday with a box of chocolates in the basket over his handlebars.

That the bride's father was also proprietor of the local newspaper means that we are blessed by a detailed account of the nuptials at St Paul's Church on 17 September 1913. The *Romsey Examiner* usually devoted no more than a terse paragraph to local marriages; on the wedding of his daughter, Henry White lavished almost a column of tiny type itemising every wedding gift. To the service conducted by her uncle, the Reverend Charlton Brazier, the new Mrs Edith Iverson wore an ivory satin charmeuse with court train, overdressed in Limerick lace, a handsome net and point brace bridal veil adorned with a wreath of orange blossoms and a shower bouquet of white flowers. Harry's gift to Edith was an arctic fox fur, Edith's to Harry a dressing case, while the seventy-seven guests chipped in everything from a painted table centre to an aquamarine necklet.

Harry's best man was his friend Frank Carolan—an estate agent in Carlton's Lygon Street with his father's firm Carolan Bros—accompanied by Mary Hayes, his intended. Otherwise the guest list was drawn almost exclusively from the bride's side, the *Examiner* referring vaguely to the groom's relatives being 'too far away to attend'; a euphemistic description, one suspects, of the abiding family rift. After a reception at the local Mechanics Institute, the happy couple headed 'by motor' to the coastal resort of Lorne for their honeymoon.

Harry and Ede Iverson's first matrimonial home was at 10 Langridge Street, Middle Park, a residence called Carinya. It was while there on 13 June 1914 that their first child was born: a daughter Mary Joyce, to be known in the family as Joy. As families in those days seldom stopped at one, the Iversons then sought a larger property: a red brick cottage at 1 Longmore Street, St Kilda. And it was here on 27 July 1915 that their second child was born: a son, John Bryan. He would be known to the cricket world as Jack.

THREE

By the time of Jack Iverson's birth, Australia had been at war almost a year. It had 75,000 troops overseas, a further 17,000 in training, and had suffered 12,000 dead or wounded. St Kilda, moreover, was a war-minded suburb. Its main arterial avenue Beaconsfield Parade had been lain as a military road against possible Russian invasion, while the seven members of a local contingent who died in the Boer War were commemorated in a beachfront memorial. At news of the World War I declaration on 5 August 1914, council members had interrupted their proceedings to sing 'God Save the King'. After voting a £200 donation to the Patriotic Fund on 24 August, they sang it again. When news arrived that HMAS *Sydney* had sunk the German surface raider *Emden* in the Indian Ocean on 9 November, they adjourned their deliberations over the vexed issue of mixed bathing to belt it out once more.

Locals had formed branches of the Red Cross and the Patriotic League within a month of the commencement of hostilities, and numerous events were held in furtherance of the war effort. Three days after Jack Iverson's birth, attorney-general Billy Hughes was guest of honour at a soul-stirring Town Hall recruiting drive where a band played martial and loyal airs beneath a large shield inscribed with the legend 'Duty' while women knitted socks for soldiers at the front. A profusion of similar occasions round the state must have done the trick. In the month that Jack was born, 21,698 Victorians enlisted of an Australian total of 36,575: the highest monthly figure of the war.

Pushing her perambulator round the avenues neighbouring Longmore Street, Ede Iverson would have seen many young men in uniform. St Kilda was a favoured stopping-off point for servicemen on leave, especially after the St Kilda Soldiers Lounge was opened on the Lower Esplanade in December 1915: 30,000 visited during its first six months. Her husband, however, was not among them. This was not necessarily notable: 60 per cent of Australians between the ages of eighteen and forty-four did not enlist, and perhaps Harry Iverson felt his duties lay closer to home. But there is also the possibility he felt inhibited by his German parentage. It was not an easy time in Australia for anyone or anything with the faintest Teutonic taint. Anti-German leagues had sprung up, and none were safe from their denunciations; not even John Monash—wilfully misspelt by his enemies as Monasch—whose father had naturalised in 1856. Anonymous correspondents to newspapers, signing themselves 'Britisher' or 'Loyal Australian', fingered neighbours or acquaintances with German surnames. German schools were closed in South Australia, and remained open in Victoria only by employing Australian teachers and teaching from Australian syllabuses. Twelve days before Jack's birth, in fact, it became an offence under the War Precautions Act for an enemy alien to anglicise their name, as the Iversons had done.

Not even place names were spared from the pervasive paranoia: the Barossa towns that Louis Iverson knew as Hahndorf, Heidelberg and Hamburg became Yantaringa, Kobandilla and Haig; the locations near Albury he visited as Germantown and German Creek became Holbrook and Empire Vale. By the time the Nomenclature Committee on Enemy Place Names had finished its work—altering *in toto* some sixty-nine names—Australia's German history had been obsessively whitewashed.

St Kilda took with a will to obliterating the enemy within. When the local football club discovered that its colours mirrored those on the German flag, mortified players stitched small but visible union jacks to their guernseys until the club's administrators legislated for a new livery. Local postmistress Matilda Rockstroh, a native-born public servant with a spotless thirty-three-year record, was stood down because of her genealogy: her parents were German gold rush immigrants. The bureaucratese accompanying this decision explained that Rockstroh's 'lineal connection with the German race' made it unlikely that 'her inclinations and proclivities, if they could be discovered and put to an enforced election, would tend towards the interests of the British empire'.

St Kilda council, furthermore, supported conscription in the October 1916 and December 1917 referenda, and the suburb voted overwhelmingly in favour. One wonders which way Harry Iverson cast his vote: he must have felt a patriotic pang for a country in which he had been able to haul himself up by the bootstraps, yet he himself had apparently no inclination to join the colours. Perhaps he was relieved that the 'no' vote prevailed. For a young man so fastidiously building a future for his family, the disruption of conscription would have been severe. And for a young man with a German father, service may have proved a particular ordeal.

When their third child Ruth was born in June 1918, Harry and Ede Iverson sought a larger dwelling. They eventually acquired a brick house with a spacious backyard not far away at 17 Burnett Street. The house, called Wymwould, is no longer there—replaced by a nondescript block of flats in a brick the shade of weak tea—although the handsome period houses that remain preserve the air of suburban gentility. Burnett Street is actually one of St Kilda's oldest thoroughfares, a relic of the 1850s when St Kilda Road was still a bush track, bushrangers roamed the Domain and itinerant Aborigines importuning residents were considered 'a great nuisance to local shopkeepers'. The street itself was named for John Alexander Burnett, then one of Melbourne's leading real estate auctioneers: auspicious nomenclature given the venture Harry Iverson was about to undertake and in which son Jack would follow.

A five-minute walk away in a street named for Burnett's employers, Dalgety, was Harry Iverson's old friend Frank

Carolan, now married and also beginning a family. Carolan had suffered an unfortunately eventful war. Invalided from the Australian Imperial Force with varicose veins, he had joined the Australian Flying Corps but been injured in a flying accident in England and returned home for a lengthy convalescence. Nonetheless, he was eager to return to the real estate business, this time under his own banner, and took Harry on as a partner.

War had provided the most concerted economic stimulus for Australia since the discovery of gold, and peace would shortly remove the remaining fetters on pent-up demand. Carolan, Iverson & Co. opened its doors at a boom time for Melbourne real estate. The city's population grew by a third in the decade after the war, bursting through a million in October 1928, and property values and commissions mushroomed as new office buildings soared and new homes multiplied. The impression was of a city straining restlessly at its tethers. Regulations set in February 1916 restricted buildings to a maximum height of 132 feet; between 1922 and 1933, no fewer than seventeen were topped out at exactly that height.

Public transport infrastructure was hastily reorganised to keep pace with shifting demographics as new sub-divisions were opened. A five-year program of electrifying the railways began in October 1918, and the disparate metropolitan tram routes were consolidated in the Melbourne and Metropolitan Tramways Board in November 1919. Hansom cabs, traps and wagons still preponderated on Melbourne's streets, but a growing number of automobiles celebrated the citizenry's newfound mobility and unself-conscious materialism. Carolan, Iverson & Co.'s office at 243 Collins Street had an ideal vantage point on the city's new bustle, almost equidistant between what a February 1923 survey found were Melbourne's two busiest corners: the intersections of Collins Street with Swanston and Elizabeth featured an hourly traffic rate of 429 and 374 cars respectively.

Carolan, Iverson & Co. quickly established itself as one of Melbourne's busiest agencies, in competition with family concerns like Baillieu Allard, K. Gardner & Lang, and Geo. M. Hume. It was strong in the city, where office space was expanding apace, and found lucrative work in the suburbs as a specialist in terrace houses. An early coup was a sub-division at the corner of Caroline and Alexandra streets in South Yarra, on which developer Harry Lawson erected some of the city's most prestigious and pricey residential addresses, which Carolan, Iverson & Co. then also sold. Frank Carolan was the salesman, an approachable and convivial 'man about town' who entertained flamboyantly at the Kelvin Club. Harry Iverson was his counterfoil, the numbers man, an assiduous book-keeper never less than sartorially immaculate with a fresh flower in his lapel.

Evidence that Carolan, Iverson & Co. was moving in increasingly exalted circles comes from an unusual source: a court case in which the firm was involved with a Queen Street property concern called Central Investments Pty Ltd in March 1927. CIPL sued Carolan, Iverson & Co. for the massive sum of £4500 in damages over its £27,000 purchase from Combined Estates Pty Ltd of a property known as Milton House in Flinders Lane in which Frank Carolan and Harry Iverson had acted as agents, contending *inter alia* that the pair had misrepresented CEPL's position that the sale price was the lowest it would accept, and that certain furniture as shown by the defendants went with the sale. Carolan, Iverson & Co. denied the allegations and counterclaimed against the plaintiffs for £250, being their commission on the sale.

A fascinating legal battle seemed in prospect in the First Civil Court. CIPL retained the services of a brilliant junior counsel, Robert Menzies, who later that year would begin his political career by announcing he would stand for the Legislative Council seat of East Yarra Province. Fighting in Carolan, Iverson & Co.'s corner was Wilfred Fullagar, later a Supreme Court judge. But the case had barely begun when Menzies informed Justice Mann that his client had capitulated: CIPL's allegations of fraud were unconditionally withdrawn and judgment entered for the defendants on the counterclaim, with the plaintiffs also agreeing to pay Carolan, Iverson & Co.'s costs of £75.

The case was clearly of great moment to Harry Iverson; he clipped a press report of the settlement from the *Argus* and glued it to a piece of cardboard as a keepsake. It found its way into his son's desk drawer when the business became his, and was still there when the firm was finally sold. Quite why, we cannot tell. Perhaps it was jubilation at having stared down a threat that would almost certainly have undone all Harry's hard work. Perhaps there was also some sort of moral lesson implied, that business if conducted ethically had nothing to fear from even the grandest legal array. For Harry prided himself on unimpeachable ethics, and would set his son stern standards by which to live.

The Iverson family was conventional in its child-rearing precept. Harry worked long hours in Collins Street, setting off just after 8am each day on the tram to St Kilda station to meet the train for town, and often arriving home after 6pm. Ede, a strong-willed and self-reliant woman in her own right, fulfilled the role of domestic carer and emotional bulwark. She bore her fourth and last child in December 1921—a third daughter, Marjorie—and set to the task of raising them. By this time, Jack was attending Scott Street Central School in St Kilda: one of a generation of Victorian primary schools, opened in June 1917 on a 2.5 hectare block.

The Iverson household was a proper one. His own upbringing having been so chaotic and uncertain, Harry favoured a life of order. The usual diurnal course involved his early departure and the children being packed off to school. Ede set to her domestic duties with the aid of a houseboy, who ran errands, polished the silver, the doorknobs and washed the car, a laundress who called weekly, and a live-in maid; the Iversons had a series, all teenage girls from the Ballarat Orphanage. The children were expected to dress for dinner, which was announced at 6.30pm daily by the ringing of a bell. All played the piano: Harry invested in a Haines upright, and liked to hear his favourites like 'Lily of Laguna' and 'Alexander's Ragtime Band'. Even Harry's recreation adhered to a fixed pattern. Every Thursday, without fail, he would play golf at Kingston Heath: a course that had attracted many estate agents, thanks to its president W. H. Allard of Baillieu Allard.

Jack was from the first a contentedly self-contained boy, polite, well-mannered, unobtrusive, a nuisance to no-one. Although from his father he kept an admiring, reverent distance, there was a strong maternal bond; according to his sister Ruth, Ede 'thought everything John did was wonderful'. He was a competent student, if never an outstanding one, and played the piano by ear rather than undertaking tuition. He later revealed a pleasant singing voice—perhaps a genetic inheritance from his musical forebears—though he was never inclined to sing at home.

While Jack lacked a male sibling, there were numerous attractions for a boy in St Kilda's suburban idyll: the St Kilda Pier was invariably lined with anglers and yacht race spectators, Luna Park fun fair had opened in 1907, the Palais de Danse in 1908. There were baths on the foreshore, and beaches that the memoirist Graham McInnes remembered on hot days being 'so crammed with prone bodies that there seemed to be more people than sand'. Wymwould was also suitable for backyard ball games, and Jack and Frank Carolan's son Ivor became regular playmates. Also in this period, Jack formed the most enduring friendship of his life with a lad whose father lived directly across the road.

Alan Meckiff was the son of a manager at the National Bank, raised by grandparents in Blackburn when his mother died in his infancy, and a boarder at Melbourne's Scotch College, but who summered with his father in Burnett Street. One day a tennis ball bounced over his fence. Jack Iverson came to fetch it, Alan returned it, and a friendship based on propinquity blossomed. Aside from family Christmases which the Iversons spent with the Whites at Romsey, the pair were inseparable in summers; fishing, playing marbles, riding their bicycles, playing in their backyards, like so many other sons of the growing Melbourne bourgeoisie. To Alan, Jack was 'quiet, very self-contained, a good companion'.

When Ivor Carolan or Alan Meckiff were away, Jack fell back on his own devices. Fortunately, while it may have been necessity made virtue, Jack always gave the appearance of enjoying his own company and manufacturing his own amusements. He had, in particular, one habit all his own. From the earliest age, he was an inveterate flicker of whatever happened to fall between his fingers: wads of paper, small stones, cherry pips. One of Wymwould's most entertaining accoutrements was the large family table tennis table in the courtyard, on which Jack swiftly became so formidable that his siblings were loath to challenge him. 'I hated playing John,' says Ruth. 'Because he always cut everything. You'd move to one side of the table, and you'd find it spinning over the other.' Yet nothing about the game, Alan Meckiff remembers, gave Jack more transparent pleasure than simply spinning the table tennis ball, especially an extraordinary trick of flicking the sphere forward but imparting such spin that it whirred straight back to him. Jack's hands, large already for his age, equipped him uniquely for these acts of conjuring.

Myriad sources repeat the accepted yarn that Jack Iverson was first bewitched by the physics of the rotating ball while in the army, but he was rehearsing the 'mystery spinner' role he could scarcely have foreseen almost two decades before he seriously took cricket up. For although Alan Meckiff recalls that his friend always bowled a sound length in their childhood games, he says that Jack was otherwise indifferent to cricket and derived far greater enjoyment from his father's game of golf.

What makes the story all the more unusual is that table tennis was not then a pastime of note, even among Australia's fad-friendly middle-classes. Table tennis had originated in Victorian Britain, emerging from university common rooms and officers' messes to become a popular parlour game, though with widespread variation in the absence of strict codification. What we would recognise today as a table-tennis ball was actually a celluloid toy ball from the United States introduced to one variation of the game called Gossima about a century ago by a British cross-country athlete, James Gibb; the sound the ball made on a table and then on a hollow vellum racquet gave rise to the onomatopoeic name Ping Pong subsequently adopted by the American toys and hobbies firm Parker Bros in their version of the pastime. But there were many other mutations, such as Whiff Whaff and Flim Flam, with balls made of string, rubber or cork, and bats carved from cardboard or wood covered in either parchment or leather.

Table tennis first came to Australia late in its global vogue—ping pong championships were staged in South Australia in 1898, a short-lived association created in New South Wales with the Lord Mayor as patron—and then only briefly. For, as the game outwore its novelty in Britain and the USA, it also virtually disappeared in Australia. It did not resurface until 1921 when a group of Britons formed what was called the Ping Pong Association, subsequently renamed the English Table Tennis Association, which inspired a European revival and led to standardisation of rules and equipment in 1926. The conventional bat surface agreed upon was allegedly an invention of an Englishman called E. C. Goode who, visiting an apothecary for a migraine cure, noted a studded rubber cash mat on the counter and concluded that it might enhance his spin and control at ping pong. The blinding flash, legend has it, not only improved his table tennis but spontaneously dispelled his headache.

So here is the strangest of mischances. Comparatively few Melbourne households in the mid-1920s would have contained such an artefact of a short-lived turn-of-the-century craze that was at the time only just making a comeback abroad. Yet Wymwould did, and that table tennis ball would accompany Jack everywhere for the next two decades, until his experiments in gyrostatics achieved their greatest application.

FOUR

When Jack turned ten, his father Harry decided to send him to board at Geelong College. A believer in self-direction and self-discipline, Harry perhaps had in mind his son experiencing some of the character-building loneliness that had been part of his own youth. Indeed, Harry seems to have believed in the efficacy of boarding schools in general; he had already sent his oldest daughter Joy to Geelong's leading girls' school, the Hermitage.

Ede Iverson appears to have been at least ambivalent. She would recall as one of her saddest moments the day she deposited Jack for his first term. For whatever reason, the school was virtually deserted on their arrival. She was able to glimpse in the rear-vision mirror of her Singer motor car as she drove away the receding figure of Jack standing in the

quadrangle, cap tugged down, long legs bare, alone. The image
was indelible enough for Ede to recall it many years later to
her granddaughter Sherry.

Geelong College was then a small public school of fewer
than 250 boys, but steeped nonetheless in the English educa-
tional presumption that young men should not only be able to
recite their *hic, haec, hocs* but also execute a decent cover drive.
In the school magazine, *Pegasus*, correspondents debated
subjects like 'Is refinement effeminate?' and 'Why communism
would ruin Australia'. They submitted such poems as 'To the
Commander of the R101 Who Stayed At His Position Among
Flames Until the End'.

Sport mattered at all the members of the Associated Public
Schools, especially the annual Head of the River boat race,
which craved the prestige of an antipodean Henley Regatta.
Newcomers, in fact, were often startled by the grave importance attached to athletic endeavour. When the young
Englishman James Darling came from Charterhouse in 1930
to become principal of Geelong Grammar and expressed
surprise at such earnestness, his sportsmaster hissed through
gritted teeth: 'The trouble with you Englishmen is that you
don't know the difference between games and sport.'

College's principal, Reverend Francis Rolland, knew the
difference. A Presbyterian minister who had won a Military
Cross while serving as a chaplain in the Australian Imperial
Force, he was revered by boys who nicknamed him 'the Cocoa
King': legend had it that among his wartime exploits had been
conveying mugs of cocoa to frontline soldiers of the 14th
Battalion during bombardments. Trying to revive the school
after a period of wartime austerity, Rolland regarded sport as

a priority; not because he felt sporting success should be an end in itself, but because College's long-term record of sporting failure was such a psychological retardant. For College's trophy cabinet was bare. Its first XI's record at the time Jack Iverson arrived was particularly parlous, amounting to four victories in the fifteen preceding years.

Rolland oversaw marked improvements to grounds and facilities, and the recruitment of outstanding coaches. He cultivated competition between the four houses—Morrison, Shannon, Calvert and Warrinn—through intra-school events. One school song even borrowed directly from Newbolt to exhort:

> Sons of the school who are there today
> You must exalt her name
> In study and on fields of play
> Play up and play the game.

Rolland's particular joy was tennis: he seemed always to have a racquet with him ready for a game with one of his students. But College also became a school where one could learn a lifetime allegiance to cricket. Its grounds were picturesque, lovingly-maintained, and could have been the backdrop to a novel by R. F. Delderfield. Revered coach Percival Lloyd Williams, a painstaking science master from Wesley College, ran nets five nights a week. The school hero was an omnicompetent athlete called Lindsay Hassett, for five seasons a member of the College first XI, as well as captain of football and tennis. The College historian records that even A. H. MacRoberts, Rolland's rigid and feared deputy, known to the boys as 'Boop', was softened by on-field feats:

> His weekly inspections of the boys' records caused even bravest hearts to quail. As flagellator-in-chief he had

a remarkable eye for multiple underwear. To the last he loved cricket, however, and the boys who made a good score in a Public School match would possibly be called to the 'bookroom', not for the usual dread purpose, but to receive a ten-shilling note.

The more I examined the extant records, however, the less likely it seemed that Jack Iverson would have benefited from such largesse. Only the ghostliest traces of him remained.

As a sportsman, he was evidently no great shakes. *Pegasus* for February 1929 noted him as captain of the under-15 B-section cricket team that played on what was called the cow paddock: an unenclosed pasture that the boys used for their daily sports and pastimes. But this was no great distinction: cow paddock cricket was the pastime of those not quite good enough to grace the soft and splendid turf of the main oval.

Jack bowled medium pace for a couple of seasons in the school's second XI and occasionally hit hard: in one fixture witnessed by his mother at Melbourne Grammar's junior school Grimwade House, he long-handled an undefeated 52 from two overs. On the basis of this performance, he was selected to open in a trial game for Hassett's first XI against Wesley College. It proved an inspired stroke of miscasting: he was stumped first ball by Ross Gregory, the dashing stroke-player who would earn two Australian caps in the 1936–37 Ashes series before perishing on active service as a pilot in June 1942.

Apart from playing it, Jack displayed little interest in cricket. When selected to play for Australia, he would recall having attended only one day of Test cricket in his life: a Melbourne match in the 1928–29 Ashes series from which his only recollection was—neither the batting of Bradman or Hammond, nor the bowling of Grimmett or Larwood— 'Douglas Jardine's harlequin cap'.

As a student, Jack's record was similarly inconspicuous. There was one musical interlude in September 1927 when he played the title role in an adaptation of *The Mikado* called *The Wandering Minstrel*. In a cast photograph, he is the one figure with his hands behind his back, a shy smile on his lips. But the written record for this medium-pace bowler and medium-pace scholar expired with the valete for December 1933, which mentioned no honours either academic or sporting.

There had to be more. Was there anyone, I wondered, who might remember Jack from his school years? As it happened, the College had recently hosted a luncheon for those old boys who had left the school fifty-five years or more earlier and kindly made their guest list available. I sent a form letter to the thirty or so whose years had overlapped with Jack's and hoped for the best. In a school as small as College had been then, the prospects seemed good.

Over the next few weeks, responses began arriving. One telephone caller confided a memory of 'Jack Iverson playing a game of cricket on the cow paddock and standing at square leg wearing his overcoat'. He seemed to think this detail so salacious that he doggedly declined to identify himself. Others who did identify themselves offered a little more: that Jack enjoyed playing Peter Dawson records on the boarding house phonograph, that Jack would conserve his penny tramfare when returning from football matches at Corio Oval by walking the five kilometres back to College. But the only genuinely useful and uniform intelligence cited by more than a couple of respondents was Jack's infatuation with table tennis balls. A little white sphere was produced at College at every opportunity, squirted from his oversized fingers, made to jink and jag about the boarding house corridors, bounced off the old eighteen-pounder cannons in the school grounds. It had effaced in the minds of contemporaries almost all else.

Finally, however, I discovered in Barwon Heads a man called Jim Carstairs. He had known Jack, known him well. His first memory, in fact, was of an enchanting singing voice at the auditions for *The Wandering Minstrel*. 'I sang one line and they said: "Out!" Then this other fella comes in and sings with this beautiful voice and gets the part: John Iverson.'

The Jack that Jim Carstairs recalled chimed with Alan Meckiff's earlier recollections: 'Quiet, reserved, not outgoing, never the life of the party, quite shy really. Which is probably why we got on, because I was a bit the same, didn't make friends easily at school.' Shared shyness did not, of course, prevent the pair collaborating in some traditional schoolboy mischief-making, usually involving sport. One day the boys were hitting a golf ball across the cow paddock towards the corrugated iron lavatories neighbouring the school's tennis courts when 'Boop' MacRoberts appeared. Too late; Jack had essayed his drive. Fortunately, MacRoberts was in the process of closing the door to the masters' one-holer just as the projectile clanged against it. By the time the deputy principal had reopened the door in search of the malefactor, both Jim and Jack had made themselves scarce.

On another occasion, the pair even indulged in something

a little more subversive at the expense of their unpopular mathematics master, C. C. Shinkfield:

> Shinkfield was always immaculate, beautifully turned out, matching tie, shirt and suit. Used to queen around the place, and we used to think he was a bit of queen. Anyway, one day we were playing on the cow paddock and Shinkfield decides he's going to walk right across the field, through the middle of the game, not looking left or right. When he went past, John goes: 'I'll give you an easy one. See if you can get him.' And he bowled me this absolute sitter which I hit up in the air and right into the small of Shinkfield's back. He turned around and shook his fist at us. Think I got one of my many canings for that!

Of course, Jim remembered the table tennis ball, with the addendum that Jack was little less prodigious using a tennis ball, flicking the ball out with a rotation so fierce that it bounced first one way then the other. The boys also became close enough to spend summer holidays together. One summer, Jim took Jack to stay with his family at Streatham where his father managed a property called Blytheway for the Wetherley family. Another, Jack brought Jim to stay with him at Wymwould. Jim enjoyed the visit, although it struck him in hindsight how little Jack had to do with his father. Harry was very obviously the master of his household and, though Jack was well provided for, their relationship seemed formal, perhaps even remote. Jim recalls:

> I remember a day we played at Kingston Heath. There was the old man playing up ahead with the club champion and the state amateur champion, a fella called Ryan, with me

and John trailing behind. I can think of some fathers who might have had us playing together as a four.

There might also have been an element in the son of the father, for Jim Carstairs' recollections proceeded little further. Close as they had been at school, their friendship tapered away afterwards, apart from a brief reunion in 1950 when by sheer coincidence Jim found himself owning a Sale property neighbouring Alan Meckiff's. As we talked in Jim's living room at Barwon Heads, a tone of regret entered his voice:

> I know I was very pleased for him when he played for Australia. It was a great thrill to know someone playing Test cricket. I wrote to congratulate him and he wrote back. Then Alan Meckiff reintroduced us and it seemed like we'd gone straight back to our old friendship. And, you know, sometimes you catch up with people some years after school and you re-establish the friendship. We'd been as close as any two boys at school. But it just didn't happen. I don't really know why.

I should have felt disappointed to have come away from researching Jack's schooldays with so little. Yet, perversely, it was almost gratifying; there was something about this virtual anonymity that endeared him further to me. The sheer insubstance of Jack Iverson's trail seemed to make him all the more extraordinary and separate: perhaps no Test cricketer has had a junior record so mediocre. Figures like Jack inhabit every school generation, indistinct, blurring with the years until they can scarcely be identified in class photographs, the vaguely recalled extras in the cast. As a rule, they do not play cricket for their countries.

Jack's record, consequently, offers a reflection on the way sporting lives are often written. A maxim beloved of biographers runs: 'Life must be lived forwards, but can only be understood backwards.' With cricketers, this often means superimposing a sense of predestiny: when nine, Bill Batsman scored a century on a bumping pitch in a blinding light against the biggest boy from a rival school and announced himself a prodigy; at ten, Bob Bowler was shouldered from the field after a match-winning hat-trick and vowed to play for his country.

Yet there are so many prodigies and so many vows made in the headiness of youthful success, and so few yield anything beyond cherished memories in adulthood of a time when everything seemed within one's grasp. One of cricket's most beguiling and confounding qualities is that it grants almost everyone a brief glimpse of the possible: a brilliant catch, a clean-hit stroke, an unexpectedly hostile delivery. As E. V. Lucas put it in *English Leaves*: 'There is no other game at which the confirmed duffer is so persistent and undepressed.' But, more often than not, those glimpses foretell nothing. When he reached the Test stage, Iverson would reminisce of only one boyhood game: an intra-school match against Shannon House where he dismissed the school hero Hassett with the complicity of an inside edge. He cited it as one of his happiest moments on a cricket field. There is, however, no extant scorebook or confirmatory recollection from Hassett. And had Jack continued the rather mundane path he'd begun at school, it would have remained no more than a cherished private memory, of a piece with so many others. Indeed, this might almost have been the end of Jack's cricketing days. For the thirteen years after leaving school, he played little. His table tennis ball, however, would continue to accompany him.

FIVE

It can be deduced from Jack's seven years at Geelong College that Harry's business career was continuing to flourish. College fees at the time were £48 a term, while the boys were apportioned a shilling a week in pocket money (of which threepence was designated for the church collection plate on Sundays). This proved too steep for many parents as the bitter years of the Depression unfolded, and many boys left the school prematurely between 1930 and 1933. The town of Geelong itself was buffeted by the economic shockwave, to the extent that new mayor Oswald Hearne inaugurated a relief fund called wryly 'Mother Hubbard's Cupboard'. Harry Iverson, by contrast, saw all four of his children through private schools: Joy at the Hermitage, Jack at the College, Ruth and Marjorie at St Margaret's.

This cannot have been easy. Melbourne property prices ebbed dramatically during the Depression. The most active end of the market was the rather grisly one of dissolving bankrupt estates on behalf of desperate creditors, often at knockdown prices. Even with the long-term relationships he had struck with the University of Melbourne and the Church of England, managing their property portfolios, Harry would have been hard-pressed sustaining the cash flow from his rent rolls as straitened tenants struggled to meet their obligations.

There was the further disruption in 1932 from the dissolution of Harry's partnership with Frank Carolan. The circumstances of this are mysterious. One story has it that a dispute developed over Carolan's use of funds from the agent's trust account, but Frank's son Ivor would say no more than: 'It was a mistake. A big mistake, but a mistake.' Whatever the case, the partners were irrevocably estranged, setting up independent businesses and living independent lives; as had been the case with his siblings, Harry knew no half-measures once disappointed. Carolan & Co. remained at 243 Collins Street. H. W. Iverson, promoting itself as a 'Real Estate Investment Specialist', opened at 271 Collins Street, the chambers then and now of the National Bank. The families, meanwhile, having been so intimate, socialised no further. Ivor Carolan never saw again the man he referred to as 'Uncle Harry'.

Getting started again would have proved difficult. Setting up as an agent was expensive: the Real Estate and Stock Institute required the posting of sizeable fidelity bonds with the clerk of petty sessions before it would issue a licence (£500 for an individual, £1000 for a corporation). Harry would also have been acutely conscious of the many competitors round him scrabbling for the puny amounts of good business available. A random shot fired in Collins Street in those days, if not intercepted by a stockbroker, would probably have hit an estate agent: there was Syd Arnold, Best & Co. at 145, Geo. M. Hume at 220, H. P. Knight at 315, J. W. Styles at 340, Baillieu Allard at 360, W. B. Simson at 379, K. Gardner & Lang at 400, H. C. Costello at 405 and J. R. Buxton at 443.

Nonetheless, again to judge by Harry's circumstances, he put his best foot forward. As the effects of the Depression lifted and the real estate market improved, the Iverson family moved a little further up in the world. Wymwould was placed on the market then sold in November 1935, and the family moved for three months into St Kilda's George Hotel while Harry sought a new home. In the end, he refrained from buying: a business acquaintance, W. E. Carr, was intending to relocate his family to England for an extended period and wanted to rent his house at 257 St Kilda Street in Brighton to someone he knew.

Brighton was, and remains, one of Melbourne's ritziest addresses: smart, snug and not a little smug. For another young Melburnian of the time, Graham McInnes, then growing up in suburban Malvern, it represented that 'far-off unattainable pleasure dome by the dreamy sea'. Harry Iverson had now attained it, and in some style: Kuring-gai was a handsome and imposing three-storey mansion right on the beachfront and neighbouring the Royal Brighton Yacht Club, complete with six telephones to the outside and a further seven handsets for internal communication. Though his name was not on the title, Harry Iverson could nonetheless feel satisfied that he was making comfortable social progress.

For much of this period, again, Jack Iverson would be far away. He returned from school a strapping figure, towering over his siblings, nudging six foot, broad and deep in the chest. A set of photographs from 1934 evidence his adolescent growth spurt: eighteen-year-old Jack is bursting from his old College blazer, and standing tall in riding boots that suggest a country squire. And this, indeed, was his destination, if not his station.

Jack's going 'on the land' may have been his father's notion: as it was imagined to inculcate rural hardiness and self-discipline, becoming a station hand or labourer was at the time an informal finishing school for many young Australian and English males. But the idea may also have been Jack's: both Alan Meckiff and Jim Carstairs became jackaroos after completing their secondary education, excited about farm life by their conversations with graziers' sons in their respective boarding houses. Jack had also enjoyed his summers at Blytheway, the property managed by Jim's father, and his sister Ruth feels that he 'loved the thought of country life'.

Here again, however, information is scant, almost derisory. The most extensive biographical portrait of Jack, written by Bob Coleman in the Victorian Cricket Association history *Seasons in the Sun*, contains no more than the sentence: 'From the age of nine [sic] to eighteen, he was a boarder at Geelong College, after which he sought the wider horizons of station life, working as a jackaroo in the Mallee and western Victoria.' But where under those wider horizons was I to find him?

Alan Meckiff volunteered that he thought Jack had gone first to a wheat farm in the Mallee, so I pored for days over the electoral rolls of the area for 1934 and 1935; although not yet old enough to vote, there was the faintest chance that he would be picked up. There were Ivers and Ivisons, but no trace of an Iverson. I consulted Sands and McDougall directories: for areas outside Melbourne, alas, they documented commercial residences rather than residential ones. Perhaps Jack had notified the Geelong College old boys' association of an address. No such luck. I sat in the State Library of Victoria for a few more days, leafing with growing despondency through books about the Mallee, and finally had a heart-to-heart with the staffer in the genealogy section. He confirmed my suspicion. Looking for an itinerant teenage labourer in the Mallee in the mid-1930s was 'searching for a needle in a haystack'; an apposite cliche given the rural setting.

I mention this because I suspect it was hereabouts that what had begun as a project took on the qualities of a quest. That Jack's fugitive figure had shrunken almost to vanishing point gave him an unexpected additional dimension: the quality of the unrecorded everyman, a solitary figure among the numberless millions swallowed by time and territory. I wanted to find where Jack Iverson had been in the years 1934 and 1935, not only because it might prove germane to my research, but to see if it was possible to disentangle a single thread from that tight-woven tapestry of undifferentiated consciousnesses. And there was still one clue I had not followed up.

Both Coleman's *Seasons in the Sun* and Peter Pierce's entry on Jack Iverson in the *Australian Dictionary of Biography* mentioned *en passant* that he had won a golf title in the Victorian town of

Maldon: Coleman said 1935, Pierce 1936. I contacted both writers, but neither could help: the former couldn't remember, the latter couldn't even remember having made the reference and suspected its insertion by editors. An inquiry to Canberra's National Dictionary Centre brought by return mail an October 1953 press clipping from Melbourne's *Herald* dating the tournament as the 'club championship at Maldon in 1936'. The small item was written in such a way that suggested its source could only have been Jack himself.

Maldon, in central Victoria, about 140 kilometres north of Melbourne in the orbit of Castlemaine, seemed a curious place for Jack to have gone after school. In its pomp at Christmas 1853, this old gold town had been home to 20,000 souls. Eighty years later, its population had withered to 732, following the closure of the last mine in 1926. Maldon's future appeared so clouded that, in the years leading up to and during the Depression, nearly half its houses were relocated, many to Castlemaine, some as far as Melbourne, carried on the back of timber jinkers. From the lookout tower about 500 metres above sea level on nearby Mount Tarrengower, according to a guidebook of the 1930s, 'the fortunate visitor will feel very silent and overwhelmed by the beauty of it all, and that for a while he has been near to the heart of things'. The visitor would also have noticed the increasing abundance of vacant lots, lending some streets the look of a gap-toothed smile.

Maldon had, however, one attraction: it enjoyed—if that is the right word—the lowest cost of living in Australia. A vacant lot cost no more than £10. Houses could be bought from £180, bluestone cottages from £140. Indeed, the modern visitor might nearly be living in the town as it was then. Thanks to its listing as Australia's first 'notable town' in 1965 by the National Trust, Maldon's peculiar streetscapes of cottages and out-buildings in wattle and daub, mud-brick and timber slats, remain untouched, as if preserved beneath a laboratory's bell jar.

The town's golf club was founded in August 1908 as a six-hole course of 1581 metres carved from virgin bushland, then relocated and refurbished five years later as a nine-hole course measuring 2355 metres across a cluster of leased paddocks by the road to Dunolly. In Jack's day, it would have been wild indeed: posts connected by wire protected the sand scrapes from grazing sheep, while the clubhouse was a galvanised iron shed in a town without electricity. But I still could not deter-mine out *which* day had been Jack's: perversely, the club's honour boards and minute books extended back no further than 1937, and the name Iverson was conspicuous by its absence.

There was nothing for it but to read every issue of the *Tarrengower Times* for the years 1934, 1935 and 1936. Reading the first year was actually no hardship: one could feel the bristling communal pride that a son of Maldon, Bill Woodfull, was captaining Australia in the Ashes tour of that year, inspir-ing a vigorous local score-guessing contest, the Diabolo Cream Separator Test Cricket Competition. There remained, however, no trace of my subject. The *Tarrengower Times* published full scores of both the Maldon Golf Club and the Castlemaine Cricket Association, but the name Iverson leapt from neither.

Nor was there a hint of Jack when I skipped to 1936—the year the *Herald* had given for his championship victory—and seeing the same advertisements for constipation tablets and the results from agricultural festivals was beginning to gnaw my patience. And as I turned back to 1935 this alley seemed disconcertingly blind. But then, at last, so difficult to make out on the white-on-black microfiche print that I almost missed it, a tiny entry appeared at the foot of a page: 'The competition conducted at Baringhup on the night of the school concert for the 10/- note was won by Mr J. Iverson, Baringhup East.'

So, at last, I had a location. Baringhup, on the Loddon River eleven kilometres from Maldon, was no more than a speck on the map in the mid-1930s: a post office converted from the old Cobb & Co. guesthouse, the Loddon Hotel, a Presbyterian church and a general store serving the surrounding farms. Its last policeman had retired in 1990 and was not replaced. In all likelihood, I'd be unable to narrow my search further: sixty-four years later, what chance existed that original inhabitants of a rural hamlet might survive with remembrance of an itinerant worker who hit a mean golf ball? But I felt lucky. On the advice of the Castlemaine Historical Society, I had a long, meandering conversation with Sam Palmer, a genealogist at the Maldon Museum which turned into a long, meandering letter from me to her concerning Jack. Another kitchen window, another knock, but after five weeks the door opened, and I spoke to Jack Iverson's one-time next-door neighbour.

Neil Neilson was eight years old when Jack Iverson came to Baringhup East, but remembered it like yesterday. For a while, he guessed, Jack had been his boyhood hero, something of a sporting Adonis.

He was a very tall man, fit and strong; a lovely man, too, very decent, and I never heard anything different. So, yes, he was a bit of an idol, I suppose. When I was a kid, he was very good to me. If he was off up the paddock he often let me go with him, and I tagged along with him for many a mile.

Jack worked for Mrs Olive Glover on a 486-hectare sheep farm called Blue Hills, set in a gently sloping valley. She had two grown-up sons, Tom and Harry, but need of a jackaroo because her husband Fred was often absent on his rounds as a commercial traveller. Neil and his sister lived 300 metres up the incline with their parents Charlie and Ivy.

Mother Glover and her boys lived in a newish five-room cement brick homestead that still stands at Blue Hills, while Jack bedded down in their former dwelling: a smaller shack of split planks, buttressed by hessian and paper. Maldon's winters are classically country-cold, damp and hoarfrosted, so it was little wonder that Jack often strolled up the road for the favour of the Neilsons' hearth and hospitality. And when Jack wasn't patrolling the acreages of Blue Hills—rounding up sheep, seeding pasture, distributing feed, fencing—he would often drop in on the Neilsons for another purpose. He'd accept a cup of tea, have a bit of a yarn, then stake out a patch of grass with a pile of golf balls and steadily drive them down the hill into the backyard of Blue Hills; a goodly drive, even with the downward gradient, and worth at least a par-4 hole at Kingston Heath. The nineteen-year-old six-footer with the lazy, looping swing; how quickly that ball soared from view.

Gazing about the largely unchanged setting and sampling some of its abiding quietude, it was not difficult to recreate the scene and Jack's contentment in it. No longer was he the lad who scrubbed up for dinner at 6.30pm, no longer was he the shy and gawky boarding schoolboy. Here was a place to appreciate the simple physical sensations of threading together a fence, the muscle-tautening strain of shifting a hay bale, the sweet pang of striking a golf ball into space. Here even was the unfamiliar experience of affection—if from a callow boy—for his sporting prowess. And Neil Neilson's respect for his childhood hero was still evident in his voice as I spoke to him. He repeated the phrase 'a very good man' in such a way that it had obviously meant much to him that their paths had crossed. His admiration must have been keener still sixty-four years ago, when Jack troubled to carve him his own wooden golf club from the limb of a tree.

Neil never saw Jack again after the latter moved on from Baringhup East. But he flushed with pride when he read of Jack playing cricket for Australia fifteen years later, and kept that wooden golf club a good while, although, sorry, he didn't have it now. 'No, golf wasn't for me. Couldn't get the hang of it. But Jack, my word he could hit a ball.' And by this stage, I had some further evidence of that capability. On 8 June 1935, Jack Iverson teed off at Maldon Golf Club for the first time and recorded an 84 off the stick.

On the scores from the *Tarrengower Times*, Jack Iverson must have created quite a stir. He played off a handicap of fourteen, easily the lowest in a club that seems to have had its share of golf bandits: brothers Syd and Ed Rewell, for example, both played off thirty-two. As the club's leading official and chief benefactor, respectively, one suspects that these examiners were entitled to indulge themselves.

Jack played every Saturday in June, recording progressively lower scores as the club championship impended. This began with three consecutive Saturdays in July to determine a final eight on the basis of the contestants' best two rounds; Jack missed the first qualifying round, but recorded the best scores in the next two weekends to make the cut.

First play-off in August, Jack eliminated one A. Wilkinson seven-up. Next weekend, not part of the championship, he streeted the field with a 77 to shave two strokes off the course record set by club captain A. E. House. In the final two rounds of the championship, he then rolled title-holder S. Rowe five and four, and the previous year's runner-up H. Ware six and five. Reported the *Tarrengower Times* of the final duel:

> From the outset both players were on their toes and the first series of holes were well fought out, Iverson being two up at the ninth. After that, he steadily increased his lead and was five up at the twelfth and shortly after had the match in his keeping.

There were a few other golf scores—Jack's handicap having been reduced to ten—and the last fixture listed for him to be played on 21 September 1935 contained a match-up to stir the imagination: J. Iverson v S. Warne. Sadly, no scores were recorded.

Confirmation that Jack had lingered long enough in the Maldon area to leave a boy with a lasting memory and to win a long-forgotten golf trophy was of no great moment. But I savoured it. This indistinct figure had escaped official records and standard source works, slipped census takers and rate collectors, faded to a cipher citizen. But he had, nonetheless, through the medium of sport, left a tiny trace that said: 'I was here.'

SIX

About the mid-1930s, according to Alf Batchelder's entry on Iverson in the *Oxford Companion to Australian Cricket*, Jack's pastoral peregrinations took him to a property called Landscape, situated on the Goulburn River three kilometres east of Tallarook and just over eighty kilometres north of Melbourne along the old Sydney Highway. And of this period, there seemed a fair chance that some detail had been preserved, for the pastoral homestead had a most distinguished owner: Essington Lewis, one of Australia's few captains of industry worth the title.

In three decades at the Broken Hill Proprietary Company, South Australian Lewis had worked his way up from shift boss in a zinc plant to undisputed chief and presiding genius of the whole corporation, Australia's largest. Thick-set, snub-nosed, alert and restless, he had by the mid-1930s transformed BHP into a fully-integrated steel monopoly, by buying out its chief domestic rival, investing in collieries to fuel its coke batteries, and sponsoring downstream steel-oriented industries. He would go on in May 1940 to be perhaps the most powerful businessman in the nation's history as director-general of munitions, having industries employing as many as 150,000 people under his jurisdiction.

To his managers and engineers, Lewis was often a martinet, endlessly pedantic about cleanliness, waste and punctuality. He annotated working papers in lead pencil with one of three words—'yes,' 'no' or 'why?'—and had a mind harder to change than a $1000 note. Unfortunate victims of the Depression he divided into the poor and the deserving poor. The former were unworthy of sympathy, the latter to be encouraged only within reason: a pavement fruit seller that Lewis met near BHP's headquarters who needed £2 to stock his barrow was issued not a handout but a loan, complete with contract obliging him to fortnightly repayments. Yet Lewis himself disdained personal wealth and felt most at home among working men: in the words of his biographer, Geoffrey Blainey, 'they personified his own cult of action'. Touring a steelworks with him was often laborious; he seemed to know and have a line of banter for almost every man. In social situations, where he often felt self-conscious, he expressed his unease by mopping his brow with a grey workman's sweatrag.

A paradox of this arch-technocrat was his unaffected joy in the bush. Having aspired at one stage to a life on the land, he was boundlessly enthusiastic about silviculture, and in his lifetime probably oversaw the planting of more trees than any other Australian. In his biography of Lewis, *The Steelmaster*, Geoffrey Blainey offers this view of the industrial archetype at Landscape during the mid-1930s:

> From the windows and doorways of this large brick homestead he could see the swift, cold ripples of the Goulburn River, the narrow river flats that were so green in spring, and round hills rising steeply to south and north. When he was driven there at the end of a hard week in his President Studebaker Eight sedan, and the car came up the white gravel drive to the rambling house with its manicured lawns and flower beds and orchard, he began to relax...So many of his memories were seen through a rural frame, and he loved trees and was fond of animals and was less demanding of them than people; the landscape almost had the effect of a tranquilliser.

Did Jack Iverson work for this most remarkable Australian? Lewis's papers are lodged with the University of Melbourne Archives. At first glance, at least where the many boxes of Landscape ephemera were concerned, they appeared a frightful mess: from one folder, for instance, fell a note to Lewis from his son Robert ('Good soaking rain. 80 points since Thursday'), quotes on a truck, a dishwasher and table ironer, and a recipe for curry. Yet there were also minute books, ledgers, audit reports and cash books in meticulous order—some of which seemed to have lain unopened for sixty years—and finally on a cream page dated 2 February 1936 was the handwritten inscription 'J. B. Iverson 2/8/8': his first monthly wage. There were only a few more entries: four months later, perhaps for concision's sake, the book-keeper responsible for the property's accounts aggregated salaries for all staff. I felt again absurdly thrilled; had the accounts adopted the new treatment a quarter earlier, there might have been no trace of Jack to discover.

Even better news came presently, when I made contact with one of Lewis's daughters, Jane Nevile. Yes, she remembered Jack, and she and her sister Mary Munckton would be pleased to show me round Landscape and share their recollections. As we drove there, Jane passed me a stapled, typewritten document whose details I could not at first make out. 'I thought you might be interested in this,' she said. 'It's the station journal that we used to keep.' I flipped hesitantly to the back page and glanced at the signature. The hand was neat and legible: 'With compliments from John B. Iverson.'

By the time Lewis acquired Landscape on 5 October 1933, it had more than a century of history behind it. The first whites to traverse the area were the explorers Hume and Hovell; indeed, the pair had spent Christmas in 1824 there to allow Hume's mare to recover from snakebite. They were followed south from Sydney by the so-called 'overlanders', including the rangy and resolute frontiersman Joseph Hawdon who took up squatter's rights over the 11,118-hectare Tallarook Run and held them for twenty years.

The estate that Lewis eventually acquired had been built largely by two subsequent owners: Englishman Thomas Brooke, who planted what became its skyscraping bunyah pines, and James McCormack, who named the homestead Landscape because of the verandahs on all sides of his art nouveau residence. During Brooke's ownership, the region had been crisscrossed by bushrangers including Harry Power and a youthful Ned Kelly, who bailed up Seymour's Colonial Bank. During McCormack's, a cave overlooking the property was inhabited by a shaggy and bewhiskered itinerant known as 'The Wild Man of Tallarook' whose illicit whisky still brought so many folk from near that they were followed by police from far.

After his purchase, Lewis spent two years extensively refurbishing the 1512-hectare property, recruiting labourers from Whyalla to erect a mighty stone stable complex out of granite hewn from the surrounding hills, and expanding livestock numbers. A detailed audit for shire rates from the period enumerates Landscape's features as: thirteen acres of oats, fifty acres of lucerne, seventeen horses, eight dairy cows, eighty-one rams, 3181 ewes, 685 wethers and 383 lambs producing 29,000 bales of sheep's wool, 400 pounds of butter, thirty-five tons of oats, and fifty tons of lucerne. As Blainey put it, Lewis 'seems to have looked upon idle lands with the same uneasiness that he regarded idle people; he wanted to make them useful.'

In November 1935, a local work gang commenced the digging of a swimming pool with the assistance of two draught horses; their names, reflecting the era's sporting preoccupations, were Bradman and Larwood. Jack signed on just as excavations were ending on 3 January 1936, and a photograph from that day includes him at the extreme right holding a wheelbarrow; he is unmistakable for being, as so often in group photographs, half a head taller than anybody else.

It is unlikely that Lewis himself hired Jack. That task was usually delegated to one of his personal assistants, the interview often at Scotts Hotel, a historic hostelry at 444 Collins

Street favoured by country dwellers visiting Melbourne. Nonetheless, Lewis would have approved of Jack's career choice. He himself had left school to become a station hand at fifteen, and had recently withdrawn his eldest son Jim from Geelong Grammar in order to send him jackarooing for a year at Bon Bon in South Australia. His principal lamentation about the impact of the Depression, too, was that young men coming from school could so rarely find worthwhile positions.

Lewis was present at Landscape, moreover, even in absence; his insistence on rising early and working hard and systematically was always respectfully observed. Chores round the homestead began at 6am, when the frost on its paddocks crackled underfoot. A bell rang at 7.55am to signal five minutes to breakfast, and at 8am to signal its commencement. Porridge, kidneys, sausages and eggs sustained the staff of overseers, gardeners, yardmen, rabbiters and Jack the jackaroo for their extensive daily chores: clearing, planting, altering, erecting the incinerator, concreting the new garage floor, and fencing any one of the property's thirty-five paddocks. At the time Jack joined the staff, the surrounding countryside was also tinder-dry from summer, and his diary records several summonses to fight bushfires at neighbouring Habbies Howe and Sharpes.

Lewis's signature, his lateral mind and undeviating attention to detail, are discernible at Landscape even today. He once noticed while horseriding, for instance, that flies seldom settled as avidly on blue shirts as on those of white or khaki. Interiors of the milking shed, laundry and loose box were accordingly painted blue. One of his chief annoyances was being unable to lay his hand on a tool or implement at the moment he needed it. Thus a conspicuous feature of the stables, machinery shed and workshop are elaborate and sturdy shadow boards of green where silhouettes of the property's equipment have been stencilled in red. There they are in elegant and precise outline, often with a calligraphed explanatory legend: from pincers to curry combs, horseshoes to harrows, rivets to rags, saws, drill-bits and jars with contents ranging from nails and screws to turpentine and blowfly oil. Nothing, of course, is as it was when every Saturday morning was devoted to a cleaning bee under the owner's invigilation, but the shadow boards survive as a testament to Lewis's teeming technical mind. One almost feels the presence of a ghostly squadron of tools awaiting the return of this great apostle of work.

Even under a boss of Lewis's Stakhanovite zeal, however, there were opportunities for leisure. There was a cinema at Woodend, a Mechanics Institute and a pub at Tallarook. Seymour hosted an annual show every September, Tallarook an annual sports day every February: at the first Jack attended, he and station manager 'Boots' Taylor won the 'bending race' (a peculiar local derby in which participants manoeuvred a car round an obstacle course).

Landscape was involved in a local tri-cornered cricket competition against Trawool and Tallarook, which took place on Shed paddock, a sizeable block of land 300 metres from the Goulburn River. In Jack's first season, the homestead emerged triumphant despite being able to field only ten men. Lewis's daughters were both keen on filling in, but there was no question of permission: the men preferred relying on Jeff the sheepdog as a substitute fieldsman, despite the fact that he was often less than willing to surrender the ball after retrieving it. Lewis's son Robert also remembers spontaneous games organised against visitors, including a match that Landscape's team played against a road gang from Trawool on a paddock whose gradient was so steep that an uphill boundary was worth six and a downhill boundary worth two.

Jack's typewritten station journal chronicled daily events in microscopic detail. Having perhaps inherited some of his father's meticulousness, Jack the jackaroo even looked up from his work long enough on 17 November 1937 to watch Lewis fly overhead in his new Lockheed 12A called the 'Silver City'—the epithet of Broken Hill—on the inaugural non-stop flight from Melbourne to Newcastle. Jack documented the pilot, co-pilot, engineer and passengers, the flight time (two hours, forty-five minutes) and the flight path ('The above plane circled twice over Landscape in its flight').

So detailed is the diary, in fact, that it is tempting to turn its pages with another finger in *Wisden*, into whose pages Jack's name would be entered a dozen years later. The day that Australia retained the Ashes in March 1937, for instance, staff at Landscape were busy laying superphosphate at Habbies Howe and throwing out rye seed, while preparing to take Rosebud the dairy cow to Melbourne. As Stan McCabe made his legendary 232 at Trent Bridge against England in June 1938, Jack was helping to erect a gate on Camp Hill and making a 'cat feeder'. These two worlds, so distant, so distinct, yet Jack would eventually find a way to bridge them.

There was no upstairs–downstairs division between the Lewis family and their employees. Lewis himself loved to tinker in the blacksmith's shop. On one occasion, he was visited by the Apostolic Delegate who failed to recognise this vision of grimy toil as Australia's foremost industrialist. 'You work out here?' inquired the cleric.

'Yes,' Lewis replied drily, 'but they don't pay me much.'

For the most part, family and staff ate and amused themselves together, while Jack lived in a bare but comfortable room on the homestead's south-east corner that shared a bathroom with Robert Lewis. In the evenings, the children and the station hands repaired to the dining room where a partners table contained cards, tiddly-winks, a gramophone and knuckle bones for jacks. There was a pianola and a piano, which Jack could play by ear, and on which he picked out popular tunes like 'The Desert Song' and 'Lily of Laguna' (his father's favourite, as it happens). The girls were inclined to mischievous practical jokes, on one occasion stealing into Jack's room to secrete thorny bunyah fronds in his bed. Jack apparently took this in good part, contenting himself with acts of revenge on the family's jarrah ping pong table.

So there it was again: that table tennis ball in which Jack had delighted for ten years or more, still his constant companion, to the degree where it had almost effaced all other of Jane Nevile's recollections:

> My main memory of Jack is of him standing at the table in the dining room spinning this ping pong ball incessantly with the fingers of his right hand. I don't remember him actually propelling it, but he was always spinning it, like a set of worry beads. It was almost an obsession with him.

In actual games of ping pong and blow pong—a variant of the game where competitors crouch at each end of the table puffing for supremacy—Mary Munckton recalls the jackaroo as invincible:

I reckoned I was pretty good at ping pong, and later on I won a few trophies for it while travelling to England on ships. But Jack would spot me twenty points and still beat me, with monotonous regularity, and it used to make my blood boil.

It was a cloudless and sunny day without a breath of wind when I visited Landscape, the sort that I could imagine Jack cherishing even amid his daily toil. In a photograph that survives of him standing by the machinery shed, he looks fit, cheerful, relaxed; nothing like the quiet son of a real estate agent or the shy boarder he had been. There is a small lump in one of his jacket pockets; perhaps the ping pong ball waiting for the playful grasp of hands that Robert Lewis remembers being 'as big as tennis racquets'. Jack's sister Ruth remembers that he always spoke glowingly of the Lewis family's kindnesses, and believes that her brother was never happier than during his years at Landscape. 'He had a wonderful time, doing what he loved doing most, and his life with them was a very happy one.'

By the time Jack made his last diary entry on 3 September 1938, however, that happy time had almost expired. Whether at his own instigation or paternal behest, Jack left a week before Christmas, this time bound for the family home at Kuring-gai, and a different life altogether.

SEVEN

Three weeks after Christmas 1938 was Harry's fifty-fourth birthday. He had worked hard his entire life and was doubtless thinking dynastic thoughts. Although he'd had junior partners in H. W. Iverson, the business had remained essentially a family concern, and it was only natural that Harry anticipated his son following him in it. Whether Jack's future career was determined by negotiation or command, he entered the records of the Real Estate and Stock Institute as a licensed sub-agent for H. W. Iverson on 9 May 1939. Most in the industry at the time were thus classified: under the Real Estate Agents Act, a sub-agent could perform all the functions of a registered agent providing that they were 'lawfully authorised in writing' to do so.

By the time the licence was renewed on 1 January 1940,

however, circumstances had altered. Australia was again at war. Two divisions of Australian troops were bound for North Africa; another two would be established that year. Policy guidelines on enlistment were published in newspapers: the ideal recruit of the 2nd Australian Imperial Force was to be between twenty and thirty-five years, at least five feet six inches tall, A1 at a medical examination and not in a reserved occupation. Twenty-four-year-old, six-foot-two-inch Jack Iverson fulfilled all these criteria when he passed his medical at Caulfield RRD on 15 June 1940 and assumed the guise of VX23811. The only additional detail his enlistment form notes are distinguishing features—a burn scar at the base of his left index finger and another scar on his right thigh—perhaps legacies of his time on the land.

Jack was allocated to 2/2 Anti-Aircraft Regiment (Heavy)— a new unit then establishing its headquarters under Lt-Colonel E. M. Neylan at Puckapanyal Training Camp near Seymour— which divided into 4, 5 and 6 Battery, of which Jack joined the last. It was a curious juncture in what was still a European conflict. Price controls had been introduced but few commodities were rationed, and foodstuffs and petrol remained plentiful. Though the Australian Golf Open and Sheffield Shield were about to be suspended, takings at the 1940 Melbourne Cup would break records.

Hitler's conquest of Holland and Belgium and invasion of France the previous month had jolted Australian complacency, but the transition to a war economy was proving anything but seamless. Munitions were in short supply. When 2/2 commenced rather desultory training on the unit's weapon of choice, the 3.7-inch gun, it had to husband its ammunition carefully, and ensure against overtaxing the relatively few skilled trainers. Six Battery's first assignment was a month in the Melbourne suburb of Maribyrnong, ostensibly to provide air defence for the ordnance and explosives factory there, but it did not fire a live round until a practice shoot at Werribee at the end of September. There was ample time to enjoy the picture shows in the YMCA tent, concerts in the RSL tent, to thumb through the unit newspaper *Ack-Ack* and to anticipate the visit the regiment received from wrestler Big Chief Little Wolf.

Other, more formal, visitors reminded the new soldiers of their common purpose. Prime minister Robert Menzies reviewed the troops on 28 June and the governor-general did the same on 23 August. The unit diary proudly recorded the latter's response: 'He subsequently commented very favourably on the parade and was particularly impressed by the steadiness of the men.' And VX23811 seems to have been a typically steady man, becoming a 1st Class Driver on 25 September, and gaining promotion to Lance-Bombardier on 12 December.

In the ranks of 2/2, there were a few familiar faces; by coincidence, both his old friend Alan Meckiff and his school-boy contemporary Lindsay Hassett were members of the same unit. Both the countryside and the regimentation of the routine also reminded Jack of his years at Landscape; reveille at 0630 hours would have been no hardship for one who had risen half an hour earlier at the sound of Essington Lewis's bell. When he spent Christmas Day 1940 fighting bushfires round the camp, Jack would have found the sensations familiar indeed.

After a sea journey of five weeks on the *Mauretania*, 2/2 Anti-Aircraft Regiment (Heavy) arrived in Gaza on 17 March 1941. Camp was struck at Khassa, a huge tent city in Palestine already home to many other units. A rumour at once swept 2/2 that it was to be diverted to Greece. 'There were all sorts of threats about going there,' recalls Alan Meckiff. 'We had our gear packed ready to leave.' But, when the British commander-in-chief General Wavell designated 60,000 British, Australian and New Zealand troops to compose its defensive garrison on 5 April, the new arrivals were not among them. Over the next fifty-six days, as the Germans swept both Greece and Crete, the men of 2/2 would have considered themselves fortunate.

At the time, Wavell was stretched thin by a host of demands on his limited manpower: there was insurrection in Syria, a pro-German coup in Iraq, and an Italian army in Ethiopia to neutralise. Worst of all, German forces in the desert were now under the command of the adroit field-marshal Erwin Rommel. Even as Wavell was siphoning off troops to Greece, Rommel's Afrika Korps was sweeping more than 320 kilometres across the north coast of Cyrenaica as far as Bardia and Sollum in barely a fortnight. Then, however, Rommel was forced to halt, both by supply difficulties and by the thorn in his side posed by Australian soldiers from the 9th Division in the fortified enclave of Tobruk. The war in North Africa lapsed into an uneasy stalemate, the respective armies like exhausted boxers in need of a bucket and sponge. They would grapple with each other for almost a year without either achieving a decisive breakthrough.

It was, in all aspects, a most unusual theatre of war, the antagonists intermeshing for the most part like frictionless gears, only occasionally rubbing against each other to spin off a stream of sparks. Alan Moorehead, the gifted Australian war correspondent of the *Daily Express*, imagined it like sea warfare on land:

> Men moved by compass. No position was static. There were few if any forts to be held. Each truck or tank was as individual as a destroyer, and each squadron of tanks or guns made great sweeps across the desert as a battle-squadron at sea will vanish over the horizon. One did not occupy the desert any more than one occupied the sea...There were no trenches. There was no front line. We might patrol five hundred miles into Libya and call the country ours. The Italians might as easily have patrolled as far into the Egyptian desert without being seen. These patrols in terms of territory conquered meant nothing.

The way the desert enveloped both friend and foe made for protracted periods of idleness and, having come so far, 2/2 became part of that general inactivity. Khassa was almost as much conurbation as camp, its occupants almost as much settlers as soldiers. The main threat to their welfare became, not some abstracted enemy, evidence of which they seldom saw, but the desert itself. Gunners were unprepared for the enervating heat and fierce glare, reflected off the sand. Drivers and convoy managers, of whom Jack was one, contended with rutted and treacherous roads that snapped axles like matchsticks and sand that seemed to impregnate every pore. As Keith Douglas put it in his classic desert war memoir *Alamein to Zem-Zem*:

> On the main tracks, marked with crude replicas of a hat, a bottle, a boat, cut out of petrol tins, lorries appeared like

ships, plunging their bows into drifts of dust and rearing up suddenly over crests like waves. Their wheels were continually hidden in dust clouds; the ordinary sand being pulverised by so much traffic into a substance almost liquid, sticky to the touch, into which the feet of men walking sank to the knee. Every man had a white mask of dust in which, if he wore no goggles, his eyes showed like a clown's eyes...Trucks and their loads became a uniform dust colour before they had travelled twenty yards; even with a handkerchief tied like a cowboy's over nose and mouth, it was difficult to breathe.

Disease, too, exacted a steady toll; diarrhoea was rife, and no-one was spared the 'wog' sores that followed exposure to the air of cuts and burns. And, like scores of others in 2/2, Jack had a spell at 1 Australian Corps Rest Station recuperating from sandfly fever. He would have been careful henceforward to observe instructions for the application of the repellent Flysol: 1 ounce per 2000 cubic feet released in the tent twice a day, at dawn and dusk, and allowed fifteen minutes to settle.

Otherwise, Jack's time was occupied with guard duties and the camp's varieties of recreation. There was a cinema, a range of approved cafes and hotels, even donkey races. There were games of rugby and cricket—indeed, the regiment had an unusual number of good cricketers, including Australian players Hassett, Alec Hurwood and Ted White—although Jack seldom played and did not make the regimental team. It would have been an existence at once busy and tedious and, as inactivity is so frequently the enemy of military discipline, a flavour of camp life is detectable in the records of courts martial published in Lt-Colonel Neylan's daily orders detailing offences for which soldiers were disciplined: the private who, told to 'pick up the step', asked: 'What bloody step?'; the gunner who 'on being ordered to rise from his bed did continue lying therein'; the soldier who on being warned about grinning on parade replied: 'This is my night in the clink, put me under arrest' (in fact, he was fined £1).

Sporadic air activity occasionally enlivened affairs. The unit recorded its first kill on 10 June 1941, which was chalked up to 4 Battery at Ir Gannim near Haifa, and 5 Battery also subsequently had a busy time at Suez. But when 6 Battery finally embarked on its first posting on 28 July, it was to Beirut, actually one of the Middle East's quieter corners. The soldiers' digs were relatively commodious at the Caserne Joffre and Quartier Foch barracks on the Rue de Verdun in the west of the city, and the war had left the city virtually untouched. Gendarmes still directed traffic, cars observed a 15 miles per hour speed limit, and articulated trams threaded the main drag, the Place des Martyres. The town was a military melting pot: the Australian soldiers cohabiting with units of the Free French and British sailors from the destroyers *Hasty* and *Kingston* that swung at anchor in the harbour. But there was no sense of siege or, when the occasional air raid warning was heard, of panic. Shopkeepers methodically drew their shutters and joined the rest of the civilian population heading for shelters, only to emerge half an hour or so later when the siren proved a false alarm.

Six Battery accommodated one change, taking control of a bunch of 75mm anti-aircraft guns surrendered to the Australians as part of the armistice with French forces. They also spent inordinate amounts of time excavating elaborate gun emplacements, dugouts and command posts camouflaged with hessian and dummy trees. But they had little confidence in their new weapons, which dated from World War I, when finally they fired them more than three months after their arrival on 1 November 1941 at an unidentified aircraft flying overhead from west to east. The crews of 6 Battery loaded with impressive speed, after nearly eighteen months of training, but fired with unimpressive accuracy, the French weapons proving cumbrous and difficult to aim. Which was just as well for, after a score or so rounds, the scream was heard: 'Cease fire!' They had been firing on an RAF Hawker Hurricane.

The exercise was repeated the following day with another unidentified insurgent, this time probably a German aircraft, but out of range. The unit diary put the best face on it: 'The fifty-two rounds fired by the battery on the first two nights of the month have made the men keener than ever'. But Jack's first Christmas overseas would have been notable largely for snow: the first in Lebanon for twenty-two years and probably the first he had seen in his life.

By the beginning of 1942, the business of war had grown more earnest. Russia, the United States and Japan had entered hostilities. The strange and artificial stalemate persisted in North Africa, but the Afrika Korps had retaken Benghazi and further hemmed in Tobruk. In a rearrangement of AIF forces following the recall to Australia of the 6th and 7th Divisions, a new anti-aircraft unit was to be formed as part of 9th Division under the command of Lieut. Col. Paul Chalmers. This was the 2/4 Light Anti-Aircraft Regiment, composed of soldiers from the three pre-existing anti-aircraft units in the Middle East: 2/1, 2/2 and 2/3. Those designated began arriving at Beit Jirja in Palestine on 16 January. Jack Iverson and many colleagues from 6 Battery were among about four hundred troops taken on strength that day. He became part of 11 Battery, commanded by Captain John Bloomfield.

Jack seems to have fitted in well with his new mates. 'He was a nice fellow,' says Bert Davey, then a bombardier in 11 Battery. 'Happy, you could have a good laugh with him about things, and he told a good story.' But it was Captain Bloomfield who became the most significant figure in Jack Iverson's military life. A forty-year-old barrister from Armadale and an alumnus of 2/2's 6 Battery himself, he was an enthusiastic officer with an avuncular manner that led to his nickname of 'Uncle John', or 'UFJ' when his men became a little peevish. An unflagging monitor of morale, he distributed among his NCOs a dissertation on their duties comprising no fewer than fifty-one points, many of them accented towards 'spirit' and 'initiative'. Ken Noldt, who became troop clerk in 11 Battery, recalls:

> He was actually a rather wonderful man. Never meant to be a soldier, and not meant really to be an officer either, in the sense that he was never above the other ranks. He was always with us. I can still see him marching along, one gaiter in his trousers and one gaiter out. A few fellows detested him, of course, but I think underneath everyone respected him.

Bloomfield took an unusual interest in Jack, promoting him to bombardier, and recommending him upon return to Beit Jirja as supervisor of 2/4's MT School, which held courses on map reading, convoy administration and maintenance. Jack would eventually be responsible for all 11 Battery's transport fleet—thirty-seven vehicles, ranging from tractors to haul guns through lorries to move men—which was no mean achievement for one whose principal claim to driving fame was victory in the bending race at Tallarook six years earlier. Jack returned Bloomfield's regard and appreciated his confidence; it was the first time in his life that he had been entrusted with a responsible position. Other members of 11 Battery noted that Jack was unusually 'tight' with the CO, ascribing it to their both being private school boys: Jack from Geelong College, Bloomfield from Geelong Grammar. 'There were a lot of officers from public schools,' says Bill Carmody, an 11 Battery gunner. 'But not a lot of the enlisted men were, so that would have made Jack a bit unusual.' It would be stretching definitions to call it a friendship—officers and other ranks could never truly regard themselves as friends—but it was a mutual regard. Much later, in July 1953, when Bloomfield was endorsed Liberal candidate for the seat of Malvern, Jack helped in his campaign and ran his transport pool. When Bloomfield became Victorian minister for education between 1956 and 1962, the families exchanged Christmas cards.

In the Middle East, Bloomfield appreciated a reliable underling like VX23811. As did other battery commanders, he frequently had his hands full with disciplinary matters. When 2/4 finally gathered for exercises in the Syrian desert in the first week of June 1942, the results were dreadful. 'Discipline on the whole was poor,' noted the unit diary. 'Too much talking and swearing went on round the sites and a general tendency to lounge, even in the presence of officers, was noticeable.' Records of courts martial enumerate a vast range of offences, while the sentences convey some sense of the vagaries of military justice: for trafficking hashish, thirty-two days in the stockade; for pawning a military vehicle, sixty days; for selling a pair of boots, ninety days; for rather carelessly shooting an Arab child while on sentry duty, nothing at all.

Discipline, however, was now imperative. In July, at last, 2/4 was blooded as a fighting unit. With the unit briefly disaggregated to provide cover for field artillery trying unsuccessfully to dislodge German units on Tel El Eisa Ridge near the coastal town of Alamein, it fought a series of short but sharp engagements costing seven lives but in which it could claim ten enemy aircraft shot down. It was a promising baptism, and providential, for there was clearly far more fighting to come. When Churchill appointed new management for Allied forces in North Africa the following month—commander-in-chief General Alexander and his field commander General Montgomery—rumours circulated of a long-awaited 'big push' to evict the Germans from the region.

After a profusion of offensives and counter-offensives, the Allied and Axis armies were staring at each other across a defensive line drawn sixty or so kilometres from Alamein to the Qattara depression, a salt marsh lying below sea level. Something had to give. Throughout the lull in fighting in August and September, regimental orders became stricter and more hectoring. Thriftlessness about supplies, once condoned, was replaced by orders to conserve oil, re-use cooking fat, and collect jam tins. Even stationery was rationed: letters home had to use both sides of paper, single-spaced. Censorship was strictly enforced: of their activities in July, soldiers were limited to the statement 'I have been in battle'.

In the 'big push' codenamed 'Lightfoot'—which Montgomery foresaw 'hitting the Germans for six'—2/4's role was again to provide anti-aircraft cover for designated artillery units; in the case of 11 Battery to shepherd 2/12 and 2/7 Field Regiments from positions south of the main road and west of the Qattara Track. The logistics behind the assault were formidable. Much of the physical moving was to occur under cover of darkness, and driving by night in the desert could be hairy. Vehicles had to black out most of their lights in order to avoid attracting enemy attention and it was easy to stray from the barely marked paths that counted as roads. Once lost, drivers could have the devil's own job re-establishing contact with their comrades. Part of the MT School course that Jack led involved recourse under such circumstances to Cassiopeia: a chair-shaped group of stars on the opposite side of the Pole star to the Plough. When not swathed by clouds, the stars were a natural navigation beacon.

As 'Lightfoot' commenced at 9.40pm on 23 October across the full sixty kilometres of front, there was no trouble seeing anything. With the racket of 908 field guns and artillery pieces sounding across the sky like the crack of doom, the light was for fifteen minutes so brilliant that one could have read a newspaper in the forward positions. Darkness and an unearthly silence then followed in a five-minute pause, before a creeping barrage began, peppered with tracers, to protect and steer the advance of the Eighth Army infantry. Marching at a mandatory seventy-five yards per minute on either side of guide parties navigating the minefields, thousands of soldiers weighed down with kit, rations, shovels and sandbags dropped stakes every 100 yards with rearward facing torches that shone different coloured lights designating different units towards their own lines. 'You've never heard such a noise in all your life,' recalls Bert Davey. 'And you've never seen a fireworks display like it.'

For the next eight days, as they traced their artillery units forward, 2/4's batteries were kept busy by a succession of air raids. Eleven Battery even had the experience of being strafed by RAF Hurricanes, luckily without casualties. During the day, the glare was such that aircraft were often heard before they were seen. During the night, the flash from their guns would momentarily render targets invisible. Nonetheless, the guiding principle of anti-aircraft warfare was to keep firing, no matter what. Even if a battery could not score a hit, the intensity of their discharge should discourage accurate attack by forcing aircraft to disgorge their bombs too soon. And 2/4 kept up its rate of fire, loosing off 12,000 rounds before the first day without raids on 3 November, and suffering only two dead and ten wounded. As the sand settled on Alamein, it emerged that Montgomery's Eighth Army had put its enemies to flight, capturing 30,000 men including nine generals. The British commander's ebullient summary was read to 2/4, as it was to all units, on 12 November: 'When we began the Battle of Egypt on 23 October, I said that together we would hit the Germans and Italians for six right out of North Africa...Today, there are no German and Italian soldiers on Egyptian territory except prisoners.'

'God,' wrote one soldier, 'was good to the regiment.' It had seen its share of fighting, but suffered only eleven dead in a strength of almost 900, and was now leaving the desert behind. After leave and Christmas, a truck convoy from El Bureij camp in Palestine began a week-long journey across the Sinai desert to Port Tewfik for embarkation on the *Ile de France*, a 47,000-tonne French liner.

Jack returned to Melbourne in February 1943 enervated and underweight, and spent much of his leave with his family. Harry, Ede and his sisters had moved from palatial Kuring-gai eighteen months earlier after buying a similarly spacious two-storey residence called Moana about half a mile down the road at 148 The Esplanade. Jack moved into a bedroom there.

The war was now in full swing, and hard to escape from. Part of Jack's convalescent ritual was strolling over the road, often with a book, to laze on the beach; he had a favourite spot, a few metres from a flight of bluestone steps that led down to the sand.

One day, he returned from his daily beach sojourn and went upstairs to Moana's sunroom. 'Had a nice thing done to me today,' he told his assembled family. 'When I went down to my spot on the sand, someone had stuck a white feather there.' A self-righteous watcher had apparently mistaken Jack for a civilian layabout neglecting his duty. Jack's sister Ruth, who recalls the story, could not tell whether her brother was upset or merely reporting a fact: 'That was John. You never knew if he was really bothered about something.'

EIGHT

'War,' wrote the American jurist Oliver Wendell Holmes, 'is an organised bore.' His experience was of the American Civil War, but his observation held true eight decades later as Allied and Axis armies groped about in search of one another across the vastnesses of Africa and the Pacific. Indeed, only a sixth of Australian servicemen in World War II experienced active combat first-hand.

Nonetheless, whether they were exhilarated by fear or numbed by boredom, the lives of countless soldiers, sailors and airmen were irrevocably changed. Had he not been a brave RAAF pilot placing his life at risk, David Campbell might not have had the nerve and need to begin submitting his evocative lyric verse to Douglas Stewart at the *Bulletin* in 1942. Had they not been underemployed vassals in the peculiar bolthole of Alf

Conlon's Directorate of Research and Civil Affairs, Lieutenant James McAuley and Corporal Harold Stewart might never have arrived at the impish notion of inventing the poet 'Ern Malley' to puncture Max Harris's modernist bubble. Young official war artists like Albert Tucker and Ivor Hele were destined to become painters of great renown. Service experiences would inform the works of writers as varied as Robin Boyd, Ivan Southall, Jon Cleary, Russell Braddon, Paul Brickhill and Rohan Rivett. An underemployed RAF intelligence officer in the desert, Patrick White felt that 'detached from my past, real life, and with no clue of the future, I was temporarily a free being'.

For Jack Iverson, VX23811, the experience was also of temporary freedom. Had it not been for World War II, chances are he'd never have bowled a cricket ball in anger. Before his enlistment, his life and career had appeared predestined. Whatever his ambitions were, he sublimated them so effectively that nobody was aware of them. But war changed everything, and did so by being 'an organised bore'.

By the third week of April, 2/4 LAA Regiment had regathered at Kairi in Queensland's Atherton Tablelands, the 9th Division training area. Or, at least, most of it did. Twenty-one soldiers were absent without leave, compelling its new commanding officer, Lieut. Col. 'Bullet' Myers, to issue a stern directive: 'Attention is directed to the fact that the seriousness of the offence of absence without leave is not properly appreciated and that the commital of this offence has become very prevalent.' The prodigals eventually returned, though this did not stifle the constant cadging for leave. Two soldiers wrote slyly to their wives, for instance, soliciting letters saying that their children were ill, rather forgetful of the fact that all mail went via censors.

The unit would spend two months at Kairi. There was no clue to its next destination aside from the training regimen: a great deal of marching, which blistered feet softened by leave, experimentation with the loading of equipment and stores, and a mock amphibious landing at Trinity Beach at Cairns. For 11 Battery, there was the new discipline of becoming a so-called 'airborne battery', which involved endless stop-watched practices at Mareeba Airport shoving the components of their guns into fuselages of derelict DC2s and DC3s. But for Jack Iverson, the most significant aspect of his spell at Kairi was that for the first time in uniform he began playing cricket regularly.

Evidence for this is actually in Jack's own hand. A type-written screed survives on which, in seven columns, Jack enumerated his individual performances in every wartime match in which he participated. It is a remarkable document, as it could scarcely have been compiled retrospectively, and must be thought of as almost unique: few soldiers would have bothered to document their services sport in such detail.

Jack, of course, had long had this sedulous streak; much like his father, a trained accountant. His detailed station diary at Landscape testifies to an orderly and retentive mind and, if his few surviving colleagues have any recollection of Jack apart from being 'tall', it is of his meticulous and methodical manner and habit. 'Oh, yes, he was a meticulous man, Jack,' says Ken Noldt. 'Wouldn't have been running transport if he hadn't been.' Bill Carmody recalls one unusual faculty: 'When we played football, Jack would always be waiting at the end of the game to tell you how many kicks and marks you'd had. I suppose he must have kept statistics.'

Jack certainly kept them for cricket, and his documentary proof shows his interest dawning at Kairi. Up to his spell on the Atherton Tablelands, he had played only half a dozen intra-unit games spaced over three years. Despite the Kairi training schedule, he now played another half a dozen for 11 Battery, including four in a fortnight. The results would have pleased him, even if his three hat-tricks in consecutive games imply a rather poor standard of competition. If he managed to hit the ball with any success—and he did not score more than 21 at Kairi—he lovingly appended to his record the number of 'sixers' he struck.

In matches at Kairi, Jack seems merely to have been reproducing his schoolboy medium pace. Max Scott, a gunner in 12 Battery, recalls:

> My only real memory of Iverson is getting out to him. We were having a match to select a regimental team. I wasn't a regular cricketer, more of a footballer, but Iverson gave me a short one on leg stump. I thought: 'Hello. Here's one to clout.' What did I do? I hooked him straight to square leg.

Nonetheless, in Jack's statistical *vade mecum* is at last a hint of his future.

Jack's regiment was bound for Port Moresby, and began its staged embarkation by air from Mareeba Airport on 12 July 1943. Transport units shipped out from Townsville on the *Taroona* a month later. They were headed for another unusual theatre of war, as far removed from the parched sandscapes of North Africa as could be imagined.

New Guinea had assumed vital strategic significance within weeks of Pearl Harbor. Port Moresby, with its secure and protected Fairfax Harbour, was the ideal location from which to launch an invasion of Australia's vulnerable north, and the prospect of the Japanese flag fluttering over it had seemed for a time unpalatably real. The first bombs had fallen on the town on 3 February 1942 and, though the Battle of the Coral Sea on 15 May had turned back a planned seaborne invasion on the south coast, Japanese soldiers crossing the Owen Stanley Ranges from the north had come within twenty-five miles of the town by September.

Increasingly desperate fighting had averted the immediate threat, but the island remained unstable, 'the loose front step on Australia's porch'. Moresby assuredly looked like a town in the teeth of war, littered with bomb craters and with a civilian population a fraction the size of its prewar level of about 400 whites and 1000 natives. Even Fairfax Harbour testified to Japanese offensive force, featuring the devastated hulk of the old Burns Philp steamer *Macdhui* bombed to blazes in June 1942. The clouded Owen Stanleys that loomed to the north, meanwhile, betokened an interior of almost impenetrable mystery. So uncharted was the range at the commencement of the war that two American officers seeking the remains of a downed aircraft had discovered two entire mountains unmarked on maps: Mount Rennels and Mount Graves still bear their names.

Soldiers of 2/4 had to acclimatise swiftly to this alien landscape. Again, there were strict instructions to minimise the risk of myriad diseases: malaria, impetigo bullusa, tinea pedis. The kunai grass that grew as tall as a man hid the threat of scrub typhus inflicted by tiny red mites. As hand-to-hand combat with the enemy was finally in prospect, soldiers were instructed in some none-too-polite conversational Japanese: *susume* (advance), *shitsumoni kotaite kudasai* (answer my questions) and the essential *watashi wa nihongo ga wakarimasen* (I cannot understand Japanese). They even had to get used to a sight to which few Australians in 1943 would have been accustomed: black faces, on their valued native bearers. On 13 August, 'Bullet' Myers enjoined his soldiers to remember: 'The natives do not like to be called "George". The correct term is "boy".'

It was to be the busiest and most gruelling period of 2/4's war, and simultaneously the dullest of Jack's. A fortnight after Myers' imprecation, 10 and 12 Battery sailed with the 9th Division for two months of often torrid action around Lae and Finschhafen-Langemak. In particular, on 17–18 October, they helped see off an attempted Japanese landing at Scarlet Beach. Eleven Battery saw far less action, being peripherally involved in a 7th Division assault on Nadzab, and Jack little if any, having remained with two detachments in Moresby. Though he didn't know it, his war was virtually over. And, though he would scarcely have realised this either, his cricket career was dawning.

Life in the desert had often been harsh, but at least there had been the prospect of a little leave in the exotic surrounds of Alexandria, Cairo or Beirut. Moresby, by contrast, was pokey and isolated, a crumbling colonial outpost with a soporific tropical climate, few entertainments beyond a solitary cinema and mostly soldiers for company. Many Australian servicemen posted there loathed it, a gunner in another anti-aircraft unit turning his thoughts into verse:

> If you can live in Moresby
> Settle down with some old gin
> Then you can say, you're a better man
> Than I am, Gunga Din

Stationed at Pom Pom Park neighbouring the airfield, with its steel-plate airstrips, the members of 11 Battery left behind by their regiment took to the unlikeliest of amusements. Although he had no training or special interest in entomology, for instance, Ken Noldt chased and collected butterflies: 'They were huge there, and just beautiful. And otherwise there was very jolly little to do.'

Many soldiers when bored headed for Pom Pom Park's well-stocked YMCA tent, with its hampers of minor luxuries from the Australian Comforts Fund. Generations of soldiers had done much the same. Tents provided by the Young Men's Christian Association had been features of military life since the American Civil War, while emissaries of the Australian YMCA had travelled abroad with Australian servicemen as early as the Boer War and the Boxer Rebellion. There had been a YMCA dugout on Gallipoli, with a red YMCA triangle on its tarpaulin roof to discourage Turkish aircraft. There was now one at the Australian prisoner-of-war camp at Changi, its two volunteers having accepted voluntary incarceration and created the 'Changi University' where soldiers were distracted from their hardships by such initiatives as debating, drama and a music appreciation class.

About 150 YMCA personnel were now overseas, many in New Guinea, distributing sporting gear, stationery, toothpaste, chocolate, coffee and Christmas cards under their charter which was 'to organise and provide for the social and recreation facilities and the moral agencies' of the soldier. Some, indeed, were as brave as any soldier. Ron Bain produced the *Busu Beaut*, a daily news-sheet composed from radio bulletins, for his corps of engineers. George Trenholme created capacious Christmas stockings from mosquito nets for his machine gun battalion. Leslie Taylor ran a roving boxing school with the same verve as he gave to a Christian address. The 'YM bloke' never carried a rifle, but would sometimes carry one for a soldier who was evidently struggling, and they recognised the risks they were running. Taylor, for instance, would always take his turn as a sentry: 'I felt more comfortable when I was watching than when I was lying and listening, and if a Jap had sneaked up on us he would not have said "Oh, YMCA? So sorry" and passed on to drop his grenade on the next fellow.'

Jack had been a habitue of 2/4's YMCA tent in the Middle East, for one reason in particular. The unit's first shipment of sporting goods from the Australian Comforts Fund in January 1942 had included *inter alia* two dozen table tennis balls, and Jack had played the game incessantly with two others from 11 Battery HQ, Bombardier Bert Davey from South Australia and Gunner Max Mulligan from Western Australia. Jack's party piece, of course, was spinning it, so that it swerved round in the air and jinked round corners. 'God, he could spin it,' says Davey. 'There wasn't anything he couldn't do.'

It was the same at Pom Pom Park. A ball would appear from his pocket at any opportunity, and feature in a variety of amusements, including spontaneous games of French cricket. As Jack explained to the sports writer R. S. Whitington for an article published six years later in *Sporting Life*:

> The idea was to try and spin the ping pong ball to beat the bat—the 12-inch ruler—and hit the pole. I found that by flicking the ball (as one does with a marble) with the thumb across the index and second finger, I could send it up straight, but could not impart any spin.
>
> Then I got the idea of doubling the second finger of my hand back into the palm, placing the ping pong ball on the back of that finger and holding the ball in position with my thumb. With this grip I did not have to use my index, third or fourth fingers. My second finger became a lever or spring and by releasing that finger I found I could get an abnormal amount of spin.
>
> I also found that if I held my thumb horizontally to the left I could flick the ball far to the leg side of the tent pole and make it break terrifically towards the pole.
>
> Under the rules of our French cricket we weren't allowed to lift our elbow and bowl overarm, so I could not reverse the process and point the thumb to the right or leg side and deliver an off break or 'wrong 'un' as it is called.
>
> So I started flicking the leg spinner. I found that I could flick the ping pong ball about six feet in the air with this one. It would drop quickly and bounce two feet in front of where the batsman played for it. I got a lot of catches at silly mid on and silly point with this ball. Also, with this action, the ball would come in as an inswinger and when it pitched turn very sharply from the leg.

This gave me the idea of trying to bowl the same type of ball with a tennis ball overarm. The peculiar thing was, though, that when I flicked it underarm with a ping pong ball I got an inswinging leg break but when I bowled it overarm with a tennis ball it gave me a natural wrong 'un. It was a wrong 'un, too, bowled with the wrist over the ball which caused it to appear to the batsman as an ordinary leg break.

This last factor was actually not peculiar at all; a leg break underarm would naturally become an off spinner overarm. But as diversion from the tedium of being in the rear of a war now fast being won, it was a bewitching discovery.

Jack's other distraction was cricket itself, which he was now playing with the zeal of a convert. According to his own digest, he featured between December 1943 and December 1944 in fifty-three matches. It is now hard to guess at their quality. The regiment featured some handy cricketers—Bombardier Stan Semmens later turned out in sub-district ranks for Brunswick and Gunner Duncan McKenzie played after the war for North Melbourne—although Jack's scratchings in his personal *Wisden* suggest that the standard varied quite widely.

Jack represented 11 Battery, captained by Warrant Officer Steve Henderson from Melbourne. The majority of games were played at Pom Pom Park itself, whose ground was flattened earth largely encircled by kunai grass and on whose matting pitch he often appears to have been lethal: in four weeks alone, from mid-January to mid-February 1944, he picked up 52 wickets. In one game against the 7th Division at

Dumpu, he also notes a score of 52 with '7 sixers'.

Yet occasionally, just very occasionally, Jack's enthusiasms—the abiding one of spinning spheres, the recent one of cricket—began to intersect. Exactly why is not immediately clear. Jack himself left behind two explanations. One, contained in an interview he granted Bert Oldfield for the great keeper's 1953 textbook *The Rattle of the Stumps*, was laziness:

> I stuck at the fast bowling until the heat became enough 'to make your bloomin' eyebrows crawl', as Kipling poetically put it. And being an Aussie and not averse to a bit of 'bludging' if it came my way, I looked around for a more comfortable means of delivering the ball.
>
> It was then I made what proved to be a rather lucky decision. Remembering the odd ways I used to kill time by flicking oddities about, I tried the grip on the cricket ball in a match against an Artillery regiment. For that over, our wicketkeeper became a mere spectator. My first delivery was hit out of sight and the ball lost in the jungle grass. This cavalier treatment continued, and the fieldsmen had leather-hunting enough to last the innings. Tropical heat, perspiration and leg weariness prompted the captain to bellow: 'For Pete's sake, bowl the ball! We've enough runs to chase as it is!' This should have been the end of the experiment. But I still got too hot when fast bowling, and to cool off would revert to the two-finger exercise.

This is a delightful passage. Although Oldfield probably added a few of the more ornate flourishes, there is a tang of Jack in it, the snatch of Kipling perhaps a remnant of that Geelong College education. But the implication that Jack's 'lucky decision' was purely adventitious smacks of undue modesty. Jack had always loved spinning a ball. He had belatedly come to a pleasure in cricket. That they should have combined would, one must suspect, have been a more conscious decision.

As it happens, Jack had already let slip an alternative explanation, almost *entre nous*, in his aforementioned 1950 interview with Whitington. The writer narrated his own version of that very first delivery that was deposited in the kunai grass:

> His army team captain, Sergeant [sic] Steve Henderson, of Melbourne, became rather terse at the time. 'Stick to your fast-mediums,' he told Iverson. 'We'll have quite enough runs to get even then.'
>
> Iverson says: 'I suppose I have always been a bit of a rebel though and I used to send down one of the specials once in a while.'

The content of the two explanations is obviously quite different, and so, more subtly, is the voice. Talking to Oldfield, Jack sounds more ingenuous, even sympathetic with his long-suffering skipper thinking of the runs being surrendered. He describes his new-style deliveries as 'oddities'; no wonder, really, that the skipper was distrustful.

In his conversation with Whitington, by contrast, Iverson sets up a situation with slightly more feeling, and ascribes to Henderson a slightly crueller comment. His new toy is called the 'special', and his persistence with it in the face of his captain's sarcasm related with a childlike delight.

The accuracy of Jack's paraphrase is unimportant: Henderson probably made neither of the remarks attributed to him. The significant element is what registered in Jack's mind's ear, and how it altered. There is an obvious explanation for the variation. Oldfield dates his talk with Jack as 'some time after the 1950–1951 season'. By that time, he had scaled cricket's heights, starred in an Ashes series, and a certain sporting sardonicism probably seemed in order. The Whitington interview predates that same Ashes series, a time when Jack would still have felt protective of his 'special', and when Jack might also have sensed doubters of whom he made Henderson an epitome.

The comments to Whitington, therefore, seem to reflect more truly Jack's feelings at the time of his exploratory efforts. Only one aspect jars: Jack's description of himself as 'always a bit of a rebel'. A rebel? Jack? The real estate agent's son, the reserved boarding-school boy, the likeable young jackaroo, the methodical soldier? I paused over this stray remark when I read it the first time, and many times after. Jack could hardly be said to have struck anyone as 'a bit of a rebel' in his travels. Yet was it the way Jack perceived himself?

NINE

The only period of 1944 in which Jack was not playing cricket was a twelve-week spell from May to August, for the good reason that he was getting married while on leave. The arrangements for Jack's wedding were made mostly in his absence, and he needed to scurry. Most of 2/4 LAA Regiment sailed from Moresby to Brisbane on 25 May aboard the *Klipfontein*, and dispersed a week later from Kalinga Transit Camp. Jack could not leave on the *Ormiston* until his transport detachment had secured their vehicles and handed over their workshop. He did not make landfall in Townsville until 8 June, and arrived in Melbourne only a fortnight in advance of the 1 July ceremony at St John's Anglican Church, Toorak.

Jack had not hurried into marriage. He was just a few weeks short of his twenty-ninth birthday—three years older than the male median age for marriage—and had resisted well-meaning attempts in the past to find him possible life-partners. Jack's sister Ruth, for instance, had introduced him hopefully to a young and eligible friend of hers from Hampton, Julie Austin, and 'tried very hard to foster a romance', but without success. Julie married another man, Jeffrey Harris.

Once his mind was made up, however, he wasted little time: Dorothy Jean de Tracy, two years younger than Jack, was the one for him. They were introduced in February 1942 by a friend of his sister Joy, Amy Griffith, who met Jean while working in the dining hall at Melbourne's Myer Emporium; Amy as a hostess, Jean as a waitress. Amy remembers:

> Johnny was a very fine man, tall, very handsome. Rather quiet, not very boisterous, and I liked him a lot. As a matter of fact, I was rather keen on him myself, but we were great friends. Jean was very attractive, too, brown hair, blue eyes, always very helpful to everybody, liked to tell everyone what to do. [laughing] Including Johnny.

After a brief courtship, the couple quickly settled on marriage. And despite the sense of surprise, it was generally agreed a suitable match; Jack, reserved and thoughtful, needed a wife as outgoing and organised as Jean. She was, moreover, from a family fit to pass Harry Iverson's scrutiny; Jean's father William de Tracy was a civil engineer, who lived with his wife Alice in Culshaw Avenue in the well-to-do Melbourne suburb of Toorak. Jack and Jean cut an eye-catching couple when walking out together. On one occasion when they were promenading down Brighton's Church Street, two young women passing them paused to evaluate Jack's tall and well-proportioned figure. To her delight, Jean heard one of the women confide to the other: 'Gee, ain't he a lolly.'

Family lore has it that it was a struggle to find clothes to fit the groom. Jack had sweated about nine kilograms away in the tropics, and one could have fitted two fingers between his neck and the collar of his uniform. Jean, with rationing in force, had to make do with a blue wedding dress. Nonetheless, it was a pleasing ceremony in the handsome old bluestone church. Friends came from far and near: Amy, who had since herself married, came all the way from Townsville to admire her handiwork.

The matrimonial photograph published in the *Leader*'s 'Weddings of the Week' on 5 July is almost indistinguishable from the others on the page, and could be any one of thousands from World War II: slightly stiff-looking uniformed groom, beaming bride leaning into him, framed by a church archway, flanked by a bridal party. Jean's matron of honour was her sister Marjorie. Jack's best man, Gunner Peter Robinson, appears to have been a last-minute inclusion; his best friend Alan Meckiff was on duty with 2/2 AA Regiment at the time. Before embarking on a short honeymoon at the seaside resort of Sorrento, Jean, with the fastidiousness that was her hallmark, collected a piece of wedding cake and a half-bottle of champagne as keepsakes.

It was not long before the couple were parted once more. Less than three weeks after his wedding, Jack had to rejoin his unit at Wongabel in Queensland, while Jean went to live with her in-laws and continued her job as a typist in a city secretarial pool. For the newlyweds, it would have been a strain. They could write, but telephone time was restricted by order: 'Before any telephone conversation, each caller will make notes on subjects to which he will refer. Verbosity, circumlocution and chatter will be avoided.' Nonetheless, Jack was suitably uxorious. When Alan Meckiff told his friend he was about to go on leave, Jack asked that he deliver Jean the largest bouquet of red roses available. On another occasion, Ruth Iverson opened the door to find a sailor holding a bunch of flowers for Jean as an emissary for Jack. Jean, meanwhile, learned to recognise 2/4's shoulder patch and made a point of conversing with soldiers wearing it on the off-chance they might bear some news. The couple soon evolved pet names for one another: to Jean, Jack was usually Johnny; to Jack, Jean was variously Dot, Trace and Polly.

Jack must have felt listless during his last year in 2/4. The string of exercises and shoots had about them the sense of busy work. Nobody now expected another tour of duty, and the battery dances, film evenings and weekly newspaper *Sports & Digs* could hardly have absorbed all Jack's surplus time. Members of 11 Battery were especially irked when sent to dismantle a vacated camp at Ravenshoe so that the building materials could be recycled by the Dutch in the rebuilding of the East Indies. After a few days pulling nails from wood so that touchy wharfies would handle them, one member wrote: 'I don't feel I have gone through the war to become a labourer.'

Jack killed time with a two-week transport course, but otherwise would have pined for the day he could return to home and hearth. When finally he obtained leave again at the end of July 1945, he joined Jean on a holiday revisiting their honeymoon destination. The couple were relaxing on the balcony of the Sorrento Hotel on 15 August, gazing across Port Phillip Bay at the Melbourne skyline, when they heard the sounds of a gathering commotion—excited voices, car horns, lights—and sought an explanation. Didn't they know? The war was over. And in that case, so was the military career of Lance-Sergeant J. B. Iverson.

Jack 'marched in for discharge' from 2/4 LAA Regiment on 1 September 1945, six years to the day that Hitler had invaded Poland, and sixty-three months since his enlistment. Closing the various folders that documented his war service, and perusing the glimpses of Jack in uniform obtained from interviews, I still found it difficult to ascertain exactly what sort of war he had experienced.

Jack Iverson seldom spoke of his wartime experiences. The few anecdotes he related were humorous and self-deprecatory. He told of diving for cover during an air-raid into, of all places, a stack of land mines. He told of wanting to duck out to the horse races while on guard duty, probably in Beirut, and locking his one compliant prisoner in the guardhouse. In itself, this was not unusual. Even Lindsay Hassett, otherwise the blithest of cricket spirits, seldom indulged in war stories. According to biographer Jack McHarg: 'Losses of life in the smaller wars that followed World War II distressed him.' But the question of whether Jack suffered any residual trauma from the war was consequently very difficult to determine. His wartime letters home to his parents are no longer in existence, and in their place are mainly impressions and conjectures. Some of these, while offered in all sincerity, proved to be red herrings. During the preliminary stages of my research, for instance, four separate interviewees told me confidentially that

Jack had been court-martialled in the army, and had never got over the shame and sense of injustice. There is no evidence for this whatsoever. Indeed, Jack's war record proved quite spotless.

Of other questions, it was harder to be definitive. In her first letter to me, his sister Ruth commented: 'The war claimed him for six years—and on his return, he came home—and it took him many, many months to recover from experiences of what he had been through during those years of trauma.' Jean Iverson herself confided to her daughters when they were grown up that there were nights when their marital bed shook as Jack, in his sleep, apparently relived junctures of his service. The recollections were obviously trustworthy, but were they significant?

That war took physical toll of Jack should not really surprise. Soldiers returning from the enervating heat of the desert and tropics were often underweight. Jack, a tall man, would have appeared especially elongated in his roomier pre-war wardrobe. As for mental anguish, the evidence of its possible source is scarce. From what can be known of Jack's service through records, he cannot be said to have had a war in the teeth of conflict, and we must be wary of what the military historian Michael McKernan has described as the modern tendency 'to regard every elderly man now wearing an RSL badge as a war hero'. Not that Jack had a cushy or cloistered military service; no-one in the theatres in which he served could have had such a thing. But the demands on a transport sergeant in an anti-aircraft regiment and those on a combat infantryman are quite different. Indeed, in some senses, we might think of Jack having had a classical war in the context of the global, mechanised and long-distance business it was becoming.

The possibility still exists that Jack harboured quite vivid, perhaps even scarifying recollections of a few phases of his service, for even fleeting exposures to bombardment and air attack left their marks. After 2/4 LAA Regiment's exposure to both at Tel El Eisa and Alamein, it reported nineteen cases of what were described as 'anxiety neuroses', of whom fourteen were typed B-class (suitable for discharge). As the unit diary commented: 'If a man cracks up badly, he seldom becomes fit again for frontline service.' Nor need symptoms of psychological disturbance have shown up immediately, for delayed cases of mental problems related to service arose in numbers for many years after the cessation of hostilities. In a letter to a friend of November 1950, for instance, the novelist Miles Franklin described the family impact of such a case eloquently:

> I have no more strength and I have to live in a disorganised litter, no strength for writing. I got your letter in March but have not replied because I've been swamped. Had a sick nephew—war neurosis case—who kept me up night and day without sleep until he went to the repat hospital.

For many men the war did not stop neatly in 1945, but for one very good reason Jack does not seem to have been among them. In fact, his first life-changing decision as a civilian points us in quite the opposite direction. It was not the choice of a man oppressed by intolerable memories. Rather, it was the act of someone who was 'a bit of a rebel'.

TEN

Jack Iverson's life to the age of thirty was typical for a man of his time. Boarding school, the land, the armed forces; one might be referring to his pals Alan Meckiff or Jim Carstairs; one might be describing Essington Lewis's son Jim or even the Nobel Prize-winning novelist Patrick White. Grandson of immigrants, son of a self-made man and destined to follow in the family business; in 1945 such a reckoning would have applied to thousands beyond counting.

War changed that in general, and one other event in particular. The story, often retold, was first reported in Jack's 1950 interview with Whitington. According to the writer and, we must consequently believe, according to his subject, Jack all but abandoned thought of his idiosyncratic bowling experiments in New Guinea as he reassimilated into civilian life. But he then had a chance meeting on Jolimont Park, which neighbours the Melbourne Cricket Ground, while walking with his wife. There before them was a match involving cricketers from the Melbourne School for the Blind. As Whitington told the readers of *Sporting Life*:

> The courage and persevering determination of those blind players began a train of thought and resolve working in Iverson's mind. 'If those chaps with all their handicap can do as well as that, I'm going to give my bowling discovery a go,' muttered Jack, more to the nearest oak tree and the summer air than to his wife.
>
> 'And Johnny, if you take it up, I know you well enough to be certain you will finish in there,' said Jean Iverson, pointing to the adjoining MCG.

Whitington described the story of Iverson's epiphany as 'one of the sporting romances of the decade', and the following year included it in his book *Catch!* It has since been credulously reprinted countless times and—now that Jack, Jean and Whitington are dead—there is no real way today to ascertain its veracity. Nonetheless, as it is almost the fulcrum of the Iverson story, some aspects of it implore investigation.

We flatter ourselves that it is only in our generation that the disabled have been able to lead fulfilling lives, so it comes as a surprise to learn that blind cricket was played as long ago as 1945. In fact, it dates as far back as 1922, when employees of the Royal Victorian Institute for the Blind began to play amongst themselves. They were later joined by ex-servicemen who had lost their sight in World War I, and the first interstate blind game took place between Victoria and New South Wales in January 1928.

In 1945, blind cricket was re-establishing itself after the war. Many blind people had found employment during wartime labour shortages, in jobs like telephony for the PMG and with manufacturing companies including Petersville Sleigh and Kodak, and this had starved the competition of players. Now with the outbreak of peace, many past players were returning, as cricket is an ideal game for the sightless or visually impaired: a non-contact sport that nonetheless occurs at close quarters. Four teams played one another for supremacy: the RVIB, the Association for the Blind, the Braille Library and the Blind Institute Royals.

After beginning as an improvised game with the bowlers propelling a jam tin filled with pebbles that batsmen swung at the sound of, blind cricket had by 1945 also become sufficiently serious to merit specialised equipment. Charlie Bradley, a basketmaker at the institute who had been a fine athlete before being partially blinded while trying to undo his shoelace with a fork, began producing durable balls from cane and filled with bottle tops and lead. These would be soaked in water for twenty-four hours before a game, with the result that innings tended to favour the bowlers first, then tilt as the ball dried towards the batsmen. Dick Wyatt, a veteran of the immediate postwar era, told me that the games were often very competitive: 'After all, it was the only game we had.'

I spoke to Dick Wyatt for far longer than I really needed to. But why not? Writing about Jack had already tugged me many places I'd never dreamt of going. Dick was a genuine character. He explained how he'd taken up the game after losing his sight at twenty-one in a fox-hunting accident near Beechworth. 'When I had my sight, my game was tennis,' he said. 'But after I became blind, I didn't really want to know about that anymore.' In 1947, he met a girl scorer called Jean Hall at a blind cricket match. They married, are still, and have four children. Dick urged me to go down to watch a game: 'You might find a wife.'

So I did, to the RVIB in Kooyong that Saturday, where two games were in progress on a sloping strip of land the size of a hockey field. It was a strangely haunting spectacle. The batsmen stooped over their bats, stiff but vigilant. Most fielders stood within ten metres of the bat, close enough to make off with the batsman's wallet. It might have been a pastiche, had the participants not been so obviously earnest, or a mime, had they not been so noisy; because the players navigate by sound, the air was thick with cries, like the cawing of a flock of gulls. Bowler and wicketkeeper were especially vocal, involved in a kind of a catechism, calling each other's names, so that the bowler knew where to direct his underarm delivery. The pace was slow—as one can imagine, bowlers can lose direction and struggle to recover it—but not leisured: if concentration and patience are useful virtues for cricket, in the blind game they border on the indispensable.

Was this what Jack had seen? If so, I could understand why he was arrested by it. A newly married man just returned from five years in uniform would have counted himself fortunate, and the glimpse of others less so might have made the challenge of persevering with his 'bowling discovery' seem less quixotic. Repatriation literature after World War II stressed the virtues of self-reliance. As one 1945 army rehabilitation pamphlet put it: 'You have in your hands to shape for yourself in civilian life a career no less worthy than that which you leave now.' And, in his huge hands, Iverson had powers of prestidigitation he must have realised were beyond the ordinary.

The conversation around the ground was much like you would hear around any cricket club, a lot of good-humoured banter, leg-pulling and yarning. Several of the players had just returned from the inaugural Blind World Cup in Delhi, lamenting their semi-final defeat by Pakistan, but brimming with stories about the exotic east and its passion for cricket in any form. Being hemmed in by autograph hunters and offered money for their caps were not experiences to which any blind Australian cricketer had been accustomed.

Suddenly, the conversation turned to someone called 'The Freak'. My ears pricked; this, of course, was Jack's sobriquet. In fact, the man under discussion was the batsman, Garry Stinchcombe, a World Cup representative so aurally acute that he has been known to take outfield catches by hearing alone. I had to wait until he was dismissed before speaking to him— and, as I should have expected of 'The Freak', he made me wait a while—but finally I was able to introduce myself.

Garry did not lose his sight until the age of nine, and believes that the memory of vision has advantaged him in spatial understanding. He reads the play by listening to the side of the pitch down which the ball is travelling, and anticipating strokes. How did he feel about being called 'The Freak'? He smiled broadly: 'It's not the most politically correct nickname in disability circles.'

Not so long ago, Garry decided to give the game away. He has two children, eight and five, and a secondary school teaching certificate which he uses at the RVIB. He told the state association secretary Doug Sloan he probably wouldn't have time to play again:

> Doug said: 'Keep your locker key. You never know.' So I did and, at the start of the season, they called me up and said: 'Can you come down? We're a man short.' Well, of course, I've played in every game since, gone to New South Wales and Queensland, made the Australian team, been to New Delhi. I guess I'm hooked. It's a great game, isn't it?

I found it a poignant comment. Here was one 'Freak', a blind man, but who could not give up the game. Meanwhile, I was writing of another 'Freak', sighted, fit and talented, who slipped from the game all too easily.

One fact I learned from this interlude was enlightening. When I asked Dick and Jean Wyatt about playing at Jolimont Park, they were both adamant: blind cricket was never played there. At a pinch, they suggested that the odd, very infrequent social game might have been convened in the shadow of the MCG, but even then they considered it unlikely.

What did this mean? Perhaps Whitington simply got the place wrong; but then he would surely only have reproduced what Jack had told him. I could not overlook the possibility of journalistic invention and embellishment, for Whitington, as anyone who has relied on him as a source could tell you, had his flights of imaginative fancy; yet surely no-one would have confected such a fiction, neither Jack nor his Boswell. Perhaps it was a case of a rare, long-forgotten social game that the Wyatts conceded was a faint possibility; in which case, it was an amazing coincidence that Jack was in the area when such a sight was on show.

At once, this jot of detail seemed immensely consequent and terribly trivial. Important in the sense that it challenged the authenticity of Whitington's long-accepted reportage; unimportant in that it did not alter the fact that Jack believed in the story and its inspirational properties. And on reflection, the story's absolute veracity may be less important than what it tells us about Jack. By that which stirs a man we might judge him. The story Jack wove round those blind cricketers is, perhaps, a tiny aperture on the undiscoverable innermost man. Indeed, it was not the only occasion in Jack's life where he was moved by stoicism in the face of their disability. Jack's daughter, Sherry Holt, would later recall for me an episode in her father's career as an ABC broadcaster:

> I remember Dad telling me one day that this lady had brought her son in to the commentary box, and this little boy was blind but loved cricket and loved my father's voice on the radio. So she'd gotten permission to come in and introduce them, and Dad told me about how he'd run his fingers all over Dad's face and the console and the headphones. That really affected Dad. He thought it was amazing.

The story of Jack Iverson's chance meeting with a troupe of blind cricketers, precipitating the climacteric that made him a Test bowler, is one of cricket's loveliest. As they say, it 'should be true'. In concluding that faith was permissible, of course, I could not ignore my own sentimentality. I wanted to believe. But then again, I think, so did Jack.

From the very beginning, Jack's aspirations as a cricketer would be constrained by conditions. Much had changed in the Iverson household during his wartime absences. Jack's older sister Joy had married Horrie 'Hock' Wood, a liquor merchant, and borne their first child Janis in October 1944. Jack's younger sister Marjorie had married Bill Quintell, a sales representative for Remington-Rand, and borne their first child Robyn in July 1945. Only Harry, Ede and Ruth remained at Moana when, on his demobilisation, Jack joined Jean there.

In Jack's absence in the Army, too, his future as an estate agent had been mapped out. Had circumstances been even slightly different, Harry might not have been so keen for Jack to follow him as proprietor of H. W. Iverson. Had Harry Iverson still been in partnership with Frank Carolan, for instance, or had his brood contained another son, Jack may have been freer to choose his own career path. But the reality of the situation—and Jack's father believed in a stern reality—decreed the response. Like about three-quarters of Australian ex-servicemen, Jack resumed on becoming a civilian his pre-war employment.

Nobody in the family believes Jack had any real desire to follow his father into real estate. Their sense was and remains that he rather coveted returning to the land after the war, and that he accepted his ordained role out of filial piety; a point to which we shall return. But however Jack may have chafed within himself, he showed no instinct here to be 'a bit of a rebel'. In official records of the Real Estate and Stock Institute, he turns up recommencing as a licensed sub-agent at H. W. Iverson on 1 January 1947.

It was prosperous period for agents. Demand for housing

after the war far outstripped supply, leading a postwar boom in property prices and therefore commissions. Jack need only have glanced at the classified columns of his local newspaper, the *Brighton News*, to get a flavour of the keenness, even desperation, with which returned servicemen were seeking lodgings:

> Airman and English bride desperately in need of flat, furnished or unfurnished. Reply Parke's Newsagency.
>
> Returned soldier, wife and young baby urgently require unfurnished self-contained flat or house between Black Rock and Brighton.
>
> Wanted urgently, house, half-house or flat for discharged AIF officer, wife and child.
>
> 1000 cigarettes for information resulting in advertiser (returned serviceman) obtaining self-contained flat or house. Reply 'serviceman'.
>
> Wanted to buy: bricks, new or secondhand. Also cricket bat, college size, 23 Arranmore Avenue, Black Rock.

While often busy, however, real estate was actually not a bad career, nor was it one completely irreconcilable with sporting ambitions. The postwar market was a curious mix of the *laissez-faire*, in the sense that only money was required for a licence and there was no expectation of training, and red tape, in the form of extensive and formal regulations. Land sale controls required government gazetting for price, pegged at 1942 valuations, overseen by the Valuation Board in Queen Street. There were protected rents for ex-servicemen supervised by the Fair Rents Board. Commissions were as fixed as the speed of light by the Real Estate and Stock Institute at 2.5 per cent, with a sliding scale as a property increased in value, and there were a great many more private sales than auctions.

The RESI also had a twenty-five-point code of ethics, some requirements of which make quaint reading in a modern era where they are honoured more often in the breach. The agent was required, for instance, to offer a property 'solely on merit, without exaggeration, concealment, or any form of deception or misleading representation'. He was counselled against the overuse of signs 'as such practices tend to cheapen both property and agents in the estimation of the general public'. He was also firmly advised not to 'wilfully permit any property in his charge to be used for illegal or immoral purposes' and encouraged 'to avoid introducing to a neighbourhood characters of property or occupancy or any individuals whose presence will clearly be detrimental to property values'.

Such regulations protected both the public and the agents; no-one could move too fast in an environment of regulated procedures and fixed commissions, and the club-like atmosphere would continue many years yet. Indeed, it was said that any fool could make money in real estate and many fools did. Which for the time being was helpful to Jack. Jack was no fool, but had other things on his mind.

ELEVEN

The first was a child. Jack and Jean's first, Sherry, was born on 10 July 1946, at hospital in Armadale. Sherry was a bonny infant, Jack a devoted father from the first. In their first photograph together, which shows Jack bathing Sherry at the seaside across the road from Moana, he is a picture of doting gentleness.

After the child, next most important was Jack's brainchild. He would explain that, after his epiphany in the park with the blind cricketers, he rehearsed for tackling cricket by bowling a tennis ball at Jean in the garden at Moana. If this is the case, she must either have made a remarkable recovery from the strain of childbirth, or been an uncommonly devoted consort; one suspects the latter. He considered joining one of the local church competitions but decided—probably for no better reason than that its practices took place just a five-minute walk from The Esplanade—to try his luck at Brighton Cricket Club, a member of Melbourne's sub-district competition.

Jack's account and club records suggest that it was on Tuesday evening, 1 October 1946, at about 5pm, that he began that short stroll for the first time. It had been an overcast day, but the threat of rain had held off. The suburban reserve Brighton Beach Oval would have appeared invitingly picturesque with its rambling stand and 180-degree view of the bay.

Jack admitted later to a certain anxiety on that stroll; he was, after all, thirty-one years old, and had never voluntarily been a member of other than the most informal XI. He arrived early, something he'd done 'on purpose'. It may have been in his mind that, if things didn't work out, he might make good his escape before too many people were round. He was wearing his old grey bags and an ordinary shirt, too, even though he actually had a pair of flannels. Perhaps he didn't want to be thought too serious in case he embarrassed himself.

The first few cricketers were arriving for the twice-weekly practice, while club secretary Charles Berriman rolled the pitch. The owner of a local mixed business store, Berriman had been secretary for thirteen years and attended to everything from the club's accounts to the cleaning of the pavilion; the sort of yeoman servant on which every club depends. When Jack accosted him asking for a bowl, he replied: 'Certainly, feller, have a go by all means.' Berriman would have issued this proforma welcome to dozens of newcomers over the years, but never have seen anyone tackle their task like this one; rolling in off a run of arbitrary length, his massive fingers coiled round the ball as though for an outsized game of marbles.

Nobody could quite figure what the new arrival was doing with his fingers, but he was certainly accurate and even bowled a couple of reputable club batsmen out. As practice broke up with the sun setting over the bay, Berriman asked him to return on Thursday for selection night. There the committee picked him to play on the coming weekend in Brighton's third XI, which competed in the Victorian Junior Cricket Association (later the Victorian Turf Cricket Association), in a game against its most proximate rival Sandringham.

This team was only a year old, formed essentially to soak up surplus players, and played its home games on a rough track at the corner of St Kilda and Head streets. Nonetheless, there was considerable excitement at Moana; as Jack put it, 'a great to-do'. He squeezed into creams he hadn't worn for thirteen years and bowled a few more in the garden with a tennis ball just to make sure he had the knack. Jean dug out an old pair of sandshoes and ironed a fresh white shirt. He must have cut a distinctive figure, this quiet, craggy giant bursting his flannels at the seams, but his arrival at the bowling crease had the same effect as the appearance of a fox in a farmyard chicken run: the game was over in a few hours with Jack taking 15 wickets for 25 runs.

Sadly, no scorecard or real details of the game survive beyond this record: the grade seems to have been considered too inferior for newspaper coverage. But it's not difficult to imagine the scene; batsmen groping like those blind cricketers Jack had seen, the big man accepting the backpats and handshakes of colleagues whose names he could hardly have known, the disoriented Sandringham players packing their club kit and muttering that they'd never been ambushed by a bowler like this before.

Jack took 27 wickets at an average of 5.5 in three games for Brighton's third XI: a forceful case for promotion. Club lore has it that he was actually considered first for an incremental elevation to its second XI, but that its earnest, teetotal skipper Bill Easton felt an obligation to his own two spinners and wouldn't hear of their replacement. If so, it was a costly piece of selection table loyalty, for Jack would scarcely look back.

Sub-district cricket is self-explanatory: it was and is a subsidiary competition of Melbourne's district game, set up in 1908. In the summer of 1946–47, it was only just getting back on its feet after a long and taxing war in which 800 of its players had enlisted. As its president E. Glen Roberts—an octogenarian who had played cricket for Kew as far back as 1884—commented in its annual report: 'Many of these gallant lads have paid the supreme sacrifice, many still languish as prisoners in enemy hands—we remember them all.'

Brighton was more fortunate than most in the competition: it owned its home ground, which it leased in winter to the State Savings Bank for a princely £2 2s for use by senior and reserves football. It had furthermore a proud history, stretching back more than a century. Among its alumni were six Test cricketers, two of whom had captained Australia: Jack Blackham, the peerless wicketkeeper; Harry Trott, the postman turned Test all-rounder. Between the wars, its star had been Lisle Nagel, a medium-pace bowler of subtle variation with a lofty air to match his 198 centimetres whom Sir Jack Hobbs had classed among the best of his kind.

Brighton had not, however, won a premiership since the

halcyon days of Lisle Nagel and his twin brother Vern, and had recently sought to hire a player-coach from outside. Thirty-three-year-old all-rounder Dudley Fitzmaurice from South Melbourne had played four times for Victoria with a top score of 102; part of a generation of Victorian cricketers unlucky to coincide with a period of uncommon state strength, when its first-string team had regularly been composed entirely of present or future Test cricketers. At an annual fee of £50, he was a cheap acquisition, a repository of great experience and the owner into the bargain of an excellent baritone voice. And though he wouldn't have known it, Fitzmaurice was also now captain of the world's most extraordinary slow bowler.

Fitzmaurice's chief recommendation to his new spinner was practice; Jack should do a minimum ten hours a week, against a wall if he could not find batsmen to act as guinea pigs. Fitzmaurice also preached the value of fitness, of the sort favoured in those days; Jack should run three laps at the end of each net session. Brimful of a novitiate's enthusiasm, Jack complied, and became an insatiable net bowler, always first at the ground on weeknights toiling in a vacant net until someone put the pads on. Indeed, after the diffidence of his initial approach, Jack was suddenly bordering on the impatient. Former teammate Col Shipley recalls that, on Jack's debut for Brighton's first XI against Elsternwick, he prowled round the field awaiting his turn at crease, and finally remarked: 'What does a fella have to do to get a bowl round here?' When eventually Fitzmaurice called him into the attack, Jack took two wickets in his first over and finished with 4–25 as the opposition crumbled to 114 all out and a 110-run defeat.

Jack was right to be impatient. He was improving at each outing: the statistical progression of 4–56 against Yarraville, 4–55 against Brunswick and 5–47 against Preston culminated in a deadly dozen overs at Kew in which he finished with 9–33. So quickly was he done against Kew, indeed, that his feat made the stop press of the weekly *Sporting Globe* and earned a short citation in the pages of the local *Sandringham News* for 8 February 1947:

> Kew lost their opener run-out for 4, but the next partnership was beginning to look dangerous until Iverson got it on the spot and committed a sustained effort of devastating bowling. No batsman was comfortable against him and he claimed victim after victim with well-concealed spinners.

Well-concealed they were for, as Jack revealed much later, his quiver at that stage contained but a single arrow: a top spinner flicked straight down the pitch by his middle finger, like a man disposing of a cigarette, the spin imparted coinciding with the line of flight from wicket to wicket. And though his figures of 38 wickets at 11.1 for 1946–47 were the best in the competition, Jack was still a figure of some obscurity even in sub-district ranks: the Sub-District Cricket Association's annual report ascribed his 9–33, the best bag of the season, to 'R. Iverson (Brighton)'. It was clear that he was unorthodox, but few understood his gift or its origins, and not even Jack himself foresaw his future trajectory.

It was in the winter of 1947, Jack would explain, that he 'took the bit between the teeth'. He wanted to bowl a 'break', that is, to make the ball deviate off the pitch from its direct flight. The toppie's haste onto the bat had been sufficient to discompose sub-district batsman at first encounter but—even on the basis of his limited experience—Jack realised that such a method risked losing its novelty. He found that by changing the position of his arm so that the thumb was turned to the right-hand side, or the leg side for a right-hander, the delivery that squirted out spun clockwise, both viciously and naturally.

What Jack had conceived was a delivery so unusual that it was not even clear what to call it. In effect, as it spun from the off, it was an off spinner; in cause, as it appeared like a wrist spinner, one might also have classified it a googly or wrong 'un. But even if you resolved what to call it, there was still the matter of playing it, and as Brighton reconvened for pre-season training in September 1947 few could resist long: it not only turned a long way but, from Jack's height and at his standard velocity of just below medium pace, often kicked armpit-high. Word got round. Even before Brighton took the field that season, the *Brighton News* sensed that something was up; in brief pen-pictures of the local team it published on 2 October, Jack was described thus: 'He is an unorthodox bowler. He bowls spinners and has an extra good length. But he also has a wrong 'un which is very hard to pick.'

For 'very hard', read next to impossible. Jack had a little trouble landing the new delivery before Christmas. Some days, he was even comparatively expensive, and when batsmen occasionally had a successful slog there was a curious sense that Jack didn't quite know what to do. In such situations, Col

Shipley recalls, Fitzmaurice was a sympathetic leader: 'The only time Jack wasn't a really good bowler was when someone got after him, hit him round. Dud would always take him off and whip someone else on for a few overs then bring Jack back later.'

His pre-Christmas record, nonetheless, was excellent; twenty-seven wickets at 12.3 placed him second in the bowling averages behind Fitzmaurice with his pawky swingers. And when everything about this exotic new bowler clicked, any batsman who survived long could expect sore legs from the repeated pummelling of his pads, and keeper Lex Tileman could anticipate a frightful day of scuttling blindly to leg as the ball jagged back. Tileman, a former fast bowler, was an infallibly cheerful character, but he was no Blackham, and dreaded Jack's wrong 'un. 'You guys should leave me out,' he would constantly moan. 'I'm the dead weight in the side.'

No-one took him seriously; there was a premiership on the horizon. Brighton soared to the top of the table just before the season's halfway mark when Jack claimed 8–56 including a hat-trick against Caulfield then 7–32 against Ivanhoe. And in the New Year, his dominance was almost absurd. Against Footscray he claimed 11–80. Against Yarraville he was introduced earlier than usual when opening bowler Ken Brinkman's boot split and, despite being slogged for 19 in one over, reduced them from 0–28 to all out 113 with a bag of 9–47. Fitzmaurice had some other handy players at his disposal—left-hander John Cooper had a touch of class, Ken Whyte was an honest all-rounder—but you'd hardly have known it. As the *Brighton News* commented of Jack on 26 January 1948: 'His recent efforts have convinced old timers that he is the classiest bowler Brighton has ever had, not excepting the Nagels.'

A home game against Williamstown loomed as critical. The team from Melbourne's western suburbs contained a number of accomplished batsmen, including their rough diamond skipper and former Test all-rounder Maurie Sievers. Sievers even indulged in a little psychological warfare in the preceding week, telling the *Southern Cross* that he was confident of getting Iverson's measure. An unheard-of crowd of more than a thousand gathered, including a number of local politicians: Brighton's mayor and town clerk plus Brigadier Ray Tovell, a former Rat of Tobruk and now a member of Victoria's Legislative Assembly.

Jack may also have sensed the growing expectation. For once, he was not keen to bowl, turning up complaining of flu and expressing doubts about his ability to land them. Fitzmaurice indulged his spinner but, when the visitors marched to 0–86, had no choice but to deploy him. And whatever his condition, Jack showed no sign of handicap when entrusted with the ball: in 9.4 overs, he claimed 7–22, including Sievers for six. 'Williamstown were reputedly a strong batting side,' reported the *Brighton News*, 'but they were made to look like novices against Iverson's inspired bowling.'

Having waited so long, it seemed that Jack could scarcely get enough cricket. He was early to every practice and the last to surrender his ball as dusk closed in, boundless in his energy for the game. The week after the Williamstown showdown, he even volunteered to stand with teammate Charlie Stevens as an umpire in a series of country week games for juniors at Brighton Beach Reserve. On one occasion when a young leg spinner hit the pads, Jack himself appealed, then gave his adjudication: 'How's that? Out!' He gave a gusty laugh as the batsman trooped off.

Jack's success was also being savoured at Moana. Upstairs every Monday morning, in the sunroom she shared with Harry, Jack's mother Ede would be found with that day's newspapers spread before her, meticulously cutting out and trimming items concerning with her son, which she pasted in a thick 180-page Conquest scrapbook. There was never any want for material. In the local press, Jack had become as big a cricket star as anyone could recall, and on par with Brighton's other sporting idols: the cyclist Jack Hoobin, hurdler Ray Weinberg, swimmers John Marshall and Judy Joy Davies, all then striving for selection in Australia's Olympic Games team for London later that year. The *Southern Cross* summed up Jack's allure on 20 February 1948 with a picture and article beneath the headline 'Brighton's Wonder Bowler'. It began:

> One spring evening in 1946, a tall, solid stranger walked over to cricket nets where Brighton sub-district players were practising and asked for a bowl. He was given one. A month later he took four for 25 for the first XI. At the end of the season he topped the competition averages.
>
> Thirty-three-year-old [sic] Jack Iverson, standing six feet three inches and weighing fourteen stone, is unaffected by his sudden spectacular success. His dominant cricket emotion seems to be a supreme confidence that Brighton will win this year's premiership.

It proved well placed. Port Melbourne prepared the slowest and deadest of pitches when they hosted Brighton in the semi-final, and their experienced left-handed captain Ian Lee, a former Sheffield Shield player, ground out a sterling 107. But Jack bowled 23 consecutive eight-ball overs to claw in 5–103, and John Cooper's 138 the following week guaranteed their team a berth in the final.

That first flag in twenty-two years now seemed Brighton's for the asking. Cooper's wife gave birth to twins on the morning of the final, played over Easter, again at Port Melbourne oval, but there was no question about his availability. There was equally no question that Iverson shaped the match with his huge hands: he claimed 6–61 and 4–47 in Brighton's eight-wicket victory, taking his seasonal harvest to 79 wickets at a cost of 10 runs each. It would have seemed to Jack the most important match he had played, but he'd already played one more significant without even noticing.

Almost four months earlier, Brighton had played a friendly at the Albert Ground with its sister club in district ranks, the Melbourne Cricket Club; an annual fixture played when the latter had a bye. On a slow pitch, Melbourne's young opener Colin McDonald had scored a poised century. But the big, tall bloke playing for Brighton caught the district players' attention by bowling...well, what exactly was he bowling? Melbourne's captain Harcourt Dowsley was at the non-striker's end when Jack began his spell, and watched as partner Jack Green struggled through a very testing over in which he was beaten several times:

> Jack and I were batting pretty well when this bloke came on, straight away hit the spot and bowled a *very* good maiden. He [Jack] came down the pitch at the end of the

over and said: 'Better watch this bloke.' I laughed: 'I can see that!'

He was tall, looked six foot three or something like that, and he just hit the spot again and again. Jack and I were both pretty good players, aggressive, we drove and pulled, and we could both cut well. But we just couldn't get down at this fellow, couldn't get him away at all. He just seemed incapable of bowling a bad delivery...I know it sounds extraordinary. But he was landing everything on a threepenny bit.

Jack Iverson took only 2–62, but the *Southern Cross* commented that he 'did not appear to have the best of luck' and the Melbourne players agreed. Green and Dowsley both talked to him at the end of play, wondered whether he might be interested in joining district ranks; Green was ex-Brighton himself, as were a number of his colleagues. Jack was circumspect, doubtless flattered by the approach, but saying no more than that he would think about it.

There were others on Jack's trail, too. Just after Christmas, Richmond's captain Jack Ledward had visited Brighton to watch this new phenomenon in action. He was also impressed, popping in on his old cobber Fitzmaurice to test the water. 'Fair go, Jack,' Fitzmaurice replied. 'He's going to win us a premiership. Come back at the end of the season and ask again.' Ledward complied.

On 2 April 1948, the phone rang at Moana for Jack. It was Vernon Ransford, secretary of the Melbourne Cricket Club, before World War I a dashing left-handed batsman and electric outfielder. A personable and softly-spoken man, he congratulated Jack on his performances that summer, then popped the question: might he be interested in coming to play at the prestigious Melbourne Club? Jack must have sorted his attitude out before the call, for he agreed on the spot. Ransford sat down that day at the club's 314 Collins Street head office— the Colonial Mutual Life Building—and dictated a letter of invitation on the club's handsome notepaper:

> Dear Sir,
> Following upon our telephone conversation today, we are pleased to extend to you an invitation to play cricket with this club.
> Heartiest congratulations on your performances at Brighton, and look forward to meeting you personally next season.
> Yours faithfully
> V. S. Ransford

The day of its arrival, Jack briefly replied:

> Dear Sir,
> I thank you for your letter of 2nd April and accept with pleasure the invitation to play cricket with your Club next season.
> Yours faithfully
> J. B. Iverson

Jack had an end-of-season function at Brighton Beach Reserve a week later, where film was screened of the 1947 Victorian Football Association Grand Final between Port Melbourne and Sandringham; presumably he told his Brighton colleagues there of his decision. Far from being displeased, the clubmen were delighted to see their star bowler following the route previously taken by Jack Blackham, the brothers Trott and Nagel. The club's annual report sent him on his way with good cheer: 'He is a truly great bowler and all club members wish him well in the coming season with Melbourne.'

The very next day, by coincidence, a letter arrived at Moana from the secretary of Richmond, P. H. Maybury, issuing Jack 'a cordial invitation' to join that club. It contained the added inducement of a season's ticket admitting the holder to all Victorian Football League games played at Punt Road, Richmond Football Club's home ground, in the winter of 1948. But Jack Ledward was too late; the bowler sent a reply that day explaining regretfully that he had already accepted Melbourne's offer. A model of probity, Jack even sent back the football tickets. On 20 April 1948, Jack became a father for a second time, when Jean gave birth to their second daughter, Beverley. Family, business, sport; at the time, satisfaction for Jack in all must have felt attainable.

TWELVE

Tackling district cricket at the age of thirty-three was a sizeable step for Jack Iverson. The competition was flush with good cricketers, many experienced players having spun their careers out because of seasons denied them by the war. Melbourne Cricket Club, the most prestigious in town, was enjoying a period of unusual depth. Including Iverson, no fewer than nine of its first-choice team at the time had played or would play for Victoria: captain Dowsley, his predecessor George Meikle, batsmen Green and Barry Stevens, opening bowlers Clive Fairbairn and Jack Daniel, brothers Col and Ian McDonald. The two Brighton newcomers, Iverson and Cooper, might not even have felt themselves sure of a game.

Eventually, both made the cut for the first game, which marked also the baptism in the competition of Footscray.

Neither had much to do. The first week at the Albert Ground, as so often in Melbourne, was washed away by rain. The second, Fairbairn took 6–27 to rout the new team for 67, and openers Col McDonald and Mac Holten knocked off the runs without loss. Jack, though, did steal in for a handful of overs and nabbed two tailenders, both stumped by Ian McDonald, for 17.

Nobody in the press picked up on this unusual new talent immediately. Indeed, for his first few weeks, Jack was only left a few crumbs by Fairbairn and Daniel, which he picked up with quiet efficiency. But batsmen even in those fleeting excursions were left wondering; what exactly *was* this tall fellow doing with the ball? On Melbourne Cup Day in November 1948, Melbourne met Prahran, who were augmented by their Test all-rounder Sam Loxton, just returned from taking a prominent role on Australia's triumphant unbeaten tour of England under Donald Bradman's captaincy. Loxton recalls:

> We'd literally just gotten off the ship in Port Melbourne, but Prahran were playing at the Albert Ground. And this fella Iverson was bowling. A few scores had been floating across the ocean, and there were signs he might be a bit of a force, but no-one really knew what the heck he was bowling. Anyway, he floats the first one down from what looks like a leg spinner's action so—I couldn't read it in the air like Braddles—I play forward. But, by crikey, it pitches, whips back and bangs into my pads. I thought: 'Dear, oh dear, what have we got here? This fella can bowl a bit.'

Jack took his first five-wicket haul for Melbourne that day, 5–27, and earned an approving nod from the *Age*'s discerning cricket correspondent Percy Beames: 'Iverson again impressed with his well-controlled googlies.' The following match, Jack impressed on Richmond what it had missed by harvesting 6–79. This time it was the *Argus*'s turn to comment: 'The feature of the match...was the bowling of young slow bowler Jack Iverson who transferred from Brighton this year.' Young? Jack might have enjoyed that.

In fact, Jack appears to have enjoyed it all, being simultaneously pleased and abashed by these small attentions. The week after his fine spell against Richmond, he was interviewed seriously for the first time by a newspaper journalist, Bruce Andrew of the weekly *Sporting Globe*. The article, which appeared on 20 November 1948 under the heading '33-Years-Old Bowling Freak', related for the first time in print how Jack had taken up cricket 'to prove a theory developed with a table tennis ball in a tent in New Guinea during the war'. Andrew's testimonial dwelt on the extraordinariness of Jack's rise, rather exaggerating how little cricket he'd played, and lavishly lauded the newcomer's general approach:

> He left school in 1933 and never touched a cricket ball for 12 years, including five and a half years with the 9th Division at Alamein and New Guinea.
>
> But it's a different story today. He has tasted success and there is no keener player in the game. Also in his favour is the fact that he has no mistaken ideas about his cricket and can be told. This fellow may cause many upsets, if encouraged.

The article caused a great sensation at Moana. Jack was so chuffed that he did something now unheard of: he wrote to the journalist to thank him:

Hope you enjoyed your holiday as much as I appreciated your article of 20 November. My wife and parents seem to have taken a new lease of life since then and are now definitely 'cricket-minded'…Your literary effort and the many offers of practical assistance have given me just what I wanted—the overcoming of that fear that a man is too old to tackle district cricket at 33…Thanks again for what you have done and I hope to see you again at one of our future matches.

Saturdays at Moana had definitely taken on a new aura. They were Jack's days, and even important family events needed reshaping to fit in. On Saturday, 11 December 1948, the Iversons gathered to celebrate Ruth's wedding to Gordon Rinder. Jack wore a suit to the 11am service, popped into the reception at Moana like a good brother, then tugged on his whites and zipped out for the Albert Ground where he claimed 7–78 against St Kilda like a good cricketer. For he was a good cricketer. Just a very unusual one.

Bruce Andrew's reference to Jack's absence of 'mistaken ideas' and that he could 'be told' would have drawn some wry smiles at Melbourne. The fact was, they knew, that Jack often *had* to 'be told'. Among the keen recreational weekend players at Brighton, Jack had fitted in well. To the tough, experienced and close-knit band of real cricketers at Melbourne, he was a distinctly unusual addition. Dowsley's team ate cricket and drank it, talked and thought it. Jack played it.

Nobody blamed him for this. All knew how late he'd come to the game, how little he'd played while growing up. No-one could be other than amazed at his technique and his talent. But his abilities were peculiarly linear. He was a negligible batsman; indeed, he did not own a bat until the club gave him a well-worn Edgar Mayne Specially Selected. He was a liability in the field: Jack Daniel nicknamed him the 'Boundary Rider', because he ran like he'd just dismounted a horse. Even when bowling, he generally went his own sweet way, expressing no interest in field placements. 'Give me a silly mid on, a silly point and a keeper,' he would say. 'You can do what you like with the rest.'

Jack was fortunate in his skipper. Dowsley, a twenty-nine-year-old alumnus of Melbourne Grammar School, was not the archetypal craggy pro then leading many other clubs. The manager of a Flinders Lane indenting firm, he had played football for Melbourne and Carlton as a centre half-back, then spent the war piloting Catalina flying boats round Morotai, Borneo and the Philippines. A thoughtful, sensitive and intelligent man, he took a deep and affectionate interest in his new bowler:

> I liked Jack very much. The other fellows regarded him as a bit of a freak, and he wasn't one of the boys. But I was a bit closer in age to him than most of the other players in the team and I got to know him more. In fact, I made it my business to know him. I found him highly intelligent, well-read, an interesting and interested man, but very shy, and very naive about team sport, especially at first. The rest of us, of course, had been round dressing-rooms since we were kids. Although he didn't have much of an idea about fields, that didn't really cause us problems, because he was such a good bowler. I told him: 'This leg trap I want to set for you.

You're just going to have to trust me with this.' I showed him where he should bowl and, I tell you, he jolly well bowled it there.

The only aspect of Jack's behaviour that Dowsley found puzzling was the bowler's apparent lack of faith in his own ability. Despite enjoying virtually unbroken success, Dowsley recalls, Jack always seemed loath to throw in his lot with cricket completely:

> Jack was always talking about giving up cricket. He'd say: 'You can leave me out next week. I'm sick of it and I've got plenty of other things to do.' Then he'd change his mind during the week and say he wanted to play. But that was fine, really. It was just Jack.

Dowsley discovered in due course, in fact, that Jack's ambivalence was not confined to cricket. When they played golf together, Dowsley noticed that it didn't take much to vex his partner:

> Jack was a very good golfer, played off six and was a member of Kingston Heath while I was a member at Victoria. But just as Jack lost confidence playing cricket easily, he lost confidence playing golf easily, too. If he hit a couple of shots badly, he'd start talking about how he wasn't much good, and how he was going to give golf up. I wouldn't pay any attention, of course, because he was just as likely to get a birdie on the next hole and forget all about what he'd said.

After Christmas 1948, Dowsley actually decided to test how serious Jack was in his equivocations. He retells the story with much fond humour:

We always used to have a dinner after practice of a Thursday night, just to get the team together and talk about who we were playing this weekend. And this night Jack says to me as usual that he was going to give it up. So I thought I'd try and needle him a bit. I said: 'That's all right Jack. I think we're going to concentrate a bit more on some of the more experienced players round the club, like Clive Fairbairn and Jack Daniel.' And, you know, he actually got bloody annoyed. You could see it. I was chuckling away to myself because by now I realised he never had any intention of giving it away. It was just his way of giving himself some cover. It came to Saturday, and he just couldn't wait to get the ball in his hand.

Melbourne needed Jack to be razor-keen that Saturday, for the game was against Collingwood at its home ground Victoria Park. Collingwood's spiky skipper Keith Stackpole snr leered sadistically as he won the toss: the pitch was flat, the day warm and clear, and Collingwood's XI contained seven state players. 'You can bat, Harc,' said Stackpole triumphantly. 'Next fucking week.'

In fact, Melbourne batted that day. Collingwood had marched to 2–70 at a run-a-minute when Dowsley threw Jack the ball. Bowling with a stiff breeze behind him, the spinner dismissed seven batsmen for six runs—four clean bowled, two stumped, one caught—including a spell of 6–1. Collingwood crumbled for 94.

Even after this affirmation, Jack remained prone to expressions of sudden disenchantment. Just three weeks after his big day out at Victoria Park, he went wicketless for the first time against North Melbourne and, conceding 56 from 11 overs, was even a touch expensive. Clive Fairbairn remembers the scene:

In the showers after the game, Jack started saying: 'I've told you blokes all along I can't bowl. That proves it. I'm not playing again.'

My mate Jack Daniel, he hears this and he gets into Jack: 'Aw c'mon. Fairy and I get it every week. You're as weak as buggery.'

In the coming week, Fairbairn took the precaution of visiting Jack at Moana to make sure he kept going. Over a cup of tea and a sandwich in the garden, he persuaded Jack he was worth his place in the side. Jack needed nine overs to break through against University the next Saturday, but it was the first of five wickets in 44 deliveries. In the last home-and-away round of the season, Jack then bowled tirelessly on a plumb MCG batting pitch to secure 5–105 against the powerful Carlton, including his 50th district wicket. And by now, if his own teammates could not convince Jack of his value, there was a growing group of pundits amplifying their praise.

Victoria was having a satisfactory Sheffield Shield season throughout 1948–49 with a bowling attack featuring four current internationals—spinners Ian Johnson and Doug Ring, pacemen Bill Johnston and Sam Loxton—but it seemed to some that a bowler of Jack Iverson's meritorious record compelled recognition. Three days after Jack's conquest of Collingwood, Percy Millard of the *Herald* wondered in print: 'What must a bowler do to get into the Victorian Sheffield Shield side?' He urged Jack's inclusion in the forthcoming Kippax–Oldfield Testimonial match at the Sydney Cricket Ground. To one line of argument against Jack's promotion—

his age—Millard pointed out that Clarrie Grimmett of magical memory had not commenced his Test career until he was thirty-three.

Jack was not picked, but invocation of the Grimmett precedent immediately became popular among other boosters, like Kevin Hogan of the *Sun*: 'Although Iverson is thirty-five [sic] and has not yet had a full season of senior cricket, his consistent success must embarrass selectors who remember that Clarrie Grimmett was older when at the height of his fame.' An anonymous letter to the editor in the same newspaper supporting Hogan was signed simply: 'Remember Grimmett (North Fitzroy)'.

Jack then received his warmest accolade yet, from someone who had not even seen him play. Keith Miller, Australian cricket's foremost all-rounder, and with Bradman's retirement its most vivid personality, devoted his widely-read column in Sydney's *Sunday Sun* to Jack's 'meteoric' rise. Quoting 'Melbourne sources', Miller wrote:

> Well-known cricketers at the MCG have told me that Iverson is one 'out of the box'.
>
> 'It's ridiculous to class him as an O'Reilly yet,' declared one former Test star.
>
> 'But I think he is the best spinner playing in Australian cricket today.'

Miller also had recourse to the Grimmett example: 'Australian cricket sorely lacks a class spinner. If age is the barrier to selection, I find that most of our class spinners of the past have not reached their peak until their thirties.'

Sterner critics withheld their approbation until, they said, Jack was able to turn his tricks in more pressured environments against better opposition. The checkpoint of the district cricket finals, into which Melbourne had only scraped, now loomed.

Having passed so many tests already, Jack was not about to fail these. Melbourne's batsmen could come up with only 107 to defend against Carlton on 12 March 1949, but its bowlers whittled their rivals away for seven runs fewer (Jack 3–29). Chasing 209 on the third day, Carlton capitulated again for 127 (Jack, despite complaining of flu, 6–27).

The final then pitted Melbourne against competition favourites South Melbourne, certainly the best batting line-up against which Jack had bowled, and including by a quirk of recruiting rules a trio of old Geelong Collegians: Jeff Hallebone and John Chambers, both destined for Sheffield Shield cricket, and Australia's newly appointed captain, Lindsay Hassett himself.

How piquant this must have felt to Jack—the prospect of a duel with the idol of his former school, and the celebrity member of his first wartime unit—and how testing. For Hassett was probably the finest player of spin in Australia at that time, his footwork nimbler than a skilful waiter weaving between tables in a Paris cafe. Hassett had even driven his great friend and rival Bill O'Reilly to distraction, on one occasion nine years earlier achieving an exquisitely symmetrical double of 122 in each innings against New South Wales.

As it happened, Hassett was destined to make the same score again—122—against Melbourne. But it spanned five hours, as Jack declined to offer him anything of driveable length. The best that Hassett could manage was to absorb himself as much of this wonder bowler as possible, a tactic that kept him grooved on 20 for more than half an hour, saw him dropped at the wicket when 64, and cost him many singles. Hassett's South

Melbourne teammate Ian Johnson remembered:

> Only Lindsay could have played a hand like that one. He was the best player of spin bowling most of us had ever seen; good footwork, beautiful soft hands. The rest of us, we couldn't make much of Jake, and Lindsay could see that, so he made sure that we spent most of our time down the other end.

When Hassett was joined by fast bowler Barry Scott at the fall of the seventh wicket almost an hour before the close of the first day, the game contracted like a huge theatre stage where only two characters are spotlit. Jack bowled, Hassett defended, or tried to secrete a two or pilfer a four. Scott did not face the spinner until almost two hours of the second day had passed, just after Hassett had finally fallen to Fairbairn, and succumbed at once, stumped, swinging wildly. Jack delivered 270 deliveries in the innings, and grudged only 59 runs for his five wickets.

For the second consecutive season of his brief and belated cricket life, Jack Iverson was in on a premiership. Melbourne began the last day at 4–40 seeking 185, with South Melbourne so confident of its destiny that it had arranged a celebratory function for the evening, but got there thanks to 96 from nineteen-year-old Wesley Collegian Barry Stevens. Jack was there at the end, an unbeaten nine, when stumps were drawn with Melbourne 70 runs ahead and already celebrating its first flag since 1936–37. And Hassett's considered opinion, offered to Hec de Lacy of the *Sporting Globe*, would have brought Jack special satisfaction: 'He's very good—very good indeed. There's not the slightest doubt that he has something out of the ordinary.'

Jack's 64 wickets at 12 in Melbourne's premiership had amply repaid the club's intuition. It had also made him famous. The story of the origins of Jack's unique finger flick in a tent in New Guinea imbued him with a special magic. Jack retold the story in interviews with Roly Barlee on radio station 3UZ's 'Spotlight on Sport' and with Harry Hopman for his 'Sports Talk' column in the *Herald*, and it was made the subject of an 'Australian Sporting Diary' on the overseas network Radio Australia by Keith Bennie. Percy Millard, continuing his *Herald* campaign, presciently classified Jack a Test star in the making and 'a threat to England in the 1950–51 Tests in Australia'.

It seems curious now that a figure like Jack Iverson could have achieved such notice from the apparent obscurity of the rank-and-file of Melbourne district cricket. Talent worthy today of the bouquet 'best spin bowler in Australia' would not drowse at a level of the game now considered too mean to merit proper newspaper coverage. But while it had long been eclipsed by various football codes as a vehicle of inter-suburban rivalry, club cricket was still a significant proving ground fifty years ago. The district final of 1948–49 drew more than 10,000 spectators, and was umpired by two Test officials in Roy Wright and Andy Barlow.

The next level of cricket in Australia—the Sheffield Shield—was of greater prestige still. Enlarged in 1947–48 to include a fifth state, Western Australia, it had in 1948–49 drawn almost 300,000 paying customers and daily crowds approaching 5000; not quite the level of its halcyon days in the 1930s, when grounds filled at word that Bradman was batting and emptied upon his dismissal, but the most buoyant since the war.

One of the salient differences from today, of course, was that international cricket had not become a commonplace attraction. Discounting the years lost to war, there had been Test matches in Australia in only three of ten preceding summers, and there would be none again in the forthcoming 1949–50 season; a team led by Lindsay Hassett was to embark on 21 September 1949 for what was only Australia's second full tour of South Africa, and from which it would not return until the following April. Nor was there any call to make Test match cricket more frequent; on the contrary, there were some critics who felt it should be less, in order to keep the sun shining over club and first-class competitions.

So there was every reason for the whispers of Jack's talent to spread, such that his reputation now preceded him. And he had some noteworthy boosters. On 9 October 1949, Johnnie Moyes lent his voice to the chorus in favour of Jack's claims for interstate selection in the *Sydney Sun*: unnamed 'competent judges in Melbourne' had told Moyes that Jack was 'the finest spin bowler discovered since Bill O'Reilly'.

This was a significant endorsement; Moyes was Australia's best-known cricket critic and an intimate of the newly-knighted national chairman of selectors Sir Donald Bradman. In fact, as Moyes revealed later in his *Australian Bowlers*, those 'competent judges', MCC secretary Vernon Ransford and former Test superluminary Bill Ponsford, went even further than his article had suggested:

> 'This chap should be in South Africa with Hassett's team', they told me. I pointed out that Iverson had not yet been

chosen for Victoria, and that the Australian selectors could scarcely select him for an Australian side until they had seen him in action in first-class cricket. But I came away convinced Iverson could bowl. Neither Ransford nor Ponsford was likely to make a mistake, for they were superb batsmen, and Ponsford has not been excelled by any Australian as a player of spin bowling.

The 'competent judges' were about to get their way. Jack started the 1949–50 district season as he had finished 1948–49, with 5–20 in 13 overs to rout Footscray at the Western Oval, and when Victoria's selectors convened a fortnight later to pick their thirty-one-member Sheffield Shield practice squad no-one doubted that the name Iverson would be on the list. On the eve of final deliberations about the make-up of the state side travelling west to play Western Australia and South Australia, Jack underscored his name with 5–25 in the grand final rematch against South Melbourne. As Jack cleared his mail at The Esplanade on 15 November, he would have found an official letter signed by Victorian Cricket Association secretary Harry Brereton beginning: 'I have pleasure to inform you that you have been selected to represent Victoria.'

THIRTEEN

If there had been a 'great to do' at The Esplanade about Jack's selection for the Brighton 3rd XI in 1946, one can imagine the commotion that followed his selection for the state; Jean ironing her husband's creams while the children played about her, Jack checking that his luggage did not exceed the specified 35 pounds, Ede crouched over the daily newspapers scissoring out items of interest for what had now become Jack's second fat scrapbook, Harry looking on indulgently and perhaps offering a congratulatory handshake. There was the event of a visit to Melbourne's ritzy Mutual Store, where a Mr Bell fitted Jack for his blazer, cap and pullover, and finally the team's assembly at 10.30am on Wednesday, 23 November 1949, at the Australian National Airways depot in Flinders Street. Jack took it all in keenly; he preserved his £50

Melbourne–Perth–Adelaide–Melbourne air ticket on the DC–4 Skymaster, and the honorary member's tickets he was issued at both the WACA Ground and Adelaide Oval.

Perth still enjoys the status of the most isolated capital city on earth, and fifty years ago it felt especially remote, a slow-moving and parochial outpost a fifth the size of Melbourne and with a third more daily sunshine. Rodney Beven's wry verse concerning Australian capital cities, 'Observation Sociologique', concluded: 'It's hardly worth/Mentioning Perth.' Paradoxically, it was a town where the biggest employer was the Swan Brewery and the most influential political lobby the temperance movement. Indeed, when an association executive tried to obtain a licence to operate public bars at the WACA Ground that season, he touched off weeks of outraged public meetings and critical correspondence in local newspapers. Nor was a beer the only thing you couldn't find at the WACA in those days; it did not even have a scoreboard, the original having been flattened in a gale in August 1948 and not replaced.

Word of one eastern phenomenon, however, had reached Perth: Jack Iverson. Knots of onlookers followed the Victorian Sheffield Shield team from its lodgings at the Criterion Hotel when they travelled to practice, and a crowd of 200 followed Jack round the net area studying his wiles. The throng made the front page of Perth's *Daily News*, with a picture of Jack, ball wedged into his mighty fingers, captioned: 'Victorian spin bowler Jack Iverson can see nothing freakish about this peculiar grip.' It described him, *faute de mieux*, as a purveyor of 'knuckle spin'.

The match began on 25 November at a sedate pace.

Victoria's captain Doug Ring won the toss and elected to bat. But medium pacer Charlie Puckett and leg spinner Morgan Herbert, fresh from success against Queensland, made good headway through the visiting ranks, being detained only by the Hawthorn-East Melbourne all-rounder Dave Kerr (79) and South Melbourne right-hander Roy Howard (72). The home batsmen, too, made an auspicious start, reaching 2–91 at lunch on the second day. Jack began his first-class bowling career with a silly mid off and short leg and gave up only 15 runs in his first seven overs, but failed to penetrate. Otherwise, he wandered round fine leg and mid on, lost beneath a big white felt hat, wondering perhaps if he was up to this next graduation in his career. When Jack relieved medium pacer John Baird to begin his second spell in the afternoon, his moment finally arrived. Ring had Lester Charlesworth caught at slip by Keith Stackpole snr to expose the Westralian middle order, and Jack did not look back.

His baptismal first-class wicket was both notable and rather odd. Wally Driver, a burly left-hander who had come west from Richmond, was a fearsome striker of the ball, news of whose arrival at the crease often emptied Perth pubs. A representative baseballer, he had held for four years a world record for the fungo hit (where a batter tosses the ball up and slugs it): 503 feet and 2 inches, far outsoaring the previous record by Big Ed Welsh of the White Sox of 447 feet. Driver arrived to his usual salutation of loyal roars from the record crowd of 10,525, and got off the mark with a cover-driven boundary. But Jack promptly zipped one away and, as Driver toppled forward, his Melbourne teammate Ian McDonald executed a snappy stumping.

The odd thing was that keeper and fielders appealed first for a catch at the wicket, which was rejected, then to square leg for the stumping, which was upheld: 'A Reverse for Driver' as the *Daily News* headline put it. Just as oddly, Jack didn't join either appeal. Photographs of the dismissal show him at the bowler's end flat-footed and inanimate throughout; cricketers were less demonstrative souls half a century ago, but perhaps the wicket was as much relief as triumph.

If so, he need not have worried. Twenty-two-year Fred Buttsworth was next, coming out to drive but poking the ball tamely to silly mid on. When the stubborn little right-hander Basil Rigg was uprooted by Ring, Jack had Herbert stumped far from home, trapped keeper Gwilym Kessey lbw and bowled Puckett. Best wicket of all was the neat and poised left-hander Alan Edwards, who had wrested 67 in two hours, caught by McDonald from a vertical slog as he hit out in the company of the tail. Jack's figures made arresting reading: 6–47 from 146 deliveries—the eighth-best by a Victorian bowler on debut—including 6–22 in his final 58. Skipper Ring let Jack lead the Victorians from the field and, as the visitors commenced their second innings with a lead of 105, no fewer than ten telegrams arrived for him in their dressing-room, including messages from his former Brighton comrades Col Shipley and Roy Kershaw, his current Melbourne teammates Harc Dowsley and Jack Green, his parents and Jean: 'Good work Johnny Very happy Keep it up Love Polly and Kids.'

Jack could not keep it up, quite. When Western Australia set off on the final morning in pursuit of the unlikely victory target of 351 in 330 minutes with eight second-innings wickets in hand, he was suddenly far less effective. In a vivid Perth heat and on a pitch getting slower, he suffered an unusual ration of punishment. Twenty-four-year-old right-hander Ron Frankish made a resolute four-hour 104, Driver used his fungo wrists to good effect in an even-time 80, while Herbert hit 46 in an hour. Jack conceded 136 from his 42 overs, including 80 in his last 16, for only two wickets.

There were mitigations. The mercury peaked at 97 degrees Fahrenheit during the day. Jack dropped Herbert off his own bowling when the tailender was one, then endured the galling sight of Howard dropping him on the boundary and the ball rebounding for six. All told, too, Victoria's eventual 22-run victory in a match of 1108 runs before an unprecedented aggregate crowd of almost 20,000 had been a splendid advertisement for Shield cricket in this recent colony of the competition, one that Ring told the *West Australian* was 'the best...I have played in.' For Jack, nonetheless, the paucity of his second-innings reward was in stark contrast to his first-innings triumph. In the dressing-room afterwards, he seemed dejected, sitting with his head bowed for a long time.

It was a strange sight, a bowler who had claimed eight wickets on his first-class debut, apparently depressed by a few brief passages of play where the tide of affairs had been against him. That, after all, was cricket. But it was not the only unusual glimpse his new state teammates would have of their new star bowler.

The Victorians left Perth that evening for Adelaide, arriving at dawn. In the Shield match against South Australia, Jack got any residual blues out of his system with a happy tailend slog, making 31 not out, then produced a virtuoso spell, claiming 7–77 from 25 overs despite conceding 25 in his last four overs. Observers were stunned by the fields Ring set for him, a quintet of catchers within ten metres of the bat, and by the fact that Jack's control meant that they were seldom threatened. Hec de Lacy wondered in the *Sporting Globe*: 'Is there another slow bowler anywhere today whose perfect length and control would allow so many fieldsmen to crowd batsmen in such confident fashion?' ABC broadcaster Victor Richardson went even further, classifying the spell as the best slow bowling he'd seen since the war: 'He's good; so good, indeed, that I'm wondering how good he can become.'

Curiously, however, Jack tended to disappear out of playing hours. Most of the Victorian players, as was the habit, pooled their match allowances in favour of a communal feed at the Oriental Hotel. Jack did not, apparently wandering off in search of a roadside or railway station cafe that served pies and peas. Indeed, this habit became so well-known that his teammates eventually dubbed him 'the Spies and Speas Man'. Jack also went wicketless in the second innings in conditions that some felt should have suited him, although this was simpler to understand; this trip was the newcomer's first taste of four-day cricket and the heat he experienced in both Perth and Adelaide would have taxed a camel.

In more familiar conditions against Queensland when the Victorians returned home, Jack's gifts became truly manifest; he claimed 9–74 from 41 overs as the hosts just failed to prosecute an outright victory. The only batsman to achieve anything like permanence at the crease was the former Australian opener Bill Brown with 94. And, granted their first sight of the state's unlikely new bowling hero, the Melbourne crowd sat in rapt amazement. His first victim, the cussed all-rounder Ken Mackay, described the scene: 'I played confidently for a leg break, but it zipped the other way and I was stranded down the wicket. How the Melbourne crowd loved it. Cushions and hats went flying in the air...Iverson was a wizard.'

The headlines chorused Jack's praises with abandon. The *Age*: 'Iverson has another big day.' The *Herald*: 'How he does it'. The *Sun* even ran a picture sequence across the top of page one revelling in Jack's unlikely past and the apparent certainty of his future: 'Jack the giant killer couldn't make College team (But now he'll play for Australia).'

Jack, of course, slipped away early every evening, to The Esplanade, far from the back-slappers. To the congratulations, he smiled and shrugged his shoulders, sometimes turning the conversation round to mention the previous match where he didn't feel he'd done so well. 'Think I'm lucky to be here,' he would say. 'Didn't bowl so well in the second innings at Adelaide.'

No-one took him seriously. That was just Jack. In fact, his Victorian teammates got to rather like him. There was an endearing ingenuousness about the way he played. On one occasion, during the South Australian match, Ring asked him to pad up on the off-chance a nightwatchman was needed. He found Jack a few moments later suitably garbed except for having neglected to remove his black street shoes.

Jack's fielding at mid on was often a source of amusement and, Ring recalls, sometimes outright hilarity:

> One day against NSW this batsman hit the ball an enormous distance into the sky and there was no-one but Jake around. We watched in awe as the ball began its

descent. Jake sized it up, circled underneath it, moved back then forward, put his hands up into the correct position. The ball fell six feet behind him.

Jack himself, teammates also found, was capable of droll humour. While batting in Adelaide, he actually executed a semi-conscious back cut; a thoroughbred stroke for such a draughthorse batsman.

'Hang on,' the South Australian captain Phil Ridings interjected from slip. 'You're not meant to be able to bat.'

'Haven't you heard?' replied Jack. 'I'm the mystery man.' Then a characteristic flash of self-deprecation: 'But I'm the worst fieldsman in the team—easily the worst.' Teammates delightedly repeated the exchange for days.

There was something about Jack, nonetheless, that seemed to hold him back, that kept him from enjoying all the fun. 'Nothing nasty about Jack,' says Col McDonald, his Melbourne and Victorian teammate. 'Couldn't find a nicer fellow, really. The only thing was I don't think he ever knew how good he was.'

Jack's coup against Queensland was sweetly-timed. The match was watched throughout by Australian selector Albert Vincent from New South Wales. When he and his colleagues Bradman and Jack Ryder of Victoria attended the fixture beginning four days later between traditional rivals New South Wales and Victoria at the MCG, their presence had transparent significance; an Australian second-string team was shortly to tour New Zealand, and this would be the last opportunity for candidates to impress.

Visitor Jim Burke made a fine hundred, but Jack and his skipper Ring held their own, taking 5–111 and 5–138 respectively in a five-wicket victory, outshining in the process the New South Wales spin pair of Fred Johnston and Richie Benaud. When the touring party for New Zealand was revealed on 4 January 1950, the selectors threw in a few surprises, like Alan Davidson, a twenty-year-old left-arm tearaway from New South Wales. But otherwise the fourteen-man squad had all the armchair expert tips covered, including four Victorians: Ring, batsmen Ken Meuleman and Roy Howard, and Jack. Melbourne newspapers, of course, left little doubt as to whose selection was the highlight; Brian Feely's story in the *Sun* was headed 'Iverson big drawcard of NZ tour.'

It was only thirty-eight months since Jack had squeezed into his old school flannels to play in Brighton's 3rd XI. Now, at least nominally, he was to play cricket for his country. His family needed to buy a third big scrapbook to keep pace with media coverage, and Jean, now apparently deputised as official historian, was soon filling it; in Victoria's return match against NSW at the SCG, Jack spun out six second-innings wickets for 30, which he followed with five second-innings scalps for 48 against Queensland at the Gabba. In the end, Victoria could not usurp NSW in the race for the Shield, but its thirty-four-year-old spin 'prodigy' had the biggest wicket harvest at the lowest average in the competition. Jack's 46 wickets at 16.6 was—and remains—a record for a debut Shield season.

On 8 February, two days after the completion of the Shield season, Brown's fourteen boarded the steamer *Wanganella* at Port Melbourne for the trans-Tasman trip to New Zealand. Jack had with him two bats, including a Denis Compton presented to him by Melbourne teammates on which to collect autographs. He had two new pairs of cricket trousers, compliments of the Sydney firm Grip-U, which made a custom of presenting its product to new Australian players. On his shoulders, too, was now the yoke borne by every new sporting sensation, that of growing expectation.

FOURTEEN

Very few now remember Australia's trip to New Zealand half a century ago. Yet for Jack it was a much-savoured pageant of triumph, his bowling record without precedent or repeat. He seems to have collected every newspaper story concerned with the tour from the local press, which all eventually found their way into a bulging 170-page scrapbook, along with ephemera from tickets to invitations. He can seldom have been so happy in cricket; it was all so wonderfully easy.

New Zealand had been a Test nation for twenty years and was still in search of its first victory; in a cricketing as well as a geographic sense, it seemed like the end of the earth. Australia had played New Zealand only once in a full international, in March 1946, though the match had only been invested with Test status retrospectively by the Imperial Cricket Conference in April 1948. The country could boast a handful of elite cricketers, probably as good as any in the world: the princely left-hander Bert Sutcliffe, bespectacled skipper Walter Hadlee, the clean-hitting apprentice all-rounder John Reid. But otherwise the game was hidebound by a sort of received Englishness, certainly quaint, but always rather leisurely and often a little eccentric.

Good light stopped play at Timaru when the tourists played South Canterbury-Ashburton, for instance, the glare from the setting sun blinding on a pitch laid from east to west. When Sutcliffe hit a six for Otago at Dunedin over the grandstand, the Australians had to join the search to find the ball; no replacements were to hand. During the Australians' unofficial Test at the same venue, play was held up for some time when a driver stopped his train behind the bowler's arm, apparently just for a look-see. At McLean Park in Napier, the pitch was so underprepared that play was delayed by the appearance of a large number of worms on a length.

Umpiring, moreover, had peculiarly local variations. At Wanganui, the official at square leg was observed to be reclining on a shooting stick. At Dunedin again, Merv Wallace was credited with a six when a spectator ran onto the field and attempted to catch the ball five metres inside the rope. The tourists regarded it all with indulgent good humour, and set about beating their hosts out of sight, winning ten and drawing four of the trip's first and second-class matches.

Jack had a slightly rocky beginning to the journey. In the first match at the Recreation Ground in Lower Hutt, the bonny twenty-one-year-old Reid greeted his arrival with a four and an enormous six over long on. As Reid explains it, it was a case of the innocence of youth; he simply didn't know who Jack Iverson was, until the Australians told him later of his record-breaking home season:

> There's quite a moral there. Iverson to me was just another bowler—but only because I was ignorant of his record. How many batsmen in all classes of cricket have played the reputation of the bowler and not the ball? A half-volley is a half-volley whether it's bowled by Alec Bedser at Lord's or Bill Bloggs in the back paddock.

Jack was momentarily baffled. He looked searchingly at Brown and admitted: 'I don't know what to bowl to this guy.'

'I think the best thing for you to do,' said Brown, 'is have a bit of spell for a while. You can always come back later.' Jack had a rest, returned when Reid was lbw to Queenslander Len Johnson for 61, and picked up three cheap wickets to finish with the day's best figures.

Brown actually proved a very good captain for Jack, sympathetic and scientific. The genial and well-spoken Queenslander had seen a lot of cricket in his seventeen-year career—this trip being a sort of superannuation benefit, ahead of his impending retirement to run a Brisbane sports store—and he took a profound interest in the unique talent under his charge. When New Zealand umpires proved loath to grant Jack lbws, he encouraged him to bowl more often the ball that turned from leg. Noticing that Jack tended to toss his top spinner higher than the wrong 'un, he sought to persuade Jack to push them both through, so that they became indistinguishable in flight. 'I use that as a bit of variation,' Jack demurred. But when Brown explained that such rigid variation actually made him simpler to pick, Jack found the logic persuasive and caught on fast.

Jack responded to Brown's interest by throwing himself into his cricket, practising sedulously. Like Clarrie Grimmett, who sought to develop 'sympathy for the ball' by tensing and flexing his fingers before bowling, and 'Ranji' Hordern, who would massage his right hand with his left as he walked down the street, Jack was fastidious in the care and maintenance of his fingers. He took to squeezing a tennis ball for half an hour a day to strengthen his grip; not merely his middle finger, all of them. The tour also saw him develop little personal training drills, which Ken Meuleman remembers:

> Every time he had a bit of time on that trip in the dressing-room he'd lie on his back on the floor, put his foot up on a bench and start spinning the ball, bouncing it off the wall and catching it. His whole hand was incredibly strong. In fact, in a couple of matches on that tour, his middle finger got sore, so he bowled with his third finger and he bowled almost as well.

Soon, it all began paying off. Jack routed Waikato at Seddon Park with 5–41 in the second innings, then dissolved Taranaki at Pukekura Park a few days later with 5–14 in the first innings. In the latter match, indeed, Jack's turn was so venomous that more than a tenth of Taranaki's innings totals of 99 and 123 accrued in byes. Keeper Stan Sismey of New South Wales recalls:

> That day at New Plymouth, he was really something. One ball came out that I remember, it looked like the wrong 'un, so I started going down the leg side. Next thing I know it's

hit the outside of off stump. Well thank God it did, otherwise it would have been another four byes.

If Jack had not been armoured with a reputation at the
tour's commencement, he fast acquired one now. Every match
seemed to bring an improvement in results, every match a
deeper degree of batting paralysis. Jack's most astounding
performance was at the expense of an unfortunate mob called
Southland, on a freezing two days at Rugby Park in
Invercargill: from 17 overs, Jack collected 11–22, and the
figures could have been even better. When Southland's skipper
came into bat, he immediately snicked Jack's leg spinner to slip
where Phil Ridings took the catch and popped the ball in his
pocket. The batsman was so befuddled that he would not
budge, however, and the umpire declined to believe that
Ridings had not had the ball in his pocket all along. Jack
promptly bowled the local captain anyway. When the last man
came in, he cast his bat to one side as Jack let the ball go and
came dancing down the pitch like a man intent on scotching a
spider. Sismey again was so troubled that he conceded 11 byes
in Southland's second innings of 67, though he did collect a
couple of stumpings.

Jack's feats earned him a cult following. The *Sports Post*
featured him in a full-size front-page cartoon, towering like
the giant he was as a transfixed batsman tried to negotiate a
ball all-but dancing the cha-cha round him. His bronzed face,
height and physique also left a forceful impression, as Bill
Brown recalls:

> I was in the lounge of our hotel one day with some friends
> and a group of young women when Jake walked through.

He was actually quite a commanding presence physically, tall, big shoulders, a fine figure of a man, and one of these young women said: 'Is that your captain?'

I said: 'No, not really.'

She said: 'Who is?'

I said: 'Well, I am actually.'

And she looked at me as if to say: 'But you're not half the man he is.'

Jack's colleague Doug Ring overshadowed him in the unofficial Test at Carisbrook in Dunedin by taking 7–88 in the first innings. Nonetheless, Jack picked up five wickets in the match for 90 from more than 50 overs, and promptly routed both Manawatu in Palmerston North with 10–49 in almost 30 overs and Hawke's Bay in Napier with 6–29. As the *Dominion* newspaper pointed out, in fact, Jack was now in sight of a record. Returning to the country of his birth with an Australian XI in 1927–28, Clarrie Grimmett had taken 74 wickets for 1027 runs in all games. With 71 for 537 already and two matches of the tour to go, said the newspaper, 'he should pass Grimmett's bag'.

Which he did. Young John Reid treated him a little harshly again on the first day of the tour's final match at Basin Reserve in the course of a two-hour 74, but Bill Brown introduced his spinner late in each innings so that he snuck away with four tailend wickets for 42. His tour read-out beggared belief: not only had Jack obtained 75 wickets at 7.7 each, but he had not been dismissed in the course of 48 runs. Indeed, of several stories from the tour Jack adopted as part of his repertoire, one favourite with a little tactful embroidery concerned his batting: he would jest that he had ensured the purity of his tour record by joining in as non-striker with the caught-behind appeal against his last partner, Don Tallon.

Teammates do not remember Jack as a conspicuous tour personality. It was a high-spirited group, many over thirty, mostly ex-serviceman, who knew how to have a good time in a different country. Jack was more in the quiet category, easier to like than to know. Roy Howard recalls him as 'a good fellow, easy to talk to, like a very pleasant farmer'. Bill Brown recalls:

> Jake was an extremely nice bloke and all the boys liked him, but he wasn't the sort of fellow who'd have a few beers with you, or get involved in all the chiacking that went on. He wouldn't come down to breakfast first thing in the morning and say: 'How are you this morning, you silly old bugger?' He was more correct in addressing you, and I think generally he took things far more seriously than we did. It was my swansong, that tour, of course, so I was enjoying everything tremendously. But Jack was not that way, not really your hail-fellow-well-met sort of chap.

The only occasion on the trip that Brown recalls Jack losing this benign demeanour, was just before Australia's fifth game at Cook's Gardens, Wanganui. Unfamiliar with the idea of players being rotated for selection according to a roster, Jack accosted his skipper seeking an explanation. Brown says:

> I said: 'We're just giving you a bit of a rest, Jake. You've played in virtually all the games on tour, and there's a few boys who haven't had a lot of cricket.'
> Jake says: 'Well, as far as I'm concerned, you've dropped me.'

Alan Davidson remembers Jack asking plaintively whether he was 'not bowling well enough', and looking throughout the next two days 'like a dog who'd lost his bone'.

Nonetheless, here was patently an enormous talent. In the span of six months, at the age of thirty-four, Jack had taken 142 wickets for Melbourne, Victoria and Australia: an Indian summer in every sense. A few batsmen had managed to hold him at bay, but none had neutralised his threat for long. With an Ashes series in the offing the following summer, word of his gifts even spread to England. The London magazine *Illustrated* ran a four-page 'magic eye' photo spread of him dismissing Queensland's Ken Mackay at the MCG, and posed the question: 'Have the Australians found another Grimmett?' When Jack was a guest on radio station 3AW's popular 'Kia-Ora Sports Parade', it was in the guise of the hottest property in Australian cricket. 'Yes, it's the new spin wizard, Jack Iverson,' chirped host Norman Banks. 'Give him a big welcome, ladies and gentlemen. [applause]'

Delightfully, a script survives of the interview. Not that it's especially enlightening or spontaneous for, in the style of the period, it was a carefully-arranged catechism:

> BANKS: I believe Bill Brown did his usual grand job as skipper?
> IVERSON REPLIES—PAY TRIBUTE TO BROWN.

There is, nonetheless, a scent of the times and the man, the exultation that Jack must have felt in his heart at his unexpected late celebrity, the joy his family must have experienced as they huddled round the radiogram. How Jack would have savoured it, how his wife and parents would have flushed with pride to hear Banks signing off:

Well, Jack, we do once again offer our congratulations on your grand performance in New Zealand and we trust that when the Englishmen arrive here, you'll be one of our Test side. All the very, very best to you, Jack Iverson! [applause]

FIFTEEN

To understand Jack Iverson in all his weirdness and wonder, it is important to grasp one of cricket's most distinctive dimensions. You will often encounter in reading about the game the phrase 'natural player'. Yet much about cricket is quite alien to normal ball skills. Give a child a bat, and his natural urge will be to swing horizontally across the line. Give a child a ball, and his instinctive response will be a furtive underarm throw. And such was cricket's original eighteenth-century formulation, on common, village green and country estate: cross bat versus underarm. Explaining how Jack Iverson arrived at cricket is actually only part of our tale; one must also appreciate how cricket arrived at Jack Iverson. The story of bowling innovation and evolution is a path paved by unusual men with unusual ideas who, like Jack, were destined neither for prolonged careers nor enduring renown. But who, also like Jack, were sensations of their time.

John Willes was a handsome and headstrong landowner, born about 220 years ago in the Kent village of Headcorn, and addicted to shooting, boxing, cricket and other 'manly sports'. Contemporary illustrations display a striking profile, curled hair and full side-whiskers, with alert eyes and a purposeful tilt of the head. He galloped his grey mare with a disdain for danger, as though 'trying to break his neck', and entertained with a disdain for creditors, leaving bottles of whisky and brandy with glasses in a pail of water outside the hall door at his Bellringham estate so that members of his Sutton Valence team could fortify themselves after a long day in the field. He even attempted to elope with a girl from Harrietsham, though she reconsidered when her coach-and-four was overtaken by her father on horseback brandishing a pistol.

No fox or rabbit was safe from Willes with his pack of hounds, and no batsman could feel comfortable when he first hazarded roundarm bowling. He may have been wakened to its potential by meeting the old Hambledonian Tom Walker, who had trialled the method in 1792 but given it up when it was 'esteemed foul play'. Others prefer to believe that Willes developed it while practising in a barn at Fonford with his sister Christina, whose hooped skirts prevented her observance of underarm convention. Whatever its origins, Willes caused an immediate sensation on Penenden Heath, playing for XXIII of Kent against XIII of England in July 1807, both with his success and with his apparent disregard for the existing niceties. As the *Sporting Magazine* reported it, roundarm 'fully proved an obstacle in getting runs, in comparison to what might have been got by the straightforward bowling'.

Willes was not the only bowler of his era to resist the gravity of precedent by raising his arm from its traditional position, but he was the most successful. He also had his champions and imitators: with a robust belief in logic and efficiency, they considered his method part of 'the march of intellect', of a piece with free trade, mechanisation and emancipation. But he had many more detractors, both high and low.

The high included, most conspicuously, the grandees of the Marylebone Cricket Club, who had by this stage in cricket's emergence assumed and been conceded the status of its law-giver. Not that the club as yet discharged this duty with any particular skill. Indeed, MCC's first attempt to obliterate roundarm resulted in an 1816 ruling called Law No 10 that is worth quoting for its virtual unintelligibility:

> The ball must be bowled (not thrown or jerked) and be delivered underhand, with the hand below the elbow. But if the ball be jerked, or the arm extended from the body horizontally, and any part of the hand be uppermost, or the hand horizontally extended when the ball is delivered, the umpire shall call 'no ball'.

The MCC was abetted in its prohibitionary ends by the lower castes who also watched the game. So much money was being wagered on matches that a bowler offending against the natural order was bound to be inflammatory. As the *Morning Herald* phrased it in May 1821:

> Mr Willes and his bowling were frequently barred in making a match and he played sometimes amidst much uproar and confusion. Still he would persevere till the ring

closed on the players, the stumps were lawlessly pulled up, and all came to a stand-still.

The climax of this schism between roundarm and round-head came on 15 July 1822 when the MCC lured Kent to Lord's. The MCC team included three of the game's most powerful potentates: William Ward MP, Reverend Lord Frederick Beauclerk and secretary Ben Aislabie. And under their undoubtedly approving gaze, exemplary justice was meted out by umpire Harry Bentley: Willes was no-balled so persistently that, in one of the most celebrated events of cricket's primordial days, he threw the ball down, stormed from the arena and galloped away on his mare swearing he would never play again.

Having won the battle, however, the underarm lobby was destined to lose the war, thanks to the inordinate skill of roundarm slow bowler William Lillywhite and the untiring advocacy of an MCC dissident George Thomas Knight. They furthered their common cause by excelling while on opposite sides in a series of three matches in July 1827 between Sussex and All England at Lord's staged to assess the wisdom of legalising roundarm bowling. Lillywhite, who obscured his humble origins as a bricklayer by favouring the old raiment of tall top hat and cotton braces, was clearly too fine a bowler to ignore. 'He bowled a hundred times better than any man did bowl,' said umpire William Caldecourt. 'It was cruel to see how he would rattle about either the knuckles or the stumps.' Knight, who had at first been censured by the MCC for his methods, became roundarm's chiefest advocate, with an eloquence befitting a nephew of Jane Austen. In a long correspondence with *Sporting Magazine*, he railed:

The whimsical caprice of umpires, arising from the faulty definition which now regulates the bowling, is so notorious to all cricketers as to need little illustration...At MCC itself the same bowler is allowed in one match and disallowed in another...Everything is in the breast of the umpires; if he fancies you, he will let you bowl, if not, he will stop you.

The cumbrous Rule No. 10 was amended in 1828 to partly accommodate the roundarm, and wholly redrafted seven years later to make Willes's the way forward. Not that it afforded him consolation: he never forgave cricket sufficiently to play it again and, his thriftlessness having caught up with him, died in 1852 in such 'fearfully reduced circumstances' that his grave was for several years unmarked.

As batsmen assimilated roundarm variations over the next quarter-century, bowlers were increasingly induced to transgress by intermittently raising their arms above the shoulder. And the second great bowling upheaval—the transition from roundarm to overarm—partly replicated the events of the first on the other side of the Thames at The Oval.

Like Willes, Edgar Willsher was from Kent. Like Willes, too, he was not the only one straining at the bounds of legality, merely the most successful. And, as in the case of the roundarm revolution, one of the chief protagonists of the overarm drama was a Lillywhite: though this time as part of the *ancien regime* rather than a member of the *sans culottes*.

Photographs of Willsher show a slight, dark, round-shouldered, rather apologetic figure, the youngest of a farmer's fourteen children. Lord Harris, in *A Few Short Runs*, described him thus:

> Willsher was said to have had only one lung from boyhood, and certainly he was an attenuated, consumptive-looking man. I do not think he had much idea of the science of the game, and beyond his bowling never struck me as taking much interest in it...He had a curious, faraway look in his eyes, and used to look up at the sky as one talked to him.

Yet Willsher bowled left-arm cutters for a quarter of a century, so waspish that the ball sometimes seemed, in the words of his contemporary Richard Daft, 'to reach one almost before it left his hand'.

Willsher bowled six deliveries in the third over of a match between England and Surrey on 27 August 1862, but none was considered legitimate by the umpire: William Lillywhite's son John. Willsher stalked from the field, followed by eight sympathetic professional teammates. Their boycott truncated the day's play.

Lillywhite was replaced by the consent of both teams the following day, permitting the match's resumption. But he had proved his point in much the same fashion as his father: the existing law was unworkable. As the Surrey professional Billy Caffyn wrote:

> There is no doubt whatever that Willsher was often in the habit of bowling above the shoulder, but then so also were nine out of every ten bowlers of that time...The old law was an absurd one, and one wonders that it should have remained in force for so long.

This time, evolution took only two years: from 10 June 1864, it became possible to raise the arm above shoulder level. Though he did not retrace Willes's fall from grace, Willsher nursed ever after an abiding grievance about that Oval *auto da fe*. In his obituary twenty-one years later in *Cricket: A Weekly Record of the Game*, umpire Robert Thoms reported:

> Willsher often pathetically remarked that he had been born too soon: and, perhaps, to a certain extent, he had cause to think so, for he lived to see chuckers, half-chuckers, windmills and pounding down bowlers have a good time of it, whilst he, a bowler with a strictly fair delivery, as regards bowling, had to be settled for occasionally delivering the ball above the shoulder.

Thus cricket transacted what Sir Donald Bradman has called 'possibly the greatest single change in the development of the game': the establishment of the basic overarm technical template for bowlers. Fast or slow, straight or crooked, wild or mild, bowlers would henceforward deliver from an essentially upright position by rotating a fully-extended and locked arm that released the ball at or near the vertical.

The convention of the straight arm, incidentally, is one of cricket's more impenetrable mysteries. Even Roland Bowen, most piercing of the game's many historians, could do no better in his *Cricket: A History of its Growth and Development throughout the World* than the remark: 'At some unknown stage, the idea took root that "cricket" bowling involved a straight arm.' It seems simply to have been enshrined by practice, a vestige of the days when bowling was literally 'bowling', and the bent arm tabooed by tradition, in a pursuit uncommonly fond of straight lines.

Such a rigid precept should inhibit variety. In the same sense that it appears composers must eventually deplete all possible permutations and combinations of notes, or that chess players with pieces that can move only in fixed iterations must finally play every possible game, it seems that there must come a point where bowling exhausts every existing variation on its basic style. Yet, as in music, as in chess, variations have proliferated and continue to do so. Two factors, in fact, make cricket unique among ball games. The first is its ball, most enduring of its appurtenances. It seems always to have been hard. In his *The Mysteries of Love* in 1658, Edward Phillips has a woman fearing that her lover will say: 'Would my eyes had been beat out of my head with a cricket ball the day before I saw thee.' It seems always to have been about as heavy. In the oldest surviving Laws of Cricket from 1744, the ball's weight is restricted to between five and six ounces. It has, almost as long, verifiably been red. In 1753, one of the first cricket versifiers, James Love, penned the lines: 'From nervous arm with force impetuous see/The crimson ball attack the destin'd mark.' And it has, for more than two centuries, possessed the distinctive aspect of a seam: four stitches in the case of the oldest extant example, dated to 1780 after it was disinterred from a house in Lewes in 1995; subsequently, and traditionally, six.

With this collection of qualities, bowlers discovered very quickly, a cricket ball could be persuaded to do amazing things. Propelled through the atmosphere with particular grips and actions, it could be induced to swing by differentials of pressure on either side, apparently through the interaction of the thin layer of air encasing the ball and the surrounding airstream. According to physicists who have sought to explain it, this aerodynamic phenomenon owes itself to the happy accident that the 0.5–1 millimetre protuberance of the seam is about the same thickness as this boundary layer, and thus at an ideal height to trip it into turbulence.

Swing and swerve are not unknown, of course, in other bat and ball games. A baseball has its own distinct physics and behaves differently at different velocities when invested with spin and spit. But cricket moves to another dimension by being played on the ground as well as in the air. Grass, with its natural give and recuperative qualities, is cricket's original and optimum surface. Turf pitches, established at twenty-two yards in those aforementioned 1744 Laws, are its natural terrain. Perhaps no game depends so profoundly on its surface for orderly conduct. As Neville Cardus observed in *English Cricket*: 'The history of cricket is one long battle between batsman and bowler, the groundsman holding the ring.' Without the medium of the pitch, we could still have swing bowling. But with it, we can also savour the subtle shades of spin.

As it is virtually impossible to release a cricket ball without imparting some sort of rotation, a form of spin bowling has been with us since cricket's cradle days. The game's underarm pioneers twigged quickly; a flick of the fingers, and the softest lob could be imbued with a concealed barb. The physics were straightforward. A ball rotated clockwise would break into a batsman's legs, a ball rotated anti-clockwise away from the groping bat. A ball spun forward would tend to hurry, a ball spun back arrive later than expected. These were absorbing phenomena for thoughtful men, and it is probably no coincidence that cricket's first instructional text in English—*Rules and Instructions for Playing the Game of Cricket, as practised by the most Eminent Players*—was published in 1801 by a slow bowler, Tom Boxall, generally regarded as the first man to bowl the underarm leg break. Boxall, a tidewaiter at Purfleet on the north side of the Thames, gave advice about appropriate grips:

> Let the bowler hold the ball with the seam across, not too near the top of fingers, nor too high in the hand, but so as the top of the finger may just reach over the seam; it will hold so better and go with more ease.

About the necessity of practice:

> A bowler can measure his ground, put up the stumps, and stick a feather where he intends to pitch his ball; always toss the ball at the feather, which must be in a straight line to the stumps.

And about the first principles of spin:

> Although the ball is tossed straight to a mark, yet it must not roll straight, if it does not it will not twist after it hits the ground: when the ball goes out of a bowler's hand he must endeavour to make it twist a little across, then after it hits the ground it will twist the same way as it rolls when it goes from the hand.

Most bowlers in cricket's embryonic days, nonetheless, bowled fast: on rough and unkempt pitches against batsmen without protective armour, it would naturally have yielded the richest dividends. And although a few resolute souls preserved spin's vital spark, many early experimenters found the transition from underarm to overarm difficult and their numbers dwindled in the 1840s and 1850s. But their cause was furthered in the second half of the century, ironically, by the improving quality of batsmanship, incarnate in the emergent W. G. Grace, and a trend towards pitches of lower and more even bounce, set most notably by Surrey's 'painstaking and thoroughly-deserving' groundsman Sam Apted. Batsmen had to be foxed out as well as frightened and, as games lengthened in the Victorian Age, the scope for environmental degradation, both of the ball and of the pitch, increased. A worn ball to grip and a deteriorating pitch to provide purchase then, as today, invited bowlers to give the ball a rip. And especially until an extra twelve inches in width was added to the bowling crease in 1902, undulations excavated by the footfall of a few days' play offered a new generation rich opportunities.

Suddenly, in the last quarter of the nineteenth century, it was fast bowling that was in eclipse. The giants of what was also the period in which Test cricket commenced bowled with a narrower band of speed from slow to medium pace, toyed with grips, manipulated their fields, played on batsmen's nerves. The cardinal rules of spin were laid out: the ball that broke in to the right-handed batsmen, the off break, was to be spun mostly by the bowler's forefinger, rotating clockwise; the delivery turning away from the right-hander, the leg break, was delivered with the wrist cocked and the first and third finger coming over the ball. A top spinner, a ball spun forward, also known at the time as a vertical spinner, which did not jag either way but might dip in flight and drop shorter than expected, also came in handy. There was no higher tribute than that a bowler 'bowled with his head'. A few even used their faces to good effect, like the South Australian George Giffen: 'A determined look might accompany one of his flightiest balls, followed by a relaxed smile to camouflage his quickest one. With a sardonic grin he could make batsmen feel the end was near.' Then, as the new century dawned, guile reached its logical conclusion: outright deceit.

SIXTEEN

Bernard James Tindal Bosanquet was a typical specimen of the gentleman cricketer around the turn of the century, an Etonian who won his blue at Oxford University for hitting hard and bowling fast. Yet it was his quite untypical technical speculations about the rotated cricket ball that were to leave an indelible imprint on the game. And it was his invention that Jack Iverson would customise a decade after his death.

The Bosanquets were an accomplished family of Huguenot descent, their family tree festooned with distinguished clerics, critics, admirals and archaeologists. Bernard Bosanquet, a relative and namesake, was garlanded by *The Times*' obituarist in February 1923 as 'the central figure in British philosophy for a generation', having introduced the tenets of German idealism to Oxford University four decades earlier with translations of R. H. Lotze's *Logic* and the Introduction of G. W. Hegel's *Philosophy of Fine Art*. This smoothed the path to the landmark text in the development of Anglo-Hegelianism: *Appearance and Reality*, published in 1893 by Bernard Bosanquet's friend and collaborator Francis Herbert Bradley.

Neatly enough, even as Bradley was writing his seminal work, appearance and reality became the preoccupation of fourteen-year-old B. J. T. Bosanquet. When the billiard table at the family home of Claysmore was being recovered, Bosanquet joined siblings in spinning a tennis ball across the slats. It set him to wondering: could one spin a ball in such a way that it appeared to be going one way but went the other? He experimented further in a family game played with a hard rubber ball and a broomstick, employing his cousin Louise as a retriever, but otherwise kept his speculations private, perhaps for fear of ridicule. For everyone knew that spin from the off came from the fingers, spin from the leg with a twist of the wrist.

At Oxford, the question recurred, in a quaint pastime called 'twisti-twosti', whose object was to bounce a tennis ball across a table so that someone sitting opposite could not catch it. Bosanquet bowled a natural leg break, but discovered that by turning his wrist over a little further at the moment of release he could alter the axis of its spin and break it back the opposite way. It was an extraordinarily difficult ball to bowl successfully, the wrist having to go first over then under the ball so that it came out of the back of the hand. But by the summer of 1899, twenty-one-year-old Bosanquet was bowling his trick delivery in the university nets to a string of famous visiting batsmen as a kind of party piece. First there would be a few disarming leg breaks, then his patented reverse break delivered with what appeared the same action. 'If this pitched in the right place it probably hit him on the knee,' Bosanquet recalled. 'Everyone shrieked with laughter, and I was led away and locked up for the day.'

'Mr B. J. T. Bosanquet', as he was typed in the format of the day reserved for amateurs, excelled for Middlesex in the county match against Leicestershire played at Lord's from 19 to 21 July 1900. His 136 out of 224 in the first innings consumed 110 minutes, his 139 out of five for 304 in the second 170 minutes, and the hosts prevailed by five wickets. But sterilised in the small print of the visitors' second innings is the beginning of a bowling revolution. Samuel Coe was two short of a century when he became the first victim of Bosanquet's sleight of hand in a first-class match, stumped rather ingloriously by William Robertson from a ball that bounced four times.

Cricket's grapevine is usually pretty effective. It rarely takes long for word to spread of a new talent, or an unusual technique. But Bosanquet's curious new weapon went undetected, partly because the bowler swore his captain Pelham Warner to secrecy, partly because what he was perpetrating was so beyond the average cricketer's ken. These were days when English amateur batsmanship was in full flower and bowlers were drudges, when crowds chorused their disapproval of leg side bowling and run-saving fields, when the seigneurial C. B. Fry felt able to complain that a spinner was unfairly tossing the ball too high so that it was coming out of the sun. The possibility that a bowler—and a gentleman at that—could have been working on a device so treacherous would have been unthinkable.

Word did eventually seep out, though even then batsmen were reluctant to acknowledge the new-fashioned spin. Some sceptics preferred to disbelieve the evidence of their own eyes and dismiss it as accidental: Bosanquet did not disabuse them. Some obscurantists muttered that the delivery 'wasn't fair' and might even be illegal: 'Not illegal,' Bosanquet demurred. 'Only immoral.'

Not all batsmen, of course, dissolved on contact with the invention. Some days, when Bosanquet's wrist recoiled from excessive contortion and accuracy deserted him, he was an expensive luxury item. 'Mr Bosanquet was often called "the best bad bowler in England",' recalled the Warwickshire keeper Arthur Lilley, 'and there was much truth in it.' The Yorkshire potentate Lord Hawke took a chance on him, nonetheless, when he left England on 12 November 1902 leading a team of eleven amateurs and two professionals on a twenty-one-match tour of New Zealand and Australia. And, although Bosanquet fared better as a batsman than as a bowler, his strange wiles fascinated the hosts. New Zealanders are often credited with baptising Bosanquet's invention the 'googly': a name of suitably enigmatic etymology thought variously to have come from Maori dialects or to have been a corruption of the Australianism 'googler' or 'googlie' applied to any high-tossed, looping delivery. And when Australians saw Bosanquet's first trick ball in Sydney confound no less than Victor Trumper, they were impressed, and a tad apprehensive. Charles Bannerman, Test cricket's first century-maker twenty-five years earlier, confided to Plum Warner: 'That leg break of his which breaks from the off might win a Test match.'

When Warner himself led an English team including Bosanquet on a five-Test tour of Australia the following season, high hopes were held. In an open letter to Warner in the *Daily Express*, C. B. Fry entreated: 'Persuade that Bosanquet of yours to practice, practice, practice those funny googlies of his.' Perhaps disconcerted by the expectations, Bosanquet's bowling veered between the mediocre and the mortifying for two months, 10 wickets costing 451 runs. With the New Year, however, came resolution: 7–168 in a losing cause in the Third Test at the Adelaide Oval, 6–51 amid a rout of Australia in the Fourth at the SCG that saw the tourists recapture the Ashes. The googly was set to go forth and multiply.

'How he manages to bowl his off break with a leg break action,' commented *Wisden Cricketers' Almanack*, 'one cannot pretend to say.' Yet many wanted to know. One of those watching Bosanquet from afar at the SCG in that Fourth Test was a twenty-year-old member of the North Sydney second XI, Herbert Hordern. A restless, questing, whimsical character, known as 'Ranji' for the resemblance his swarthy complexion lent him to the Anglo-Indian batting guru Ranjitsinhji, Hordern tutored himself privately in the googly with his nephew Frank McElhone and friend Alec Mackenzie, until one day in about October 1905 he finally cracked its code. Hordern recalled:

> I rushed up and said: 'Why didn't you hit that one, Alec?'
> And he said: 'I don't know. I just missed it.'
> But I knew then that, if such a fine player had played the wrong way for the break, I had it.

Hordern packed the googly with him when he enrolled the following year to study dentistry at the University of Pennsylvania, and bowled it when the fancy took him on friendly tours of the Caribbean and England and against visiting XIs. Teddy Wynyard, captain of an MCC side hosted by Philadelphia in 1907, was one typical victim; as Hordern's *jeu d'esprit* jagged back to cuff off stump, he exclaimed: 'My heavens, a googly!' Arriving in international cricket as the finished article in February 1911, he took 46 wickets in only seven Tests before concern that hand damage might interfere with his vocation ended his sporting career. But the title of his autobiography twenty years later conveyed Hordern's devotion as a Bosanquet disciple: *Googlies*.

As Bosanquet obtained the 'double' for Middlesex at home in 1904—1405 runs and 132 wickets—he also entranced Frank Mitchell's visiting South Africans. One of Mitchell's number, twenty-eight-year-old Reggie Schwarz, began the tour as a batsman, then decided one day at Oxford University to dabble in Bosanquet's occult leg spin with immediate results:

> When I went on I had not the slightest idea how the field should be placed, so I told them to scatter and trusted to fortune. I managed to obtain a length and, being satisfied with that did not worry too much about getting much break on. That was my first experiment with 'googlies' in a match, and all the five wickets they accounted for were bowled down.

Schwarz finished the tour a purveyor of googlies and top spinners perhaps even better than his inspiration. Leicestershire's captain, Sir Arthur Hazelrigg, embodied the confusion of batsmen faced with this new science:

For two overs Sir Arthur was in a hopeless muddle, and he was finally beaten and bowled all over the place by one that 'came the other way'. In the pavilion, the sporting baronet was just as confounded as he had been 'on the middle'. 'What a marvellous bowler your man is,' gasped Sir Arthur. 'He is uncanny. Why, the ball pitched *there*. I played *here*, and the beastly thing bowled me out round *there*.'

Schwarz proselytised so successfully at home that the South Africans would overwhelm England there eighteen months later with no fewer than four adherents of the new religion: Schwarz, Ernie Vogler, Gordon White and Aubrey Faulkner.

By then, however, the googly's progenitor had all but faded from view. Bosanquet enjoyed one more Ashes day out, at Trent Bridge on 31 May 1905, when eight Australians succumbed to him in 32 match-winning overs for 107 runs, but his powers deserted him with curious suddenness. By his own admission, some contemporary comment cut him, both from those who laughed at his expense when the gift failed him, and those maligning him as a cricketing Pandora who'd declined to bowl, in the words of the English captain Archie MacLaren, 'as God meant him to do'. Bosanquet played eighteen seasons in all, but was a bowler only a third of them, and there was a touch of hurt amid the humour when he was asked by *Wisden* to recall the googly's genesis in its 1925 edition:

> Poor old googly! It has been subjected to ridicule, contempt, abuse, incredulity, and survived them all. Nowadays one cannot read an article on cricket without finding that any deficiencies existing at the present day are attributed to the influence of the googly. If the standard of bowling falls off, it is because too many cricketers devote

their time to trying to master it, instead of carrying on with the recognised and hallowed methods of bowling. If batsmen display a marked inability to hit the ball on the off side, or anywhere in front of the wicket, it is said that the googly has made it impossible for them to adopt the old aggressive attitude and make the odd scoring stroke. But what after all is the googly? It is merely a ball with an ordinary break produced by an extraordinary method.

Well might Bosanquet have smarted for his invention. While toxic to batsmen, the googly seemed for a time almost as poisonous to its bowlers. Perhaps it was too much for a body to stand, wondered the English amateur Rockley Wilson in the 1920 edition of the Badminton Library's *Cricket*: 'A curious fact about "googly" bowlers is the shortness of their careers. No "googly" bowler hitherto has retained his skill for more than six seasons. Mr Schwarz used latterly to find his elbow very painful, and the strain of bowling the ball out of the back of the hand must be considerable.' Charles Marriott, the Kent leg spinner, described his first experiment while at school at St Columba's in Ireland:

> One day at a net I had an astonishing spell, when I struck a perfect length and had everyone completely tied up including our professional, who took a turn with the bat for the last minute or two. It went to my head. When it was time to pack up, I shouted 'one more' and ran up determined to bowl the googly to end all googlies. What actually happened was a horrible stab of pain in my right elbow, and I found myself out of the XI for the next three matches.

Marriott scarcely bowled it again. If he did, he bowled one in his first or second over, with the idea that the threat was enough. He considered that the injury 'saved me just in time' and that he 'never felt it was worth the extra effort'. The superstitious might even have sensed a sort of Tutankhamen's curse on those whom the delivery enslaved. Of those successful with it before World War I—Bosanquet, Hordern, Schwarz, Vogler, White, Faulkner—none were alive a year after the end of World War II.

By that stage, however, the googly gremlin had finally been tamed. Conceived on the pudding practice pitches of Oxford, it was perfected on the hard, dry surfaces of Australia in the wrists of a blessed trinity of slow bowlers: Arthur Mailey, Clarrie Grimmett and Bill O'Reilly. Not that this did not take time and unswerving devotion. A scruffy urchin from South Sydney, Mailey first practised the googly with an orange because he could not afford a cricket ball, and did not play Test cricket until the age of thirty-three; the wizened and parsimonious New Zealander Grimmett rehearsed his variations with only his fox terrier Joe for company and played cricket in three states before taking 11–82 in his first Test at Sydney against England at the age of thirty-five; O'Reilly, a bellicose Irishman who engulfed batsmen like a swarm of bees, taught himself to bowl with a gnarled banksia root, and played his last Test as a forty-year-old.

In a sense, Australia between the wars was the ideal habitat for this introduced species. On pitches as hard as macadam, the hard-spun googly not only turned counterintuitively, it bounced as if it had a demon inside it. The 1920s and 1930s, too, were periods of astronomical scores, providing plenty of runs for purveyors of this difficult delivery to bowl at. As though to make it more completely their own, Australians also came to know the googly by aliases: the 'bosie', in honour of its inventor, and the 'wrong 'un' (allegedly applied first in South Africa, but widely-used here).

We might think of Jack Iverson as an addition to this lineage of Mailey, Grimmett and O'Reilly. He was, after all, an Australian who bowled a googly and did not play Test cricket until late in life. But this would not be strictly accurate. For one, the googly was his stock ball, not his surprise weapon. For another, he was intent simply on the praxis of his spin, not on the surrounding philosophy. To compare Grimmett with Jack would be like comparing a Stradivarius violin to a theremin; from a distance they sound similar, but one is the acme of its traditional type, the other a queer oddity.

In this sense, Jack Iverson belongs more truly to a deviant strain of bowlers, also liberated by the googly, but related primarily by intent. For the googly was more than simply a new delivery; it was an act of apostasy, conceived to deceive. And Bosanquet's invention set cricket's community to wondering; how else might you usurp the natural order? In the decades following him, the hunt for a new shock weapon became a curious cricketing sideshow. Especially in England, there was a succession of short-lived wonder bowlers, who came and went like dance crazes and popular cocktails.

One of the most famous was Douglas 'Daddy' Carr, a roly-poly thirty-seven-year-old Kent schoolmaster with a bouncy, quickish, almost roundarm googly, whom England summoned for the Oval Test of August 1909 from the obscurity of a career largely idled away with club teams like the Band of Brothers,

Oxford Authentics and Blue Mantles. But after three quick wickets against Monty Noble's touring Australians, he was wantonly overbowled. His gifts grew exoteric and he was never selected again.

A few weeks later, for 'Shrimp' Leveson-Gower's 1909–10 touring team to South Africa, MCC picked Worcestershire amateur George Simpson-Hayward, a throwback to cricket before John Willes, who delivered underarm lobs which he could spin either way. Simpson-Hayward, who had developed his technique spinning billiard balls and small tops, proved a force on the veldt's fast matting pitches, claiming 23 wickets at 18. 'A cleverer bowler of his kind there never was,' said Pelham Warner, though he drifted from the game on returning home.

Then there was the vogue for leg-theory, the bowling of off cutters and inswingers to a stacked leg side field, which had a host of adherents before and after World War I. There was Bill Greswell, a gifted Reptonian, who perplexed Noble's Australians at Bath in June 1909, and who might have achieved far more had his father not despatched him a few months later to run the family's tea plantation in Ceylon. There was Shanghai-born Arthur Jaques, who brought a touch of the orient to the occident with his back breaks and leg slips at Hampshire, and who also might have flourished had he not perished in World War I in September 1915 at the age of twenty-seven.

After the war, the leg-theory torch was taken up most ably by Fred Root, an orthodox medium pacer of modest attainments until he developed an arsenal of in-duckers and was favoured by a sticky-fingered leg side cordon. He surpassed 100 wickets in nine consecutive seasons and, at his zenith in

June 1926, dismissed seven Australians for 42 playing for the North of England at Edgbaston and was invited to participate in a demonstration of his art at the Oxford Street emporium of the department store Selfridge's beneath the banner 'How I Did It'. Root was, however, already thirty-six, and could achieve nothing so startling in three Test matches that summer.

For all their momentary magnetism, however, none of these meteoric personalities achieved anything as wicked or wondrous as the googly. The closest cricket came was the 'flipper', a Grimmett variation on the leg break emerging from underneath the hand that skidded from the off and ultimately supplanted the googly in his repertoire, and the googly's mirror image, the 'wrong 'un' for left-arm wrist spinners. It occurs that this delivery might have been baptised the 'right 'un', but it gained the more evocative name of the 'chinaman' in honour of one of its pioneers: Ellis 'Puss' Achong of the West Indies, son of a mainly Chinese cocoa planter. When he delivered it on tour in England during 1933 as a variation on his usual stock-in-trade of left-arm finger spin, one of his victims, Walter Robins, is alleged to have fumed: 'Fancy being bowled by a bloody chinaman.' Learie Constantine's retort sealed the neologism: 'Do you mean the bowler or the ball?'

Cricket otherwise came up with fewer and more risible results from its search. One delivery that exercised a peculiar draw, for instance, was the shooter. After all, if one could bowl a delivery from a regular action that ran across the ground after pitching, it would be the deadliest delivery of all. Finding a way to bowl it in the 1920s seems to have become a kind of minor-key cricketing version of solving Fermat's Last Theorem. At one stage, a mystery man signing himself 'Yorkshireman in

London' wrote to that county's secretary Sir Frederick Toone offering to demonstrate his version. So intrigued was Toone that he arranged for the man to visit the nets at Lord's during Yorkshire's next match there under the invigilation of left-arm spinner Roy Kilner:

> After much speculation as to what would happen, quite a few hard-earned Yorkshire shillings changed hands when the man turned up. They did not expect him to come at all, but come he did, all 'got up' with the old school blazer. He accompanied three or four stolid Yorkshire cricketers to the nets where he bowled...underarm 'grubbers'. The only shooting likely then was foiled by Roy's aversity to carrying firearms.

Cricket, though, could not stop dreaming. And if cricketers themselves could find nothing so arcane as the googly again, that did not prevent other imaginations from turning the problem over.

SEVENTEEN

It's perfectly possible that cricket has still to fathom the full potentialities of the rotated ball. We may be limited only by our imaginations. Once you start thinking about it, there seems no limit to the possibilities. Bill O'Reilly was one who believed that mysteries remained to be unlocked. He told of a game on Australia's 1934 tour of England where he bowled a conventional wrong 'un that spun not to leg but to off, defeated his keeper and scuttled away for four byes. The next ball, it happened again. But, try as he might, he was never able to repeat the phenomenon.

As a septuagenarian, that incorrigible alchemist of spin Clarrie Grimmett took up the cause of this 'wrong wrong 'un', turning the wrist round so far that the ball spun like a conventional leg break. He could bowl the double negative only over a distance of about ten metres, but remained fascinated with the concept until his death.

In his 1948 primer *Grimmett on Cricket*, he also describes a breathtaking creation called, without hint of irony, the Mystery Ball: a top spinner with a possible off break, the hand pointing towards cover, the wrist bent, the ball coming over the top of the fingers. Mystery it is because, as Dr Brian Wilkins of Wellington's Victoria University says in his learned dissertation *The Bowler's Art*, it would seem an impossibility: 'I wonder very much about this ball. No one as far as I am aware, bowls it. If they do, then it must resemble the weapon of science fiction, that having destroyed its victim, self destructs to obliterate all trace of itself.'

Sometimes particular conditions conspire in favour of the unusual. Ken Archer recalls a match at Hastings in September 1954 between an England XI and a Commonwealth XI where the West Indian Sonny Ramadhin unlocked a once-in-a-lifetime phenomenon. With an identical action, he discovered he could move the ball different ways simply by slightly varying his pace: the ball spun one way and, at an infinitesimally greater speed, seamed the other, perhaps because of the seaside air. Archer never saw anything like it again, and Ramadhin was so bewitched by the ball's behaviour that he could scarcely bowl for laughing.

On other occasions, the realm of the possible has been left tantalisingly unexplored. While bowling at Bristol for Australia in May 1964, Victorian batsman Jack Potter bedazzled his colleagues with a sort of contra-googly, a leg break that seemed to come from an off break action. Keeper Wally Grout recalled:

You had no chance of detecting it from the hand and could only hope to pick the direction of spin through the air, a dicey business particularly on the many English grounds without sightscreens...[Gloucestershire's David] Allen muttered to me one day after Jack's wrong 'un had him swiping fresh air: 'What's this fellow doing?' and though equally fooled I did my best to convince David that the ball had hit something on the wicket. In later matches the appearance of Potter at the bowling crease prompted a conference among the batsmen, one I should have been allowed to join. I was as much in the dark about Jack's pet ball as they were.

Richie Benaud was disappointed that Potter, a batsman, never took his experiment further. 'If I had a ball like that,' he lamented, 'I'd be practising at Lord's before breakfast.'

In Jack Iverson, however, we have the perfect cricket wish-fulfilment: the super bowler with the impossible talent of his own invention, the answer to all those post-Bosanquet daydreams, sublime, enigmatic, magical, perhaps even prophesied.

The freak cricketer from nowhere with the unique gift is a staple of cricket's fiction. He might be a batsman, like the African chieftain in Lord Dunsany's *How Jembu Played for Cambridge*, but more often he's a bowler, such as A. G. MacDonnell's 'mystery' paceman in the Bodyline-inspired burlesque *How Like an Angel*. There are countless variations. In Geoffrey Household's 1955 thriller *Fellow Passenger*, for instance, the reason for the bowler's mysteriousness is that he's the chief protagonist fleeing nefarious forces; he insinuates himself into a village cricket game and takes 6–9 with his off spinners.

Cricket is not alone in this. The player of preternatural ability but odd habit or ambiguous origin is found in the literature of baseball, too, from Ring Lardner's 'Alibi Ike' and 'Hurry' Kane to Bernard Malamud's immortal Roy Hobbs in *The Natural*. The Americans might even be said to have more fun with the idea: in Valentine Davies' film *It Happens Every Spring* (1949), chemistry professor Ray Milland becomes a superstar pitcher by coating his baseballs with a mixture that miraculously avoids wooden bats; in George Abbott's musical *Damn Yankees* (1957), there is the Mephistophelian presence of Mr Applegate, who endows the Washington Senators with a mighty hitter in return for a frustrated fan's soul. A recent episode of 'The X-Files' even posits the idea that many baseball greats were actually aliens.

A few cricket stories, however, stand comparison with any, and three I will discuss here resonate curiously with the story of Jack Iverson. One is *The Hampdenshire Wonder*, the first work by the English novelist John Davys Beresford, published in 1911. This will seem an odd inclusion; as Gerald Brodribb says in his famous essay on cricket in fiction, it is 'not strictly a cricket novel'. Yet the remarkable Ginger Stott of Hampdenshire is a genuinely original creation, all the stranger for his incongruity in what is essentially a work of science fiction.

Stott, a widow's son, is first enchanted by cricket at the age of seventeen when he watches a match in which a tailender's stubborn defiance is crucial. He leaves thinking 'I believe I could have bowled that chap', sets to practising at home, and develops a method of bowling with a kind of finger trick quite new to cricket; until, at least, Jack Iverson's appearance:

> He [Stott] used to spin the ball with a twist of his middle finger and thumb, just as you may see a billiard professional spin a billiard ball. To do this in his manner, it is absolutely necessary not only to have a very large and muscular hand, but to have very flexible and lithe arm muscles...Given those things, the rest is merely a question of long and assiduous practice. The human mechanism is marvellously adaptable. I have seen Stott throw a cricket ball half across the room with sufficient spin on the ball to make it shoot back to him along the carpet.

Physical attribute and the process of refinement is fundamental to Stott's technique. And because his original rehearsals in bowling take place in a yard fifty-three feet in length, he develops another unique faculty: he bowls from a standing start.

> His physique was a magnificent instrument. That long, muscular body was superbly steady on short thick legs. It gave him a fulcrum, firm, apparently immovable. And those weirdly long, thin arms could move with lightning rapidity. He always stood with his hands behind him, and then— as often as not without a preliminary step—the long arm would flash round and the ball be delivered without giving the batsman any opportunity of watching his hand. You could never tell which way he was going to break.

Extraordinarily, after an ankle injury in January 1951, Jack Iverson would experiment with just such a stand-and-deliver technique. And batsmen assuredly 'could never tell which way he was going to break'.

Stott meets with immediate success; in his second match for Hampdenshire, he dismisses all ten Surrey wickets for five runs, including six in six deliveries, all clean bowled. The only occasions over the next three seasons in which Stott is less than utterly destructive, in fact, are when batsmen attack him, for Beresford describes him as the 'victim of an obsession' with his artifice, and discomfited by its maltreatment; again a touch of Jack Iverson.

At the height of Stott's fame, however, fate intervenes. A split finger on his bowling hand, ineptly treated, must be amputated. His career is ended. And hereabouts, the novel takes a turn that can only be described as 'freakish', for the Hampdenshire Wonder of the title is not Ginger but his son Victor, whom the disappointed cricketer fathers explicitly in order to train as his successor. Alas, Ginger senses quickly that the infant is abnormal, muttering uneasily to the midwife: 'Ere, I say nurse, it's...it's a wrong 'un ain't it?'

Beresford, a clergyman's son, was crippled in infancy by polio; his fiction career was to feature both a determined agnosticism and an affinity for misunderstood freaks of nature. Victor proves to be an unearthly polymath—devouring sets of encyclopedia, dictionaries and works of the most recondite philosophy from the age of four—and destined for stranger deeds than even his celebrated father. Ginger, confounded, exits my 254-page edition after 100 pages with a resentful scoff: 'Learn 'im bowling! My Gawd! It 'ud take something. No fear, that little game's off. And I coulda done it if he'd been a decent 'ornery child, 'stead of a blarsted freak.'

The second fantasy fiction which we might conceive of as premonitory of Jack Iverson is Sir Arthur Conan Doyle's classic tale *The Story of Spedegue's Dropper*. Tom Spedegue is a village clergyman of fragile physique who is discovered in the New Forest throwing cricket balls fifty feet into the air so that they just clear a cord suspended between two oaks and descend at increasing speed on the stumps: fast bowling, as it were, from above. Through a delightful chain of events, he winds up at Lord's, performing before the home selection panel, who pitch him into the decisive Test of a series against Australia. In which, of course, in the face of derision and ribaldry, he claims fifteen wickets and recaptures the Ashes for England.

Spedegue's Dropper was written in 1929, and is very tangibly a post-Bosanquet story. There is in it the same sort of yearning as one detects behind cricket's various infatuations with lobs and leg-theory; that search for the 'next big thing'. Spedegue is inspired by Bosanquet:

> Just by using his brain he thought of and worked out the idea of concealed screw on the ball. I said to myself that Nature had handicapped me with a weak heart, but not with a weak brain, and that I might think out some new thing which was in the compass of my brain.

England's chairman of selectors emits a similar sigh: 'Bosanquets don't appear every day. We want brain as well as muscle behind the ball.'

Spedegue's Dropper is also a comic counterblast from Conan Doyle at the canons of orthodoxy for, faced by the novelty, the Australians are trussed by their trust in convention:

The slogging bumpkin from the village green would have made a better job of Spedegue than did these great cricketers, to whom the orthodox method was the only way. Every rule learned, every experience endured, had in a moment become useless. How could you play a straight bat at a ball that fell from the clouds?

Spedegue is not destined to linger: 'His heart would not stand it. His doctor declared that this one match had been one match too many, and that he must stand out in the future.' But it is universally agreed that he has reintroduced to cricket the spirit of playfulness, as only a willing innocent could:

> The Australian papers were first inclined to be resentful, but then the absurdity that a man from the second XI of an unknown club should win a Test match began to soak into them, and finally Sydney and Melbourne had joined London in its appreciation of the greatest joke in the history of cricket.

In what is probably also the greatest joke in the history of cricket writing, one could easily cast Jack Iverson without too much of a stretch. He also came from beyond cricket's fold, unencumbered by preconceptions of the orthodox, to become a Test match secret weapon. In a sense, too, Jack's heart would 'not stand it'. Again, however, as a sort of fictional intertext with Jack Iverson's life, it is not quite complete. We must look further, to the heady rise of Teddy Lamb.

Teddy Lamb is chief protagonist of *Pro* by Bruce Hamilton, older brother of the novelist Patrick, most famous for the plays on which the screenplays *Gaslight* and *Rope* were based. Subtitled *An English Tragedy*, *Pro* was the seventh novel in Bruce Hamilton's rather less distinguished fiction career, crafted while he was a history teacher at Harrison College in Barbados and sold to Cresset Press in September 1943 for a princely £50.

The story is relatively straightforward. Lamb is a nondescript medium pacer from fictional Midhampton who begins a 'routine of moderately severe labour' in the County Championship in the first decade of the twentieth century before active service that is 'a series of mischances which perhaps saved him from death or disability'. Glory impends after the war, however, when he devises a new technique of attack that becomes known as Q-bowling: a kind of leg-theory made possible by Lamb's unusually strong fingers.

While it sounds simple, however, *Pro* is one of the strangest cricket books ever written. It is more melodrama than tragedy, and Patrick Hamilton's biographer Sean French describes it as 'an authentic curiosity, rather as if a sporting tale for schoolboys were to have been rewritten by Thomas Hardy in the manner of *Jude the Obscure*'. But about certain passages there is a genuine miniature drama, especially as Lamb hatches his plan and conjectures about its future:

> Suppose Teddy was to concentrate, not on outswingers but inswingers, reinforced or not by his natural off break. Suppose he was to bowl them not, as was traditional, outside the off stump and coming in to the batsman, but moving away from him to the leg side. The batsman would have to play anything pitched on the wicket, for the ball might go with the arm, or even move the other way. He could not use his pads, for the ball would generally pitch

on or near the wicket. He would have to make a stroke. And waiting for the edged ball would be an intimidating ring of fieldmen, close in on the leg side; waiting for the hook or full leg hit a couple more, judiciously placed in the deep. Would not all but the very best batsmen be paralysed, find those formerly safe pushes to leg, in many cases almost their only run-getting resource, become suddenly as dangerous as flicking at the rising ball on the off?

For morning after morning, in strict secrecy, Teddy tried out the theory...He worked out the best speed, the right length, all possible variations which would prevent such an attack from becoming stereotyped. In the end, he believed he had got hold of something.

Q-bowling is at once a sensation. Lamb routs Yorkshire, Worcestershire and Northants, and Hamilton captures nicely his Iversonesque ascent to sporting celebrity:

> The *Daily Mirror* came out with a full front page photograph of his bowling arm, illustrating his grip. Tom Webster drew cartoons depicting him as a genial wolf in lamb's clothing. Interviews, or articles under his name, on 'How I Do It' or 'Why I Do It', or 'How I Thought Of It' appeared in dailies and weeklies. The words 'Lamb Again' occurred and recurred on the evening posters.

Having created Lamb, Hamilton then just as capriciously destroys him. Injury, a *femme fatale* and a vindictive captain play their part, but in general the author regards his character as beset by 'that ill-luck, which lies in wait for all those who look for popular sports for their living, and which had always singled out Teddy as special victim'. Lamb descends through a sort of sporting Inferno—umpiring, school coaching, selling scorecards and newspapers, pulling beers, the workhouse—and is last glimpsed in his bedsit thumbing sadly through old scrapbooks wondering where it all went wrong:

> Was it perhaps that all men had only a certain reserve of energy and resistance to draw on, and that he had by ill chance and evil circumstances been compelled to expend his too prodigally? Or had the war, those shiftless dangerous years, unprofitably squandered in the critical prime of his youth, taken its belated toll?

On the spur of the moment, it seems, Lamb gasses himself. The epilogue to this bizarre novel takes the form of a mock *Wisden* obituary which, in obeisance to the genre, dwells on the subject's playing career and skirts its squalid conclusion.

The depth of common experience between Lamb and Iverson is profound: humdrum medium pacer goes to war, invents new bowling in secret, wows cricket world, disappears quickly and mysteriously, drifts to a sad and solitary end. *Pro* was even published in 1946, the very year that Jack first wended his way to the nets at Brighton Beach Oval.

Yet it's also not quite right. For Jack was an *Am*, not a *Pro*. He did not devise his style of bowling in order to rise in cricket. He did it simply because he could. What we have in the Jack Iverson story, in effect, is a synthesis: it is as if a bowler gifted like Ginger Stott with the physical attributes for the extraordinary, and bringing to the summit of the game an element of Tom Spedegue's gentle but eager unworldliness, has been deposited in the bitter world of *Pro*, with its false dawns and fleeting fames. No-one would believe such a story if it were passed off as fiction. They had trouble enough believing it as fact.

EIGHTEEN

It was not only batsmen who went away from an encounter with Jack Iverson shaking their heads. Bowlers did, too. On the way to Adelaide in December 1949, Arthur Mailey asked Jack for a demonstration and could scarce believe his eyes:

> Not having a cricket ball handy at the time, he plucked an orange from the basket of an old lady standing by and gave me a demonstration. This was particularly educational for me, but somewhat exasperating to the old lady, who probably thought we were both cuckoo. Iverson placed the orange between the first and third fingers then put his second finger under the ball and flipped it along the floor as one might flip a fly off the table cloth.

So bizarre was Jack's method, in fact, that Mailey had reservations when Jack was picked for his first Test:

Bosanquet, the creator of the 'Bosey' or 'googly' ball put his complete trust in something tangible, something which could be developed and improved upon, but I think the Iverson invention will die with the genial creator. I am not condemning the Australian selectors for choosing Iverson in preference to McCool, Ring, Benaud or Fred Johnston, but I suggest that it is dangerous to place all your confidence in a machine for which you can't buy spare parts.

Clarrie Grimmett, by contrast, was actually a huge enthusiast for Jack, for he saw parallels between the two of them. Before World War I, in Wellington, Grimmett had tried to perfect a googly spun by extending the third finger on the right hand. He had abandoned the experiment—his hand did not have the strength—and could scarcely wait to see Jack bowl that first time in Adelaide. Nonetheless, Grimmett left their first conversation profoundly puzzled, as eavesdropper Hec de Lacy of *Sporting Globe* reported:

> Clarrie the Fox had a look at the mystery finger grip adopted by Jake the Giant Killer. 'That's your leg spinner, of course,' he remarked.
>
> 'No,' replied Iverson, 'that's my wrong 'un.'
>
> 'You've got me tricked,' said Grimmett in his slow deliberate way...They fell into talking of methods and, according to Clarrie, everything that Iverson did should have had the opposite effect.
>
> 'That's the off spinner?' quizzed Clarrie.
>
> 'No that's one I'm working on,' replied Jack. 'It spins from the leg.'

A spectator as Jack limbered up to play at the Gabba three months later was Percy Hornibrook, the sage old Queensland leggie who had understudied Grimmett in England in 1930. He left doubting the evidence of his eyes. 'If this fellow's doing it right,' he commented, 'then all the rest of us have been doing it wrong.'

So exactly how did Jack Iverson bowl? One shouldn't overstate the degree of his departure from the orthodox, for he did have more conventional virtues. His run-up was straightforward: starting with hands together, as though to conceal his artifice, he approached the bowling crease diagonally off an economical seven paces. It was no thing of beauty—the Reverend David Sheppard likened it to 'a heavy rook gliding in to land'—but it was smooth, balanced and expended little energy. His delivery stride and basic action was somewhat open-chested, but he delivered from a full height, and his body-swing and follow-through were exemplary.

Jack was not a classic spin bowler in that he was quick through the air, just the slow side of medium pace, and never condescended to such niceties as air and loop. But, as a tall man, he retained the priceless assets of bounce, to snarl glove and bat handles, and an unwaveringly, almost robotic accuracy. He seldom delivered on a drivable length, and hardly ever dropped short. George Murray, a left-hander from St Kilda who often batted against Jack at state practice, recalls:

> It was his length that was so good. You'd start coming forward to Jack but, with his height and his unusual flight, it always landed about a foot shorter than you expected, then bounced so it hit high on the bat. He was a very, very remarkable bowler.

Alan Davidson, who fielded in Jack's leg trap in New Zealand, recalls:

> He was a joy to field to at short leg. It's the sort of position where, with some bowlers, you go there in fear of your life. But I can't remember him ever bowling a half-tracker or having to take evasive action. Against the best batsman in the world, you'd feel as safe as a bank.

Jack's grip, too, was not entirely without precedent. In C. B. Fry's 1906 instructional bible *Great Bowlers and Fielders: Their Methods at a Glance*, the Australian all-rounder Warwick Armstrong can be seen with the ball in a three-point grip between his first two fingers and thumb. Fry noted: 'An uncommon grip for a leg break bowler. Apparently the second finger, curled under the ball, is the one that takes the purchase when the hand is turned.'

For two reasons, however, Jack took the grip further. The first was his capacious hand, far larger than Armstrong's. The second was that ball he was using was slightly smaller, its maximum circumference having in 1927 been reduced from 24 centimetres to 22.9 centimetres. Jack could thus coil his second finger right under the ball—leaving the forefinger out of the grip altogether—and it was when this digit was extended that bounds of credulity really stretched. Jack's instructions read like nothing you'll find in the *MCC Coaching Manual*:

> Place the ball between the thumb and third finger. Then bend back the middle finger into the palm of the hand so that the first knuckle joint of that finger rests behind the seam of the ball. When the bent back finger is straightened quickly, it acts as a spring and propels the ball over the top

of the thumb in the direction it is intended to break. The index finger plays little or no part in the action.

From this grip, Jack was able to produce three different deliveries: a googly, spinning clockwise, a top spinner, rotating forwards, and a leg break, running anti-clockwise. There was no twist of the wrist; all that altered was the positioning of the arm, with the unifying principle that the ball spun whichever way the thumb pointed: for the googly, it pointed to leg; for the toppie, it pointed straight at the batsman; for the leg break, it pointed to off.

The trickiest aspect was that the googly looked to the uninitiated a lot like a conventional leg break—with the hand pointing to the leg side, the back of it facing down the pitch—and the leg break like the contrary. The challenge for the batsman, in fact, was essentially that of counterintuition: when Jack walked like a leggie, he talked like an offie and vice versa. It was apparently possible to pick what Jack was bowling from behind, either from mid off or in the nets, but batsman had less than a second to surmise which of three ways the ball would deviate. And in Jack's first four seasons, many guessed wrong: in all classes of cricket he had claimed 350 wickets at 11.4.

The challenge for cricket's nomenclaturists, meanwhile, was to find a neologism for what Jack was bowling. He wasn't a wrist spinner, for the wrist really provided no leverage. He wasn't a finger spinner, for the middle finger imparted the propulsion not the rotation. He might have been called a thumb spinner, because it was his undersung thumb that was actually the fulcrum of the delivery. But who'd ever heard of a thumb spinner?

The epithet that attached itself most easily to Jack was

'mystery spinner'. It's a redolent phrase, but technically inexact, and sums up the bowler better than the delivery. Indeed, crick-eters never really came up with anything that quite fitted the bill, and it wasn't until a few imitators came along more than a decade later that the style found a name. When the New South Welshman Barry Rothwell played a game at Gunnedah in 1965 and found himself groping about against a local bowler called John Gleeson, he passed the word. 'You know what?' he advised his partner. 'This bloke's bowling Iversons.'

There are two miracles about Jack Iverson's bowling. Firstly, the physical strain of flicking a 5.25 ounce sphere of leather, cork and twine down a twenty-two-yard pitch, both fast enough to obtain traction and precisely enough to regularly hit a perfect length, is almost unimaginable. According to Brian Elliott, a biomechanist in the human movements department at the University of Western Australia, the force required by a slow bowler to propel a cricket ball from one end of the pitch to the other is about 70 newtons: the equivalent to the effort needed to push a seven-kilogram weight. Conventional spinners impart that force with a mixture of shoulder, arm, wrist, fingers, and elbow; Jack relied predominantly on his middle finger. In fact, as Ken Meuleman has told us, he was also capable of propelling the ball with his third finger without significant deterioration in accuracy; Jack told Hec de Lacy of the *Sporting Globe* that he trialled this method in the district final of March 1949.

Speaking anatomically, Jack was relying largely on a single ligament of the eight in his middle finger: the co-lateral on the radial side (that is, towards the thumb). Interestingly, the age that he often felt was a disadvantage may actually have been in Jack's favour. According to Greg Hoy, the Melbourne surgeon who recently treated Shane Warne for his shoulder injury, young joints remodel. Junior javelin throwers, for instance, can develop in their elbows a permanently 'lax ligament' which requires extensive treatment as they age. Jack by contrast only really started with a cricket ball when he was thirty-one—by which time his radial co-lateral would have been mature, stable and strengthened by maybe twenty years of exercise with his beloved ping pong balls.

The other miracle is that this superhuman feat came to Jack so naturally that he seldom thought much about it. He never even *pretended* to think much about it. As he put it with characteristic ingenuousness to a group of schoolboys at Melbourne's Spring Street Central School: 'So you want to know something about this funny old bowling of mine. Well, there's nothing to it. It's really very simple—in fact, at times, I do not know much about it myself.' He once told a Brighton teammate, Alan Tudor, that he did not decide what to bowl until his arm was almost at the vertical. His Australian comrade, Arthur Morris, decided it was simply a freak of nature that what left Jack's hand happened to drop always on a perfect length: 'The twenty-two yards of cricket pitch suited him perfectly. Had it been twenty or twenty-four, he would have been nothing.'

In Jack's time, in fact, that strange sense of someone who played cricket but hardly understood it was a source for his contemporaries of both wonder and despair. What talent the man had. But if only he'd had a 'cricket brain'.

If I heard this expression once, I heard it a thousand times: 'cricket brain'. It is one of those cricket expressions much easier to understand than to define. It has nothing to do with basic intelligence. It is quite distinct from talent or ability. Nor is it the same as an awareness of or conversance with technique, though that is undoubtedly a part. At its simplest level, we might think of it as a sense for cricket—mingling intuition, folk wisdom, practical physics and spatial aware- ness—that helps a player decide what to do when. To use some elementary examples: it's what tells an off spinner when the pitch is turning that he should push his line towards off stump to allow the ball room to spin back; what tells a medium pacer to drop slightly shorter to a tall batsman with a longer front- foot stride; what tells a batsman facing a left-arm bowler coming from over the wicket that a ball pitching on off stump can safely be left alone as it continues on its angle; what tells a captain when his quickest bowler is operating that his long leg should be finer rather than squarer. It is acquired, essentially, through playing, and to a lesser degree by watching. And, of course, when Jack started his career proper at the age of thirty- one, he had done little of either.

I was offered myriad examples of Jack's cricket naivety, particularly in the field. Apparently, he sometimes had diffi- culty remembering the names of fielding positions—Lindsay Hassett would have to point out where he wanted Jack to stand. He also found elusive the understanding that fielders should move in as the bowlers approached—he preferred to stand still, and rarely tried to stop a ball running either side of him. On the field, he sometimes said things that to lifetime cricketers sounded a little strange. Bill Johnston recalls how, during the first Shield match he played with Jack for Victoria at the Adelaide Oval in November 1950, Jack came up to him between overs while Lance Duldig was batting and said: 'You've got to get this fellow out, Bill.'

'Hang on,' Johnston replied. 'You've got eight balls in your overs just the same as I have.'

'Well,' said Jack, 'he got a century against us last time.' Johnston walked away wondering about the assumption that a batsman who'd scored a century once would naturally do so again.

No-one ever seems to have been too fussed by Jack's idiosyncrasies, and no-one told a story against Jack more often than Jack himself. As he said to one reporter:

> Once I tried running up from behind the umpire, and I got so wide out that I was no-balled for running outside the return crease. I've had many a laugh at myself and that day I stopped and laughed out loud. It seemed too silly to get all tangled up like I did.

Nor did anyone ever regard Jack's semi-consciousness of cricket as evidence of a lack of intelligence. It was simply that, in anything other than rolling his arm over and feeling the ball spin, he wasn't interested. Asked to sum up Jack's cricket philosophy, Clive Fairbairn says simply:

> I remember once, I was standing with him just as he was coming on to bowl. I said: 'There could be a bit in this track today, Jake. How about two slips?' He said: 'Clive, you place the field. I'll bowl the ball.' That was Jake all over.

In a sense, too, Jack's mystery was almost enhanced by its sheer weirdness. The traditional job of the slow bowler has been to tax by teasing. Where the fast bowler has posed the batsman a physical challenge to reflex and courage, the spinner has offered the more directly cerebral one of judgment and patience. Bowlers like Mailey, Grimmett and O'Reilly had 'cricket brains' that wove more plots than the Borgias. The most famous story about Grimmett concerns his being taken off by his South Australian captain Victor Richardson after three probing but unavailing hours bowling at Bradman: 'Well bowled—now put on your sweater, there's a breeze getting up.'

'Are you taking me off?' Grimmett replied. 'Just as I was working out my plan.'

English captain Mike Brearley once wrote delightfully in *Punch* of the unspoken conversation involved in facing Bishen Bedi, India's slow left-arm guru. Bedi: 'Ah, I held that one back slightly and you almost played too early.' Brearley: 'You're right, but I was onto it. You won't beat me with that one again.' Yet with Jack Iverson, there was no such silent dialogue. Batsmen felt instead in the thrall of a marvellous machine; every ball thereabouts, every ball of undiscoverable, menacing nuance.

How could you thwart such a bowler? As soon as Jack arrived on the scene, a veritable Bletchley Park of batsmen set to deciphering his encryptions. When New South Wales visited Adelaide in December 1949, a fortnight after Jack had taken 7–77 against South Australia, they heard all about the strange newcomer's devices. Having played a couple of seasons before for South Australia, NSW captain Ron James was welcome in the hosts' dressing-room and took careful note. Richie Benaud, then a nineteen-year-old all-rounder who played under James at Central Cumberland, recalls how he and opener Jim Burke benefited from this advice in the subsequent match against Victoria:

> He [James] came up with the news that Iverson was very, very good but that you had to treat him purely as an off spinner, despite your brain assuring you he was bowling leg breaks...We had lost four wickets when I walked out at the MCG. Burkie and I put together a good partnership and Iverson bowled just about all the time...Burkie played Iverson brilliantly, great footwork, and never changing his game plan of 'he's an off spinner' except when he saw one that looked a bit different, and that was invariably the leg break which on good pitches went straight on.

Just occasionally, the leg break did turn. On ordinary wickets, like nets and district cricket pitches, he could make the ball break enormous distances from leg. And in New Zealand, on its slower and damper surfaces, it often spun wickedly. But on Australian first-class pitches, as Queensland all-rounder Colin McCool recorded, it gradually became an article of faith that Jack's leg break seldom did other than hold its line:

> Well, if he bowled the leg break, I never saw it, and I don't think any other Australian did either. I'd read about this delivery, of course, before I played against him, but I put that worry right out of my mind as soon as I saw his approach to the wicket. It was so open-shouldered that I knew it was physically impossible for him to bowl the leg spinner.

It occurred to some batsmen, too, that Jack's astonishing accuracy might be turned against him. In a Melbourne match with Essendon, quite without warning, Jack suddenly began releasing an uncommon ration of full tosses to Ken Meuleman. Clive Fairbairn twigged that Meuleman was taking strike forward of his ground, and suggested to teammate Jack Daniel that they let their spinner know. 'Nah, let him cop a few,' said Daniel. 'We do every week.'

Nonetheless, the word was passed: Jack should bowl a little shorter. In fact, he could not achieve this using his normal action. Meuleman's partner George Thoms recalls standing at the non-striker's end watching Jack releasing the ball from half a metre behind the bowling crease to make the adjustment.

Another factor that worked in batsmen's favour was that Jack was just as vexing to wicketkeepers. Having driven his Brighton keeper Lex Tileman to distraction, Jack often did the same to his Melbourne and Victorian keeper Ian McDonald, to the extent that McDonald sometimes asked Jack to turn a different way at the end of his run according to which ball he intended bowling. Don Tallon, the hawk-eyed Queenslander who kept to Jack in New Zealand and subsequently in his five Tests, tried watching the rotation of the ball in flight, but there were days when even he struggled.

In fact, the player Jack felt kept best of all to him was Geoff Longney, Ian McDonald's teenage understudy at Melbourne, who made a dozen stumpings from him in ten matches. Longney first kept to Jack as a sixteen-year-old in the Melbourne nets:

> The first one he bowled was a ball that looked for all the world like a leggie and it broke a yard from the off. Then a

few balls later, he bowled what seemed like an Ian Johnson off spinner down the leg side and it broke the other way and hit the off stump.

Thereafter, Longney had a simple rule of thumb for keeping to the big spinner: the more it looked like one thing, the more likely it was to be the opposite. When he kept first for Melbourne in a match against St Kilda, Longney made a stumping from this first delivery, albeit rather luckily:

> The first ball was to Jack Edwards, who was a left-hander, and it turned and bounced when he went down the track, beat the bat, hit me in the shoulder, bounced into my left glove and I took off the bails. So I had a stumping off my first ball from Jack. I don't know what would have happened to me if I'd missed it, but I was fine from then on. I think I only missed one off him after that, and Jack was kind enough to say: 'I wish Tallon could have picked me like you.'

Jack knew there were batsmen intent on cracking his code, and worked hard to keep his edge. He never missed a state squad practice session, and was always among the first there. 'I was teaching at University High, so I'd often be early and get there about 4pm,' St Kilda's George Murray recalls. 'But Jack'd always be there, waiting for someone to bowl to.' By the time most players had arrived, Jack would have his rhythm and be making the ball wobble and weave. If he beat a batsman, he would laugh gustily; not gloatingly, but out of the same unalloyed pleasure he'd taken in his ping pong ball.

Perhaps Jack was even more in his element at practice sessions than in matches, for here he could indulge his pure delight in spinning the ball in a controlled environment. Geoff Longney certainly felt that was where Jack's chief pleasure lay:

> There was a bit of the kid about Ivo. When I say that I don't mean he wasn't a great bowler, but Ivo just loved beating the bat more than anything. He'd go into the sixth net we had at Melbourne, which was for the colts and third XI where nobody could lay a bat on him, and he just loved that.

That characteristic of enjoying bowling at the poorer batsmen, in fact, was one Jack displayed for his whole career. Len Hayball, who played with Jack in the early 1960s when he returned to Brighton, recalls:

> He loved practising and he'd always be down there early, because he enjoyed bowling to the kids. Of course, he absolutely bamboozled them. It wasn't Machiavellian, like he was lording it over them. It was just that he could do this thing and loved doing it.

We might also sense in Jack's practice habits his general quest for faith in his ability. With constant rehearsal, he could justify trusting in his magic. The leg spinner Roly Jenkins of Worcestershire, who had just taken 183 wickets in the 1949 English season, was much the same. A big-hearted, convivial man, Jenkins would nonetheless reach a crisis point every season where he felt he'd lost his gift. 'I've lost my mechanics,' he would say. 'They're just not working.' He would stake out a practice net, bowl for hours with a box of balls and by constant repetition claw his confidence back. And what better way for Jack to reinforce his confidence than by befuddling a string of inferior batsmen in the nets, much like a golfer building faith in his short game by knocking in short putts to savour the soothing sensation of the ball dropping in.

The few things that annoyed Jack at practice seem similarly to have been related to his search for self-belief. If someone took to him at state squad sessions, for instance, he would unobtrusively shift to another net. He also disliked being watched too closely. When NSW turned up to practice at the MCG nets after Victoria ahead of their interstate tussle just before Christmas 1949, for instance, wicketkeeper Stan Sismey recalls how quickly Jack stopped bowling: 'Soon as we arrived, he dropped the ball and cleared off.' In Jack's mind, it was all about staying ahead, feeling in control, preserving the mystery. If he could just maintain that feeling, who knew what he might achieve?

When Freddie Brown's MCC team arrived at Fremantle Gages aboard the *Stratheden* on 9 October 1950, all was set for Jack's supreme test. In *Sporting Life*, R. S. Whitington was casting Jack as 'Australia's trump bowler against England'. In rival magazine *Sports Novels*, Doug Ring was describing Jack as 'a bowler of near-genius' and forecasting that 'very good batsmen would have as much difficulty in playing Iverson as any other bowler in the game'. The touring press corps were leery, Stephen Fagan of the *Daily Graphic* deciding it was all part of the phoney war that preceded every Ashes series: 'The latest is Iverson whose feats round Melbourne—so they tell us—surpass even the Indian rope trick. It is all part of the Australian nerve war on our youngsters. There is no doubt that Australians pride themselves they can kid us.'

Such was the publicity in advance of Victoria's tour match with the MCC at Melbourne that England's batting bellwether Len Hutton sought the advice of the *Age*'s cricket correspondent Percy Beames. 'I've never batted against him, Len, so I can't help you much,' counselled Beames. 'All I can tell you is that he's amazing. You can't pick him, he turns it a long way, and he's incredibly accurate.' Beames was not known for his hyperbole, so one can imagine how Hutton regarded such intelligence. When prime minister Robert Menzies received the teams at a Windsor Hotel reception, in fact, Hutton made a beeline for Jack. 'I don't suppose,' the Yorkshireman said wryly, 'that you'd like to show me how you hold the ball.' Jack smiled, but kept his hand coyly round his glass.

NINETEEN

The eyes of the cricket world were on Jack Iverson when his
Victorian captain Lindsay Hassett threw him the ball at the
MCG just before lunch on 3 November 1950. Jack might have
hoped for better conditions. A chill wind blew, the first-day
surface was utterly benign, and four Victorian bowlers had so
far failed to separate the English opening alliance of Hutton
and Cyril Washbrook.

Jack's first over, in fact, went for 12, an anxious and unchar-
acteristic succession of full tosses and long hops. English
journalists must have lowered their binoculars with a sense of
vindication; they had recently seen their side humbled by a
genuine mystery bowler—the mischievous West Indian Sonny
Ramadhin had been the sensation of the northern summer—
and this Iverson was evidently not of the same standard. When

rain shortly banished players from the field and brought on an early lunch, one can imagine them pooling their sceptical judgments.

They were premature. When Jack bowled again from the Members' end, he settled at once on his usual immaculate length. The googly obtained surprising purchase and, when he turned a leg break away from Washbrook that was edged just short of slip, the usually imperturbable Lancastrian looked up like a man who'd seen a ghost. When Jack then bowled to the irrepressible Denis Compton, Jack Fingleton of the *Sydney Sun* was enthralled:

> Compton came to bat as if to suggest that he would put an immediate stop to this Iverson nonsense. He walked down the pitch and hit [Ian] Johnson for an immediate 4, but the first ball from Iverson found Compton's bat a foot away from the ball and there was a loud appeal for lbw. The next ball again beat Compton completely and a very worried Compton played out the rest of the over.
>
> Compton had evidently made up his mind that he would get to grips with Iverson. He began to run out before the next ball was bowled but Iverson dropped it short on him and Compton was left floundering, several yards up the pitch. Luckily for him, the wicketkeeper [Ian McDonald] lost the ball in his pads and Compton survived. The next ball again beat Compton. I have never seen him so befuddled by any bowler.

Compton put these escapades behind him to secure a three-hour century the next day, and Jack was not destined to break through until his twenty-first over when he bowled MCC keeper Arthur McIntyre. But his figures of 31–5–77–3—the best obtained by a spinner during the match—were agreed to have been an impressive Test audition. Nobody missed the meaning when Hassett did not employ him during England's brief second innings in the drawn match; Jack was being shielded for the big games to come. The grandee of the English press gallery, E. W. Swanton, wrote home to the *Daily Telegraph*: 'One would hazard that his flight presents no problems, but anyone who can pitch a good length, with enough spin to turn the ball appreciably on the first day at Melbourne, is obviously a bowler to be reckoned with.'

'Test cricket is not a light-hearted business,' Sir Donald Bradman had written a few months earlier in his new autobiography *Farewell to Cricket*, 'especially that between England and Australia.' Jack had stepped up to the first-class game in 1949–50 with the cream of Australia's players absent in South Africa, and would have noticed the heightened seriousness of competition in his second season as the latest instalment in Test cricket's oldest rivalry impended. Australia held the coveted urn after its pageant of success in England during 1948, and teams under its flag had not suffered defeat in 94 matches and more than a decade. Yet Bradman had retired, and the mercurial New South Welshman Sid Barnes, the country's most prolific batsman besides, had at least momentarily turned his back on Test cricket for the richer pickings of punditry. Perhaps this English side under its all-action amateur skipper Freddie Brown might turn back the Australian tide. Some handsome rewards awaited the summer's stars. Sydney's *Daily Telegraph* and businessman Ron Eaton announced that they would endow the Vok Awards for the series' best player to the tune of £1000, the winner to be decided on the basis of votes awarded by Arthur Mailey and ABC broadcaster Arthur Gilligan. Rather less formally, an East Melbourne grocer, Mr Maurice Branagan, announced that he would reward the Australian cricket team in mushrooms, at 7s 6d a pound, if they won the First Test.

The ritual of the induction of a new player in this long-running Anglo-Australian saga was now time-honoured, and on 22 November 1950 it was the turn of Jack Iverson. He actually learned that he'd been selected for his first Test from a mechanic. When a reporter from Melbourne's afternoon daily, the *Herald*, rang The Esplanade that morning with the good news, he was informed that Australia's new cap had gone to a garage in Carlton to pick up his car. A photographer arrived there to capture a gang of grinning grease monkeys pumping the big man's hand, a journalist to capture Jack's response.

Interestingly, Jack's first thoughts were not of sharing the moment with his wife and children, but of going to see his father at the Collins Street office of H. W. Iverson. 'I'll go and see the old man,' he told the *Herald*. 'He might even shout me lunch today.' Jack's father had no particular interest in cricket, had neither coached nor played with him, yet his was the company, the approval, that Jack sought. In fact, the procession of well-wishers at the office became so long in the afternoon that Jack and his father decided to head back to Brighton early.

The phones wouldn't stop ringing at Moana either, and the journalists kept coming, for pictures of the new boy *en famille*: Jack and Jean, Jack and his parents, Jack reading his daughters a bedtime story. Too young quite to understand what was going on, Sherry and Beverley Iverson grasped nonetheless it was something important: Moana's sitting room was saved only for the most important occasions.

For the journalists, it was a story to revel in: four years out of Brighton's 3rd XI, big, bashful Jack Iverson had been capped by his country. His disbelief oozed out to the *Argus* as he recapitulated his career:

> I know it sounds silly, but I just wasn't interested in big cricket until a year or so ago. Actually I hadn't even thought of cricket at all until 1946. For some reason or other I wandered along to the Brighton sub-district ground one evening and asked if I could get a bowl...I got a game with the thirds, and before long found myself in the first XI. And all the time I was wondering when they would 'wake up' and kick me out of the team. I just never dreamed I would play Test cricket.

Captivated, the *Argus* looked on Jack as an Australian epitome:

> Six feet two inches in height, 14 and a half stone in weight, with a tanned, angular face, Jack Iverson is every inch the popular conception of a typical Australian...As Jack went to answer the phone for the 100th time, his mother turned to an *Argus* reporter and said softly: 'He's wonderful! He's been a pleasure to us all his life...'

Hassett. Morris. Harvey. Lindwall. Miller. Johnson. Johnston. Tallon. Loxton. Moroney. What a constellation Jack Iverson now found himself part of: nine alumni of Bradman's invincible

1948 retinue, plus Barnes' tall-scoring successor Jack Moroney from New South Wales. In one respect, he was not out of place: it was an old team. The bonny twenty-two-year-old Neil Harvey aside, the average age of the team was over thirty. Otherwise, however, Jack had little in common with his new colleagues. This was a tight-knit, hard-nosed unit whose members had played a lot of cricket together and, even had Jack been an outgoing and ebullient character, he'd have found it difficult with his lack of experience to fit in. In fact, in the only interview Jack gave of any depth after his career was finished, he confessed to some quite profound insecurities about his position.

The interview, which took place at Jack's Collins Street office some fifteen years after his Test debut, was conducted by Alan Trengove of the *Herald*, an experienced feature writer of the day. 'He was a nice man, friendly,' says Trengove. 'A typical conservative businessman of that period, but I think still a bit overwhelmed by what had happened to him, and probably rather tickled that someone remembered him.' Some caution should probably be exercised in studying the text—in the style of the time, Trengove turned his transcript into a first-person narrative—but Jack perused it before publication and must therefore have felt its judgments authentic. It begins:

> Have you ever wondered what it's like to play Test cricket with an inferiority complex? What it's like to walk on to a field in front of a huge crowd and think: 'When is someone going to wake up to me?' Nobody could have been more nervous than I was in my Test cricket debut in the 1950–51 season after only one season of Sheffield Shield cricket...

> During all this period I waited for the day when
> someone would say: 'get the hell out of here you cheeky so-
> and-so.' Every time I walked onto a field, I would think:
> 'My God, how silly can a man get?'

If the sensations lingered after a decade and half, one can
imagine how palpable they were as Jack watched his first day
of Test cricket for twenty-one years from the home dressing-
room at the Gabba on 1 December 1950. He seems to have
kept himself to himself—a couple of the surviving members of
that team had to be reminded that he'd even played—and the
only two specific recollections involve Jack's solitary off-field
ways. Both Arthur Morris and Sam Loxton remember seeing
Jack slip back into Lennon's Hotel in the evening, having
apparently scurried away on his own for a meal at a nearby
greasy spoon.

An even more enlightening glimpse of Jack's state of mind
during his Test debut also exists. It relates to his first on-field
cameo, a moment of low comedy in the closing minutes of the
first day, when Jack joined Bill Johnston with Australia struggling at 9–226. Alec Bedser retold the story in his *Following On*:

> Bill sliced a ball from me over the slips. He felt certain it
> was going to the boundary and as he ran down the pitch I
> jokingly asked, 'What sort of stroke do you call that Bill?'
>
> He replied: 'I'm sorry Alec, but really it's one of my best
> shots. I get most of my runs with it.'
>
> This conversation took place in the middle of the
> wicket. But Reg Simpson had chased the ball and retrieved
> it just before it reached the boundary. Iverson was still
> charging up and down the pitch while Bill and I were
> chatting away happily, confident that it was four. Then I

looked up and saw Simpson about to throw to Evans.

'Look out Bill,' I shouted. 'You'll be run out.'

Back rushed Bill, all arms and legs. Iverson hared for his end and the result was that not a run was scored. Bill was out next ball for a duck.

No-one among the players or the press seems to have regarded it as other than a jolly joke, even flavoursome of the friendly relations between the sides. But a few days later there appeared a curmudgeonly and quite inaccurate letter in the *Courier-Mail* from a Mr M. M. Scott of George Street, Brisbane, who retold the story as a means of criticising the Test debutant:

> Iverson's bat was struck by a ball which then travelled towards the fence, it looked like going for four. They could have made three but Johnston ran two and Iverson half a run. He then stopped to parley with Johnston in mid wicket, then both started running for the one end with Iverson turning back to where he had started without having completed a run—result nothing. Even should Iverson take all 10 wickets, the game is better than that, and the selectors should be severely censured for including in a Test a player with so little knowledge of cricket.

Johnston remembers the incident—and the admonishing correspondence—well. 'Poor old Jack,' he says. 'It was all my fault, and this fellow in the paper blamed him.' Jack didn't forget either. He cut out the letter, and included it in his scrapbooks alongside a rare handwritten annotation:

> It was Bill who stopped.
> It was Bill who hit the ball.
> I ran two runs.

Bill ran 1.

Andy Barlow called no run.

Actually 1 run should have been recorded as we crossed once and I made the crease twice.

Why should Jack have gone to the trouble of collecting such a silly and intemperate letter, and setting down such a deliberate and detailed self-exculpation? It would seem the act of a man, in Jack's own words to Alan Trengove, 'who never got over the feeling that he was an impostor'.

Jack's role in that First Test was for the first three days utterly overshadowed by events. It was, as Jack Fingleton put it, 'surely the craziest and maddest Test match of all time'. Australia was rolled on the Friday for 228—its smallest home total for thirteen years—but monsoonal weekend rain had by the resumption of play on Monday transformed the uncovered pitch into twenty-two yards of sheer batting hell. Twenty wickets tumbled for 130 runs: Freddie Brown closed England's first innings at 7–68, Hassett Australia's second innings at 7–32, and England was 6–30 by the close. About 12,000 watched the carnage, and thousands more followed it round the city on a switchboard instituted by the *Courier-Mail*, whose Arthur Richards reported:

Judging by our telephone calls, Brisbane people found yesterday the most stirring day in local Test history. From mid-morning until night, excited men, women and children rang to ask the score. Each switch-girl dealt with one inquiry every four seconds; 900 an hour.

Not even during the Jardine-Larwood bodyline series was Brisbane so athirst for news.

Jack finally bowled his first over amid this chaos at 5.33pm, just as the sun was at last breaking through the inky vault of cloud, with England 2–22 in its second innings. He hitched his trousers and waited for Hassett to set a suitably minatory field: a slip and two close leg side catchers. Jack would have been forgiven nerves, having waited so long for his chance, but in the event betrayed none: his first over was a probing maiden to England's stubborn all-rounder Trevor Bailey, Loxton at short leg performing an elaborate dumb-show of expectation as six of the eight deliveries whipped from the pitch.

When Miller torpedoed Bailey's partner John Dewes with a yorker in the next over, nightwatchman Bedser traipsed out to take guard. Jack struck twice: Bedser spooned him to cover and Bailey wellied him to backward square leg. Arthur McIntyre poached a boundary to leg, then was run out next ball on the last leg of an all-run four, Tallon collecting a wild return in mid-pitch and opportunistically demolishing the stumps with a seven-metre throw from his gloved hand: a vignette somehow in keeping with the eccentricity of the whole day. Arthur Mailey wrote: 'I have never seen so much anguish, pain, jubilation, anxiety and embarrassment in one day's cricket in my life.' Neville Cardus added: 'It is refreshing to see celebrated batsmen, mighty hunters of runs, themselves hunted and harried and baited to death by their victims—the perse-cuted bowlers.' R. C. Robertson-Glasgow believed that, had the Marx brothers been watching, they would now be planning to film *A Day at the Test*.

Jack himself could hardly have hoped for more: 3–1–8–2. Harold Larwood, guest columnist in the *Courier-Mail*, offered an approving nod: 'I've seen Jack Iverson bowl at last, and thought that he was most impressive. He was the only spinner used by either side all day. He found a length with his first ball and maintained it for his three overs.' The debutant also had a feature role on the final day, as Australia winkled out the visitors' last four in the face of some glorious and revelatory strokeplay from Len Hutton. Jack's 4–43 from 13 overs prompted the comment from Bert Oldfield in the *Sun* that the newcomer fitted in Australia's attack 'as though he had been playing Test cricket for years'. Now the successful member of a victorious Australian Test side on a pitch that should not have suited a spinner—his slow-bowling partner Ian Johnson had not even been granted an over—could Jack still have seen himself as 'an impostor'? The answer appears to be yes.

The Melbourne Test of 1950–51 was scheduled to sprawl over eight days: six of play straddling successive festive rest days on Christmas Eve and Christmas Day. It would be the biggest cricket match of Jack's brief career and, as ever, the summer's sporting social zenith. Prime Minister Menzies and the British ambassador were guests of the Melbourne Cricket Club. The chairman of the Australian Cricket Board of Control Dr Allen Robertson was hosting a lavish dinner for both teams before Christmas, Victorian Cricket Association president Dr Arnold Seitz a cocktail party at the Windsor Hotel after. Nothing, furthermore, held a candle to an Ashes contest at the MCG as an attraction for spectators. Two watchers whose presences attracted newspaper notice were nonagenarian David Henry Fox, who had not missed a first-class game in Melbourne since 1881, and RAF Squadron Leader Rex Benson, who was convalescing from injuries in an air accident at Heidelberg Repatriation Hospital and who watched the game from his head-to-foot plaster cast with the aid of a periscope.

In a tense and low-scoring match, Jack was to be Australia's most successful bowler in England's first innings and perform a crucial auxiliary role in its second. His 4–37 on the second day from eighteen overs kept the visitors to a three-run lead, and his 2–36 on the last from twenty overs helped Lindwall and Bill Johnston harry them to a 28-run defeat. In his tour book *Ashes to Hassett*, John Kay of the *Manchester Evening News* decided that Jack had 'dictated the trend of the game'. Yet Jack's own recollection of the match to Trengove fifteen years later was that he didn't do 'anything sensational', and was unsure if the performances would be sufficient to keep his place in the team.

Jack's memory of the match was probably tarnished by his unwitting role in an umpiring controversy that marred the second day. As he bowled to Hutton just before lunch, the Yorkshireman aborted a pull shot and allowed the ball to lob from his pad over his shoulder and into Tallon's gloves. Accounts disagree as to who shouted 'Catch it!'—some say Jack, others say Hassett at mid on—but the unanimous opinion was that umpire George Cooper's upholding of Jack's appeal was a miscarriage of justice. Keith Miller, who was standing at short leg, recalls how the blood drained from Hutton's face as Cooper's finger rose. Johnnie Moyes, in *The Fight for the Ashes*, wrote: 'The batsman looked as staggered as a man who has just received his income tax assessment.'

Nobody blamed Jack, but few spared Cooper. 'An umpir-ing blunder has practically ruined England's chance of Test victory,' wrote Larwood. Even Tom Goodman, the temperate and fair-minded cricket correspondent of the *Sydney Morning Herald*, was inclined to agree:

> It is distasteful to have to refer to these 'umpiring' incidents, and more so to have to criticise them. From the press box, here situated at an awkward angle, it would be wrong to offer an opinion in this case. However, the best evidence available from men on the scene—and their evidence is unchallengeable—is that Hutton was extremely unfortunate.

Jack left behind no specific recollection of the incident and his inadvertent complicity in it, but told Trengove that he was apprehensive when the Third Test began in Sydney on 5 January 1951, fearful that Hutton was 'after my scalp because he'd been given out in what some considered a doubtful decision...in the Melbourne Test', and having heard that 'one or more of the English batsmen' had made it apparent 'that they wanted to belt the daylights out of me in order to destroy the myth'. It was in Sydney, however, that he was to prove his myth a reality.

Jack's impression that some English batsmen were after him in Sydney may have some foundation. In a lengthy summary of the series for *Sporting Life*, Keith Miller wrote of a conversation he shared with Hutton on the eve of the match:

> Discussion ultimately got around to Iverson. Hutton, with a glint in his eye that suggested trouble for the bowler, said in his broad accent: 'I'll show you how to crack him before

the tour is over la-ad.'

He did not hint at his plan but knowing Hutton I knew that he had thought deeply on the matter. That is always enough to spell trouble for the bowler.

In due course, Hutton did play Jack well on the first day, pouncing on one overpitched ball early and cover-driving it for four, then winking at Miller. A couple of overs later, he came down the pitch again and straight-drove a second boundary. Miller noted that Hutton's footwork showed a streak of premeditation: 'I noticed that as Iverson was about to deliver the ball, Hutton pushed his left leg down the pitch a little ready for that overpitched ball. If the ball was too short, either he allowed it to strike his pad or just played it with a dead bat.'

There does not, however, seem to have been any concerted attempt by the English team to prepare a strategy for playing against Jack, drawing on its experiences against the West Indian Ramadhin. 'The English team did not pool knowledge as far as I remember,' recalls John Dewes. 'We did not compare Jack with Ram, as they were so different. Ram flighted the ball more and he did not have Jack's bounce.'

So the fact that Jack went wicketless in a first innings spell of only 10 overs for 25 seems to have had more to do with the sheer blandness of the first-day SCG pitch; Alec Bedser recalled it, in fact, as the slowest Sydney pitch he ever saw, due to the use of tons of sand to expedite its recovery after the rugby season. Mild disappointment *was* expressed in the press about Jack's failure to penetrate, and Bert Oldfield felt it betrayed some of his limitations: 'When Hassett dispensed with a slip it showed just how innocuous he had become. I saw him bowl one leg break—but it didn't turn an inch.' But Jack's retrospective dramatisation of his failure to break through on that first day, as related to Trengove, makes curious reading:

> In the minds of the selectors, I was on the mat in the Third Test. Sydney provided a perfect track. It was so good in the first innings that I told our captain Lindsay Hassett, 'I can't get any response at all.' He took me off and I thought, 'This is it—this is the end of the line.'

The facts were that, this brief barren spell notwithstanding, Jack had taken 10 wickets at 14 at the mid-point of his first Test series from 61 eight-ball overs; though inferior to Bill Johnston, who had claimed thirteen wickets at 13.3, this was still superior to Lindwall, Miller and Johnson. Furthermore, no bowler who might have been considered an alternative to him—Queensland's Colin McCool, Victoria's Doug Ring, New South Wales' Fred Johnston and South Australia's Jack Wilson—was at that stage of the season paying less than 30 runs a wicket. The sheer lifelessness of the Sydney surface set everything in context, as Australia replied to England's 290 by passing 400 with four first-innings wickets still standing. If there was any 'mat' on which Jack reposed as the Test entered its fourth day, it was of his own making.

Jack made another curious remark to Trengove about the circumstances of what was to transpire on 9 January 1951. In trying to explain why the fourth-day pitch at Sydney was of such different character from that which had prevailed on the three preceding days, he spoke of rain on the third evening: 'Wickets were not covered in those days and the track was different the following day.'

Trengove did not think to check this assertion—why should he?—but Jack was actually mistaken. The rain in the match fell on the evening of the rest day, taken after two days, at which time Australia was 2–110, and had little or no bearing on the match. In his *Elusive Victory*, E. W. Swanton reported:

> Half an inch of rain fell on the parched wicket on Sunday evening—fully enough to arouse English hopes. But only a few balls in the [next] morning's play did anything to indicate the odd spot of moisture remaining in the turf. A mile from the ground, the fall had been twice as heavy. On such accidents of nature do great events depend!

Which indeed they do, though the great event for which Jack was shortly to be responsible owed nothing to the elements, or to geology, or even luck. It was, hard as Jack seems to have found believing it, nothing other than the work of a great bowler.

TWENTY

As Australia took the field after lunch at the SCG on 9 January 1951, the applause was appreciative but earnest. The crowd swelling past 30,000 had so far spent the day in light-hearted enjoyment of the Australian tail's last twitchings, and in genuine sympathy for the travails of a popular touring team reduced by injury to only three bowlers. Now there was the feeling that the Ashes might be decided that day. England trailed by 136 on the first innings, and Bill Watt's pitch was now into its fourth day.

The Australians fanned out to encircle Len Hutton and Cyril Washbrook, a new ball nestling in Ray Lindwall's grip at the Paddington end, the field an intimidating formation of expert cricketers. Keith Miller and Ian Johnson, already responsible for a stand of 150 runs and seven wickets between them, lounged at slip. Harvey, Sam Loxton and Ken Archer patrolled the in-field as keenly as kelpies. Tallon behind the stumps looked as vigilant as a policeman on a stake-out.

Yet the break did not come. Hutton and Washbrook met the thrust of Lindwall and Miller adeptly for half an hour, Hutton presenting nothing but the broadest of bats, Washbrook tucking away some riskless boundaries. And the pitch: unlike the black and basalt-hard Bulli surfaces of Bradman's prewar heyday, the Sydney track was visibly a lighter shade, more like chocolate, the wear visible, the profits for pace reduced. Spin might today prove decisive. Bill Johnston replaced Miller at the Randwick end with a maiden, but the figure hibernating at mid on held out perhaps the greatest hope of all.

The crowd had seen Jack Iverson once that day already, briefly swinging his heavy bat, and again displaying his incompetence with it: having equalled his highest Test score of one, he'd been run out attempting a hopeless second. But the crowd's murmur was audible at 2.45pm when Hassett passed him the ball at the Randwick end, and there was also a sense of expectation on the field. In their brief last-wicket stand before lunch, both Miller and Iverson had seen leg spinners from England's captain Freddie Brown deviate sharply. 'You'll turn a yard on this,' Miller had muttered encouragingly. 'It's on,' Jack had said to himself.

As he watched Hassett marshal his formation, Jack felt a pang of disquiet about his off-side protection. Johnson at slip, Harvey in the covers, Arthur Morris at point; surely he could not curb the great Hutton and Washbrook with a three-six field. But he could. There was, as usual, no anxious loosener:

Washbrook stole forward to smother a first delivery of inch-perfect length that twisted back treacherously before rolling to Johnston at short fine leg. And twice in a spotless over, good lbw appeals were rejected by umpire Andy Barlow. Jack took his cap to appreciative applause.

Miller at forward short leg could see Hutton's left leg tensing as Jack bowled his second over, and wondered if the spinner's control would hold. It did. Another maiden, the Yorkshireman incarcerated in his crease, his pads absorbing the ball like a pile of sandbags, but his bat needing to be held from harm. A stillness had come over the day. Even Jack knew they were coming out well; he glanced at the scoreboard, saw no runs against his name, and felt a little flush of confidence. For the third ball of his next over, he decided to throw in that funny old leg break of his, the one that never quite worked, but on this pitch just might.

How it worked, and how he would cherish that ball in years to come. Hutton, advancing, pulled up just short of the half-volley, and felt the ball kiss his outside edge. The eye could scarcely follow what ensued: Tallon deflected the snick wide, Johnson surged forward from slip to interpose a couple of fingers and arrest its flight, the keeper arched backwards and at full stretch recaptured the rebound in his right gauntlet. Hutton, bat groping for the sanctuary of the crease, watched his dismissal, transfixed. Jack, raising his arms halfway, felt suddenly 'up in the clouds'.

Reg Simpson negotiated the maiden, and two other maidens followed before Washbrook seemed to relieve the tension by helping himself to two boundaries from Johnston. But with the sixth ball of his fifth over, Jack struck again,

Simpson helping a huge wrong 'un into Tallon's gloves down the leg side. And though singles to Washbrook and new batsman Denis Compton in his sixth over momentarily marred the purity of his analysis, there was more to come: Washbrook, groping sightlessly at a wrong 'un, was bowled by the fifth ball of Iverson's seventh over.

It was all down to confidence, Jack told Alan Trengove fifteen years later, 'because when you are completely confident some sixth sense takes over and you bowl like a demon'. He was even fielding, for him, well. The ball had harried him throughout the first innings, following him round and exposing his inelasticity. On a couple of occasions now, he stopped well-struck Compton on drives, enjoying generous rounds of applause. And by the time the umpires lifted the bails for tea at 4pm, Jack's figures read 10–5–11–3. He did his best to accept the ovation modestly, walking cap in hand and eyes front as Hassett allowed him to pass first through the gate. 'Said you'd turn it, son,' Miller said, playfully slapping his back.

With the injured Trevor Bailey and Doug Wright unlikely to bat, Compton and Gilbert Parkhouse represented effectively England's last line of resistance, and every ball Jack bowled after the break contained the whiff of a wicket. Compton would normally have swept a bowler pitching Jack's line, but the overspin on his stock ball made it simply too dangerous. His googlies struck the pads so often and so hard, in fact, that the ball had to be wiped with a rag to remove white cleaning powder. His control was so precise that Parkhouse finally ventured off on a foolish single and was thrown out by Loxton.

Having bowled unchanged for more than two hours, and conceded only 15 runs from eight overs after tea, Jack finally gave way for a breather to Johnston at 5.15pm; a typically astute piece of Hassett captaincy. Relaxing fatally, Compton stabbed to slip, and Godfrey Evans was bowled offering an over-eager swipe at Johnson. England's determination to make the 17 runs necessary to avoid the ignominy of an innings defeat was evidenced when Bailey, broken thumb in a cast, joined his skipper Brown. But Hassett whistled up Jack from his twenty-minute furlough to complete the work he'd begun, and the bowler did so in a dozen deliveries. Brown played all round a top spinner. Bedser shouldered arms to a wrong 'un pitching wide of off stump and had his leg stump disturbed— his *leg stump*, would you believe it? Last man John Warr swung dejectedly at his first delivery and immediately joined in the ritual scramble for souvenirs. The electric thrill was so great that Jack sang out to Miller at slip: 'I wouldn't mind a piece of that!' Miller smiled: 'You'll get it, son.' And as they neared the gate, the great all-rounder popped the ball in Jack's pocket with words the spinner would always remember: 'Here, you deserve this.' Local association secretary Syd Smith would arrange for its mounting in an engraved silver hoop reading: 'Presented to J. B. Iverson by the New South Wales Cricket Association to commemorate his feat in obtaining six wickets for 27 runs during the Third Test Australia v England 5 to 9 January 1951 Commonwealth Jubilee Year.'

It was 5.51pm, just over three hours since Jack Iverson had released his first ball, and now he had won a Test match for Australia ensuring the retention of the Ashes. He had, Jack Fingleton said in the *Sydney Sun*, 'bowled as well on this day as I have seen an Australian spinner bowl'. His performance would, Percy Beames told readers of the *Age*, 'completely dispel the last lingering doubts on his greatness'. He might prove, Percy Millard commented in Melbourne's *Herald*, 'Australia's greatest match-winner since Bradman.' Even the sceptical Cardus was humming a hymn of praise in the *Sydney Morning Herald*: 'I gladly eat the words of doubt I expressed the other day about his essential quality. A man is a fool, and loses not gains, if he cannot change his mind when new evidence is put before him.'

Yet perhaps the strangest event of the day was still to come. For when journalists flocked to Jack for a few quotes to line their columns for the next day, he told them he intended to retire. 'I have been wondering about whether I should continue,' Jack said, 'and even after today's enjoyment I might decide to give up the game right away.'

Jack had provided many unusual spectacles in his brief career, but his equivocations after the Sydney Test were among the most intriguing. Just as he had rushed off to see his father first on the day of his Test selection, so did he think of his father first on the day of his greatest triumph.

Jack explained to reporters that Harry had been ill with rheumatoid arthritis—in fact, both Harry and Ede were sufferers—and that he might need to make a greater commitment to H. W. Iverson. 'I love my cricket and I don't want to give it up yet,' he told Tom Goodman of the *Sydney Morning Herald*. 'But I cannot make any decision until Friday night when I'll have a long talk with my father in Melbourne.'

It cannot be determined today if there was any understanding between Jack and his father about his future, although

Jack's ready reference to his filial duties so soon after his crowning achievement suggests that they must have been a prior topic of conversation. And Harry's own statements to the press—for he was sought out for comment—carry a similar implication. When an unnamed journalist from the *Sun* called on The Esplanade on the evening of 9 January, Harry said that he was happy for his son to continue playing, but only for the time being:

> Jack's only thinking of me when he talks of retiring. I'm confident that he'll see the season through. Jack knows I'm getting on in years and he knows the state of our business. Tonight, I feel on top of the world. I can hold things together until the end of the cricket season...I'm not going to stand in his way.

This qualified endorsement had, by the time Alf Brown of the *Herald* visited H. W. Iverson the next day, turned into something rather more stern:

> I intend to take it easy from now on. He won't have time for the big stuff, although he might be able to continue with district cricket. Jack has his responsibilities and if he sticks to big cricket in spite of them, he would be very foolish.

One shouldn't wonder that Harry was keen to step back from his business. He was to turn sixty-six in a week, and it was fully twelve years since Jack had returned from Landscape to become a sub-agent with H. W. Iverson, only to be claimed first by the war and then by sport. And, for her part, Jack's daughter Sherry believes that her father *was* under pressure to give the game away:

I think my grandfather was proud of what Dad did, but I think he was saying: 'You've had five years of cricket. It's about time to settle down and make a living.' Had Dad had one or two brothers, things might have been different, but he didn't, and it wasn't, and that was the way it was.

Jack's dilemma of cricket versus career, however, was not an uncommon one in his time. For most, the game remained an amateur pursuit. The 1950–51 domestic Test match fee was a relatively attractive £60—six times average weekly earnings— but a Sheffield Shield player could expect only about £6 a match and his professional advancement to suffer as a result of the time cricket consumed.

So why did Jack consider his own situation unsustainable? Lindsay Hassett, for instance, had set up his own Melbourne sports store in February 1949, then had to leave it for six months to tour South Africa, but was still playing avidly at an age two years Jack's senior. At the other end of seniority, Jack Moroney, two years Jack's junior, was supporting a wife and four children on a teacher's salary. Jack's post-Sydney prevarications seem understandable only in two contexts: an acute sense of honour and obligation to his father, whose sacrifices in his interest he seems to have been uncommonly aware of, and an attachment to cricket rather looser than that of his peers. Jack had pursued his sporting goals too devotedly to be classified a weak man, but his public equivocations smack of a rather deferential one. They are certainly at odds with someone whose self-perception was as 'a bit of a rebel'.

In the end, Jack did play on, informing Victorian selector Jack Ryder on the morning of 13 January that he would be available for the rest of the summer, but that thereafter he would be available only for district cricket. It was ten days before the selectors were due to reconvene, and widespread relief prevailed, for this most unlikely figure was now as big a star as any in the game.

TWENTY-ONE

When Jack came down for breakfast at the Australians' hotel on the morning after the Sydney Test, he got instead a taste of his own new celebrity. Sir Donald Bradman was the only other diner, and the chairman of selectors issued him a friendly warning: 'There must be at least fifty blokes outside the front porch. They're not waiting for me. They must be waiting for you.'

For a month or so, Jack was the toast of Australian cricket. His face was in every newspaper, on a set of cricket badges produced by the *Argus*, even on a box of Duncan's Yachts safety matches. Arthur Mailey presented him with one of his famous caricatures, featuring Jack as a human corkscrew with the fond caption 'From one twister to another.' Schoolboys passing 148 The Esplanade commented that this was 'where the Test cricketer lives'. There was even a racehorse named after him: Iverson, a two-year-old bay gelding by Cold Shower from Turvo, raced by a Mr P. C. Bell. And on 16 January, he became the subject of his own newsreels, performing his repertoire for both Movietone and Cinesound at Brighton Beach Oval.

Viewing this footage—now transferred from 35mm nitrate stock to video by the National Film and Sound Archive—was one of the most delightful detours of my search. Movietone's newsreel cameras were positioned behind the batsman's stumps, a small but appreciative crowd behind the bowler's arm, as Jack rehearsed his repertoire. The toppie skidded through, the leggie turned just enough, the wrong 'un broke quite massively, and bounced like a rubber ball. And as though to deepen the mystery, the hand was obscured by a black square so that its varying attitudes could not be associated with individual deliveries: one wonders whether this was Australian caginess or Jack's proprietorial disposition towards his art.

Jack barely acknowledged the camera. Shyly but intently, he spring-loaded a ball in his fingers and squeezed it out a couple of times. The ball whirred, even seemed to hover, before settling back in that huge hand. It was like a magician producing a dove from his shirt cuff. I was dumbstruck: still photographs of Jack, entrancing in their own way, had not prepared me for the sensation of watching him bowl, however artificially. Sadly, Jack was also dumb: the original soundtrack had been lost and, when he briefly addressed the audience, there was no accompaniment to his moving lips.

The Cinesound reel, however, delivered on its promise: 'Vic Wonder Bowler Jack Iverson Shows How He Does It'. A batsman, keeper and a scattering of fieldsman, arrayed to convey the Englishmen's dilemma, went through motions narrated by announcer Charles Lawrence. 'Watch this one,' Lawrence promised. 'It's an Iverson special.' And so it was, jabbing through a batsman's gate like a fencer's foil. 'Here's one on a nasty length,' Lawrence continued as Iverson floated one down the pitch to imperil the stumps. 'And it just tips the bails...But that's good enough in a Test match as quite a few Englishmen know.' A touch of Australian *schadenfreude* that locals would doubtless have silently applauded.

Historian Alf Batchelder recalls watching the film at St Kilda's Palais theatre. As a wheeze, management invited Iverson on stage to demonstrate his bowling to a juvenile batsman protecting a box. The tennis ball bounced once one way, then another, past the probing boy and into the ersatz wicket. For more than forty years, Batchelder doubted the evidence of his own eyes, until he interviewed Jean Iverson while compiling an entry on her husband for the *Oxford Companion to Australian Cricket*. Yes, she said matter-of-factly, her husband could do that. That and so much else.

Something was now happening to Jack Iverson at the peak of his success, however, something he had perhaps foreseen, but which nonetheless would have come as a shock. Being a star cricketer introduced cares he'd not experienced; he was a bowler whose threat opposing batsmen needed to neutralise.

The day after his newsreel appearance, Jack joined Hassett's Victorian team flying to Brisbane for its match against Queensland. In 1949–50, he'd routed the northern state twice, taking 17 wickets for 175 in two matches. But in their first encounter in 1950–51, the Queensland batsmen had fared better, especially Don Tallon and Colin McCool during a brief but bright second-innings stand of 75 in forty-minutes. McCool, in particular, had concluded that Jack might wilt under sustained attack:

> His lack of experience let him down badly as soon as the batsmen started to 'tap' him. Tallon, who was a good player of spin bowling, and myself got stuck into him...Iverson just didn't know what to do. In his agitation his arms started flapping like ducks' wings as he walked back to his mark, and the harder we hit him the more his arms flapped. It was fascinating.

At this second meeting at the Gabba, the locals played Jack even better, especially the adhesive Ken Mackay, who batted almost seven hours in the match for 57 and 139 not out. On a pitch conducive to spin, Ian Johnson bagging 12–181, Jack recorded the poorest analysis of his career: 1–110 from 33 overs.

The Victoria–New South Wales Shield match that began at the SCG three days later was an even more significant reversal. Jack's figures against a strong home batting line-up were 29–5–108–3, with two of his Test teammates in delectable form: left-hander Arthur Morris, having scored 29 in his four preceding innings, made 182 in five and a quarter hours; Miller, in 99 minutes, clubbed 83. When Jack was bowling, Morris and Miller evolved a simple rule of thumb: the high-tossed ball tended to be the top spinner, the lower-trajectory delivery the wrong 'un. Only batsmen as accomplished as Morris and Miller could have profited from such an observation, but their finding was significant: they had demonstrated that, even if Jack remained unintelligible from the hand, he could be decrypted in the air.

Morris recalls the match with characteristic modesty:

> Jack was an extraordinary bowler. I always played spinners from the hand, but he was one bloke I could never pick. For the first 80 or so, I had no idea what it was going to do. But after that I suddenly realised that you could pick him in the air, which is something I'd never done before and it was probably the only time I ever did it: his off break, he spun tremendously, but the other one he just looped. And I think that surprised Jack a bit. He was the kind of fellow who, if he didn't take 5–20 every time he bowled, he thought he was a failure.

Miller's chief recollection, meanwhile, is of Jack's stupefied expression as he was deposited in the Ladies' Stand: mouth agape, bottom lip quivering, eyes uncomprehending. 'It was almost like: "You can't do that to me",' Miller said. 'Like he couldn't believe it had happened.' The Sydney newspaper headlines, so joyous in Australian victory three weeks earlier, now had a more parochial feel:

> Jack the giant killer got whacko
> NSW batsmen win first battle against Iverson
> Batsmen smash Iverson bogy

The subtext of the Morris–Miller ambush is as intriguing as the duel in the middle. Miller asserted in his 1956 book *Cricket Crossfire* that, for the duration of the Ashes series, Hassett and Ian Johnson had seen to it that Iverson never bowled to NSW batsmen at Australian practice sessions. He wrote:

> At Brisbane in 1950 Arthur Morris went out for practice
> and, as he walked into one net, Iverson left and went into
> another where a Victorian player was having a knock. The
> usually placid Morris was furious. He put on a real show in
> the dressing-room, demanding something be done about
> this sort of stupidity. 'We are representing Australia. It is
> disgraceful to let interstate considerations be carried to such
> lengths.'

The story has since been widely retold. In his *Bumpers, Boseys
and Brickbats*, most popularly, that prolific chronicler Jack
Pollard linked the two events—Hassett's ploy of preserving
Iverson's mysteries and the retaliatory assault by Morris and
Miller—as a way of evoking the ginger in Sheffield Shield
contests between NSW and Victoria:

> Morris and Miller recalled that Hassett had become
> perhaps the only Australian who could accurately predict
> what type of ball Bill O'Reilly was about to bowl by
> frequently batting against him in the nets during Australian
> team tours. They decided to frustrate Hassett's attempt to
> prevent them doing the same with Iverson by making a full-
> scale onslaught on Iverson next time NSW and Victoria
> met...This story is typical of dozens which have come out
> of the NSW–Victoria skirmishes since interstate cricket
> began in Australia with the inter-colonial matches of 1856.

Here, however, may be an example of a story too famous for
its own good. It is a quality of cricket history that, once
written, it is seldom unwritten, partly because its main
consumers are enthusiasts prepared to countenance a little

embroidery and embellishment, partly because stories are usually exaggerated for the sake of congeniality with a received image or sentiment. This is not a criticism, nor is it a remark that one would necessarily confine to cricket: goodness knows, a true history of fishing would be neither worthwhile nor popular. But it does mean that scratching for the truth in cricket can be the very devil. To give a recent example, it was not until Simon Rae's 1998 biography of W. G. Grace that two famous stories long entangled in the warp and weft of the great man's tapestry were finally proved of doubtful veracity. Rae established that the young Frederick Spofforth could not as he claimed have bowled Grace in the nets at Melbourne in 1873—being verifiably elsewhere at the time—and that A. C. Croome's story of Grace saving his life after he impaled his throat on railings surrounding the Old Trafford enclosure in 1887 was in all likelihood rather sentimentalised. Yet the disentanglement of fact from fiction took more than a century in each case, and much else besides in the Grace legend will remain forever folkloric.

Turning to Pollard's Iverson story, some of it is obviously wrong. The dates are out: he asserts that Morris's protest came 'during practice for the First Test against the West Indies at Brisbane in 1951', a Test in which Iverson did not play. *En passant*, one might also point out that Pollard gets wrong the date for the commencement of intercolonial cricket (1850 not 1856), Jack's age (out by a year), height (out by an inch), spinning finger (out by a finger) and Test record (out by six wickets).

To this, Arthur Morris adds a further intriguing postscript. He recalls that, apparently when *Cricket Crossfire* was published, Hassett telephoned him in some distress. 'Lindsay denied it absolutely,' Morris recalls. 'He said he'd never do anything like that, and Lindsay wasn't the sort to say that lightly.' Morris had transferred his suspicions to 'some other Victorian, and I won't name names', clearly implying Johnson.

One might also consider a third possibility: that it was Jack who, anxious not to overexpose his method to future opponents, had taken it upon himself to avoid the New South Welshmen in the nets. If not obsessively secretive about his technique, Jack was certainly proprietorial about it. More than a decade later, when he was playing sub-district cricket for Brighton, his friend Col Shipley as a tease used to stand behind Jack and sing out as each ball left his hand: googly, top spinner, leg break. Jack would gripe: 'Cut it out, Col. Wait till you come in.' Continuing the byplay, Shipley would say: 'Aww, don't much feel like a bat tonight, Jack.' If Jack felt that way about a friendly jest, one can imagine his sensitivity round players of the calibre of Morris and Miller. One can also imagine how disquieting their apparent penetration of his mystery must have felt.

It is the very essence of delivering a cricket ball at a lesser velocity that one invites aggressive batsmanship, and thus also overambition and indiscretion. Being hit is consequently an occupational hazard. A fast bowler can escape punishment even when bowling poorly. A spinner seldom will. Sometimes, on a benign surface against entrenched opposition, harsh treatment may have to be endured irrespective of the quality of the bowling. In his book *The Psychology of Cricket*, Graham Winter says: 'Spin bowling is arguably the most subtle art in cricket and it may be the most psychologically demanding.'

The need for spin bowlers to cop it sweet has been remarked upon since the beginning of time. As William Clarke, one of the first great proponents of underarm leg spin more than a century before Jack Iverson took up cricket seriously, put it: 'At times it's enough to make you bite your thumbs to see your best balls pulled and sky-rocketed about—all luck—but you must console yourself with "Ah, that won't last long".' Of all cricket's species, slow bowlers have been the ones most in need of that thin suit of philosophical armour against cricket's occasional unfairness. 'Ranji' Hordern, progenitor of the Australian googly, lamented:

> It is said that everybody loves a lover, but who, unless it be a big hitter, really loves a slow bowler? If he gets five or six wickets, there is no credit, because that is what he is there for. But if he gets 'pasted' the crowd howl at him, his captain is furious, and even his teammates are inclined to shun him. Medium paced and fast bowlers never get this treatment, even after a clever little effort like 0 for 100. I don't know the reason, but there it is.

There should have been consolations for Jack amid his Sydney sufferings. He actually dismissed Miller, who mistimed to mid on, and also bowled Ron James and Robert Madden. Victoria's two other international spin bowlers, Johnson and Ring, yielded almost six runs an over. Yet teammates recall him as devastated by the experience, and the unanimous opinion of those who played with and against Jack is that he was a lesser bowler from that day forward. Doubts about his ability he'd hitherto sublimated would grow increasingly evident. Here, then, was where the lack of 'cricket brain' really counted; not in his confessed and documented ignorance of the game's mechanics, but in his lack of the faith that cricket fortune is ultimately even-handed.

In a sense, it is hardly surprising that Jack Iverson found the humiliations of Sydney hard to bear. From an early age, cricketers learn to regard failure, if not as a friend, at least as an acquaintance to whom they must at times doff their caps. Without that upbringing, with a record essentially of unleavened success, Jack Iverson was always destined to be a player apart. As his Melbourne and Victorian teammate Colin McDonald comments: 'Jake had a bit of an inferiority complex when it came to other cricketers. He'd never been through the rough and tumble, never understood that some days are good and some are bad, because it had never been hard for him.'

Jack's heartfelt response to being hit might also reflect that, unlike Johnson and Ring, orthodox purveyors of spin, Jack was bowling his own invention, his 'specials'. In a very real sense, I think, his spin was a part of Jack, perhaps the nearest he had come to self-actualisation; unlike his home and his business, both his father's, Jack's cricket was completely and authentically his. So did it feel, at some sub-conscious level, as though Morris and Miller were hitting not just his bowling but *him*?

It might also be worth turning the question back on itself. If we know what Jack lacked, what do other cricketers actually have? What about the peculiar blend of stoicism, fatalism, even masochism, that cricket demands of its players? Is one of the factors that separates the great cricketer from the competent the ability to distinguish between 'failing'—a particularly wretched nought, an unusually inglorious flogging, a specially ham-handed attempt at fielding—and being 'a failure'? We might think of it as cricket's own version of the dilemma the Prince lays before Father Pirrone in Giuseppe di Lampedusa's *The Leopard*: 'The real problem is how to go on living this life of the spirit in its most sublimated forms, those moments that are most like death.'

TWENTY-TWO

Jack Iverson was selected to play in the Fourth Test against England at the Adelaide Oval from 2 February 1951. It could not have been otherwise. Yet cricket henceforward would be harder for him, and he was actually commencing a long, slow and rather troubled fade from the game.

The one little miracle of the Adelaide match for Jack was a catch, a very good one, at square leg, one-handed, from a well-struck hook by Cyril Washbrook off Lindwall in the first innings. As Lyn Wellings described it in his *No Ashes for England*: 'The ball was passing wide and high, but Iverson thrust his large right hand at it and plucked a fine catch out of the light air.' Jack would actually savour that catch, the absolute fluke that he extended his hand to interrupt the ball's passage, as much as any wicket he ever took.

With the ball, Jack was economical, but not as penetrative as Sydney: his 3–68 from 26 overs in the first innings included two tailend wickets. And just before England began a fourth-innings pursuit of more than 500, he managed to rub himself out of the rest of the game by tripping over a ball in the nets and chipping a bone in his left ankle.

The injury cost Jack only one game—Victoria's return match against the MCC—but almost certainly corroded his confidence. Foot and ankle damage has shortened a host of careers, notably those of Harold Larwood and Frank Tyson. 'In addition to the stress fractures of the left leg, there were the complications of a left ankle sprained no fewer than eight times on uneven footholds,' Tyson recalled. 'The doctor used to tell me, with a certain degree of malicious glee, that because of post-injury arthritis, my left leg would in the final analysis end up fifteen years older than my right.' Lost faith in the ability to stamp one's front foot down debilitates all bowlers, and Jack would have been no exception.

Jack proved his return to fitness when he was selected for Victoria against Western Australia at the MCG from 16 February, bowling at something near his best in tandem with Doug Ring to claim 5–32. The home side's eight-wicket victory, in fact, clinched it the Sheffield Shield for the first time since 1946–47. But when the Fifth Test of the season commenced on the same ground three days after that game, Jack had his least effective outing to date. His thirty-two overs for the match came at a cost of only 84 runs, but incorporated just two tailend wickets. Worst of all, neither Jack nor any of his comrades could abbreviate what proved the match's decisive partnership: 74 added for the last English wicket by the stubborn Reg Simpson and off spinner Roy Tattersall, extend-ing the visitors' first-innings lead from fewer than 30 to more than 100.

Simpson, an accomplished player of slow bowling, was actually trying out a little hunch of his against Jack through-out his undefeated 156 in 338 minutes, characteristic of the tactics now being applied to the conundrum of Jack's bowling:

> During my innings I experimented by batting four or five inches outside my leg stump while facing Jack Iverson, and this seemed to throw him a little. His line and length began to suffer. The most satisfying factor was that we had regained the initiative. I also happened to reach my century on my 31st birthday.

The match ended in an enjoyable farce. Hassett bowled the final over, and helped himself to an armful of souvenir stumps even as what he imagined to be the ultimate delivery of the match was in transit to Hutton. It wasn't, and the wicket had to be rebuilt. When Hutton did make the winning hit, Compton actually plucked out a stump before setting off to take the run. Jack, Morris and Jim Burke, meanwhile, were involved in a scramble for the ball, which to the delight of Jack and his hometown crowd he won.

Jack told Rex Pullen of the *Sun* the day after the game that this little episode of high spirits made the fact that this would be his last big cricket bow especially disappointing:

> I only realised how terribly sorry I am to be saying goodbye to first-class cricket when I participated in the 'horseplay' in Lindsay Hassett's over to finish the Test...I realised that after this game I would lose all personal contact with a most

wonderful bunch of chaps—English and Australian cricketers—with whom I have never had an unpleasantness.

Jack remained adamant that he had played his final first-class
fixture, and told Pullen that he was 'seriously considering'
leaving Melbourne and returning to Brighton where it had all
begun. In the span of barely eighteen months, he had claimed
118 first-class wickets at 17.4, including 21 wickets at 15.2 in
five Tests. But this was apparently enough.

The cricket world now gathered round to praise him. In his
Ashes to Hassett, John Kay thought Jack's departure rather fitting:

> Every now and again comes a man who can do the right
> thing the wrong way round. That's Jack Iverson, a likeable
> fellow, a serious student of cricket, and a man with a
> problem. His business must come first and his father's
> health is of paramount importance. Iverson could probably
> make a fortune out of cricket, but he won't. You see, Jack
> Iverson is one of nature's gentlemen, and he'll do the right
> thing by instinct.

At a dinner for the victorious Sheffield Shield side on 6 June
1951, Victoria's governor Sir Dallas Brooks singled out Jack
for praise and lamented his loss to the game:

> Jack Iverson, your name will live on in Test cricket. When
> the English team came out last season, they all asked me:
> 'Who is this Iverson? What sort of stuff does he bowl?' But
> I had to tell them I didn't know. I have seen slow bowlers
> of all countries and played against many of them. But none
> have been similar to Iverson or vice versa.

Brooks invoked an exalted name as the only parallel: England's
saturnine assassin of medium pace, Sydney Barnes. 'I would say

that Iverson was a second edition of Barnes,' said the governor. 'And it was my greatest regret that shortly after my arrival in this great state, Iverson was compelled to withdraw from cricket.'

The talk that Jack was to fold his tent and return to Brighton persisted. When the sub-district cricket association released its annual report a month later, it contained the knowing comment: 'We believe Jack Iverson may again be playing for Brighton in this coming season.' Yet it can't have been long after that something unexpected occurred; shortly after his thirty-sixth birthday, Jack Iverson had a change of heart.

For the next two years, Jack would be the Hamlet of Australian cricket, the player who could not make up his mind. Melbourne and Victoria in particular pined to have him back, which raised the prospect that he would again be a candidate for Test selection. Yet for every step forward, he reserved his right to take two back. As in his first season with Melbourne, his commitment waxed and waned until no-one was quite sure if he was serious. Perhaps Jack himself did not know.

The first correspondent to promote the prospect of an Iverson comeback was one of his initial champions, Percy Millard of the *Herald*. On 17 September, Millard foreshadowed Jack's appearance at pre-season training for Melbourne, with the intention of playing district cricket on and off. Millard added: 'Asked about the possibility of playing big cricket this season, he replied: "That will have to decide itself." There now seems a chance of Iverson—who is very keen on the game— being available for Victoria and even Australia for at least some matches this summer.'

Even more significantly, Jack made the decision to have his still-tender left ankle seen to, booking into the St Ives private hospital on 29 September for an operation with the authority of the Australian Board of Control. This would compel a four-week convalescence, but in the long term enhance his durability for five-day cricket, and his prospects of Test selection against John Goddard's touring West Indians. Indeed, when the next instalment of the breaking story appeared on 21 October in Sydney's *Sunday Herald*, Jack was quoted as saying he was a contender for the forthcoming Test series, if with a remarkable qualification:

> I am breaking my neck to have a crack at the West Indian batsmen. The other night I went down to Brighton and, despite all the doctors have said, I had to have a go. I stood at the wicket and bowled without running a stride. I got more work on the ball and had greater control than ever before. If I do play again, I'm seriously thinking of just standing there and wheeling my arm over.

A touch of Ginger Stott from *The Hampdenshire Wonder*, and perhaps only Jack could have dreamed such a novel notion. The image of him delivering the ball from a standing start so tickled *Punch* that it fantasised of cricket commentators rebelling at losing the opportunity offered by the bowlers' walk back for picturesque descriptions of the weather and ground architecture. Gradually, however, Jack must have reconsidered. When Melbourne's new skipper Jack Green tossed him the ball in his comeback match on 13 and 17 November 1951 against Hawthorn-East Melbourne, he bowled off his usual run. And brilliantly.

Jack's 6–69 from 24 overs—22 of them consecutive—put

him back in the headlines. The *Herald* considered that he had 'virtually bowled himself back into the Test side', and could be classified a certainty for Victoria's forthcoming match against the West Indies. But the state selectors still entertained doubts, overlooking him for the tour match, and Jack seemed to as well, withdrawing from the next district fixture complaining of his ankle.

Jack was back for the subsequent round taking 3–1 and 1–16 against Footscray at the Western Oval, and on 11 December attended an Australian Board medical at the Victorian Cricket Association. State selector Jack Ryder was a notorious stickler for fitness, but Jack must have convinced him, for the spinner was included the next day in the state team scheduled to play Queensland at the MCG either side of Christmas. The stakes were clear. As Jim Blake wrote in the *Sporting Globe*: 'His showing in this game will probably decide his Test future.'

The findings, however, were inconclusive. Jack resumed his first-class career where he had left off, bowling with parsimonious precision and giving up only seven runs in his first 72 deliveries. But for some unexplained reason, perhaps to do with his ankle, he then left the field, and could not cast his spell again when he returned. Queensland left-hander Ernie Toovey, who glued the innings together by batting more than three and a half hours for 63, recalls his battle with Jack that day vividly, and also a rather surprising piece of gratuitous advice:

> Jake always gave me a lot of trouble. When I came in that day, he had a field round me that was so tight it was like walking into a team meeting. And he could have had me a few times. There were about twenty-five shouts for lbw, and the only reason there weren't more was because I think

the keeper got tired of appealing. But he went off the field for about half an hour, and that helped me get established. And one guy in their team—I can't remember who—he said at one of the drinks breaks: 'Where are you batting for Jake?'

I said: 'Oh, middle and leg.' He said: 'Try batting leg stump, because he'll have to alter his line to follow you.' And that worked because, when he came back on, I was able to hit him for six over long on and get on top of him a bit.

Jack claimed 3–90 from 30 overs—satisfactory figures by most measures other than his own—and received good notices. Rex Pullen of the *Herald* said he'd come 'though a hard test with flying colours' and reported that he 'would be available for selection in the Fourth Test'. The man himself, however, spoke rather despondently of his form to the *Sporting Globe*'s Blake: 'For some unknown reason I was dropping short at times and naturally I was peppered. The wicket was a beauty and mostly it seemed anti-spin. But that's no excuse...I just had one of those days and no matter how hard I tried I couldn't make any impression.'

Jack's frustration seemed to boil over a little in the second innings, when he let fly with a bouncer at Toovey. The incident caused a minor storm, as Toovey toppled forward in avoiding the delivery and Ian McDonald pulled off a smart stumping that was given not out. 'Stumped?' read the *Argus* headline over a picture next day that appeared to show Toovey's toe in the air. 'Umpire said: "No".' The caption asked: 'What do you think?' Jack was in no doubt, adding a rare marginal annotation in his scrapbook: 'PS: He *was* "out".'

Toovey went on to make 87, Jack to take 2–124. He had the consolation of a crucial cameo appearance as a batsman on the last evening, surviving 25 deliveries from Colin McCool and Vic Raymer to help skipper Sam Loxton draw the game. He even indulged in a little gamesmanship, walking first to the wrong end, then asking to change his bat, in order to chew up a little time. But when the Fourth Test went ahead without him on New Year's Eve, Jack had another change of heart. On 8 January 1952, he announced quietly that he would be unavailable for the rest of the season, citing business reasons.

There are a host of possible explanations for the sudden decline in Jack's effectiveness in 1951–52. He was probably still troubled by his left ankle. He had now been on the first-class scene for three years, and batsmen were almost certainly getting used to him. He had also gone out on something of a limb—both with himself and his father—by trying to accommodate cricket within his broadening commercial obligations. Jack and his father effectively swapped roles from 1 February 1952, Jack becoming H. W. Iverson's licensed agent and his father a sub-agent. Sporting success, always paramount as a source of personal reinforcement, now took on additional importance as Jack's means of justifying his continued distraction from business. And as the great baseballer Ted Williams once observed: 'The minute you start looking for success in sport is the minute it stops coming.'

Having never really thought too much about his bowling, Jack was now perhaps thinking too much, and began deviating from his basic method to compensate for the responses of batsmen. That leg break of his became more and more an incubus. Ian McDonald recalls:

> Hutton actually said it within my hearing: 'I play Iverson as an off spinner.' Which is basically what he was, though

a very good one, Jim Laker-class. But it worried Jack. He started saying: 'Everybody knows I just bowl wrong 'uns. I've got to start bowling more leg spinners.' So he started to change his bowling round completely, bowling almost all leg breaks with only a few wrong 'uns thrown in. But he wasn't any good that way, wasn't half the bowler.

Jack Daniel says:

> For some reason, it became firmly imprinted in Jack's mind that batsmen were picking him. Which wasn't really true, although obviously guys who'd been playing against him for a while were getting more used to playing him. But instead of bowling maybe a couple of leg breaks an over, he started bowling five or six, and that started to nullify his effectiveness because on good batting wickets it turned very little.

Jack's decline, it should be noted, was not abject. With Melbourne, for whom he continued to play in the second half of 1951–52 even after declaring himself unavailable for Victoria, he remained formidable. Against Essendon on Australia Day, Jack claimed 4–17 including his old rival Meuleman for nought. The following match, he claimed 6–19 against University, including a hat-trick, from 11 overs. And in the district semi-final, he routed Northcote with 6–16. In the competition final against Fitzroy at South Melbourne over the first two weekends of April 1952, however, Jack's teammates would find him as difficult to read as his opponents.

The press build-up to the Melbourne versus Fitzroy district cricket final for 1951–52 was unusually intense. Both teams were at full strength, heralding a clash to conjure with: the competition's best bowler, Jack, against perhaps the country's foremost batsman, his erstwhile Test teammate Neil Harvey. Just as Jack had excelled in Melbourne's semi-final against Northcote, Harvey had towered over Fitzroy's semi-final against St Kilda with a match double of 254 not out and 126 containing no fewer than 50 boundaries. The *Herald* even sent a photographer to South Melbourne on the morning of the final to get a picture of the opponents whose duel would clearly decide the premiership: Harvey's smile is broad, Jack's rather wan, Harvey is looking at Jack, Jack is gazing ahead.

Jack Green won the toss and Melbourne batted productively, Ian Huntingdon, Barry Stevens and Jack Solomon recording half centuries in a score of 277. Jack contributed a duck as last man. But in the course of his brief innings, Jack was hit on his padded shin by Fitzroy's medium pacer and all-rounder Harold Shillinglaw, and complained during the break between innings that he was too injured to take the field.

The Melbourne players went out with twelfth man Jim Symons in Jack's stead, Jack Daniel and Ron Hill sharing the new ball. Every so often, they cast a glance at the dressing-room, hoping for Jack's appearance, but to no avail. Although thirteenth man Jeff Collins took him for a short, stiff-legged walk in the nearby park, Jack remained of the view that he was incapable of bowling. Melbourne's opponents, meanwhile, could scarcely believe their good fortune. With Neil Harvey in sparkling touch, they passed 150 for the loss of only two wickets. Fitzroy's Kevin Kearney even thought it all a ruse, that the Melbourne brains trust was deliberately shielding Jack from Harvey.

In fact, Melbourne was bordering on panic. Feeling the

match slipping away, Jack Daniel in particular was of the opinion that his teammate was swinging the lead: 'I was saying: "For Christ's sake, someone go off and get the bastard".' Ian McDonald was apparently considered most suitable for the task of persuading Jack to return—'Because I was a doctor I was meant to understand things like this'—and stole from the field a couple of times to check on Jack's condition. But it wasn't until Harvey dragged Clive Fairbairn onto his stumps to end a shimmering 76 that Jack finally stirred.

The attitude of umpires to bowlers' absences from the field was obviously liberal, for Jack had only to field for an over before Green was able to draft him into the attack. His impact was virtually instantaneous. In his third over, he trapped Lynn Straw lbw. In his fifth, with Shillinglaw on strike, Green moved Huntingdon two metres to his right at backward square leg so that he didn't have to move for the catch that came next ball. In the same over, Kearney was hit on the pads and lbw. Yet again, Jack had turned a match by his presence, though only after he had almost turned it the other way with his absence.

On the last day, with Fitzroy chasing the unlikely target of 215 in 72 minutes, Jack shone once more, scalping three batsmen in four overs after Fairbairn had again claimed the crucial wicket of Harvey for 21. His 6–40 in the match gave him 36 wickets for the season at an average of 9 in what was his third club premiership in five seasons (not to mention having played in a winning Ashes team and a victorious Sheffield Shield side). Yet he had never been more elusive, more enigmatic, more completely Jack Iverson.

TWENTY-THREE

The lingering question in 1951–52 was whether Jack Iverson would be part of Australia's Ashes defence in 1953. Wise observers held unanimously that Jack's skills would be perfectly suited to English pitches. Clive Fairbairn remembers Bill Ponsford's pronouncement:

> A lot of us at the time reckoned that Bill was the best judge of cricket and cricketers around. So I used to go see him a bit, have a cup of tea with him, rack his brains. And one day I asked him: 'What do ya reckon the big bloke'd do in England?'
>
> Bill says: 'Under a good captain, he'd rewrite the record books.'

Jack was again ambivalent. In a letter on 14 February 1952 to an English admirer, he explained: 'I have recently taken over my Father's business and this will mean the end of any ideas about making the trip to England. So you will not be seeing the "Freak" in action. It looks as though Doug Ring and Ian Johnson will be the slow attack on that trip.'

As winter set in, however, so did second thoughts. With Clive Fairbairn and Jack Daniel, he began off-season practices during July in an indoor net on the roof of the Commercial Travellers Association in Flinders Lane. Percy Millard of the *Herald* went along to watch and commented: 'He looked what he is—still one of the world's best bowlers.' As rumours spread that Jack was planning to try out for the forthcoming Test series in Australia against South Africa preparatory to seeking selection for the Ashes tour, more and more observers became excited by the prospect. Lindsay Hassett added his voice to the swelling chorus in the *Herald* on 5 August: 'For Australia's sake, I hope big Melbourne spinner Jack Iverson will be available for the Tests against South Africa and in England next year…The English wickets should suit him.'

Given Jack's history with Hassett, this clarion call would have had particular resonance. Indeed, the very next day, Jack told Rex Pullen of the *Sun* that he would indeed be having a go:

> Iverson said last night he wanted nothing more than to bowl against the South Africans and again against the Englishmen. 'Taking into account my performances in New Zealand in 1949–50, (where he took 75 wickets), I think I would be able to give a good account on the similar English wickets,' Iverson said.

At Melbourne's pre-season, Jack was back to his keenest. He practised sedulously. The 1953 trip would clearly be his only chance to get to England—he would turn thirty-eight within the span of the tour—and he gave every appearance of making it his prime objective. When the Australian Board of Control published the itinerary for the trip on 10 September 1952, he even went to the trouble of cutting it from the newspaper for inclusion in his scrapbooks. And after two district rounds, Jack was selected for Victoria's first two matches of the season: the fixture against the touring Springboks at the MCG and the subsequent Shield match against South Australia at the Adelaide Oval. The scenario could hardly have been more propitious: one game against an opposition unfamiliar with Jack's wiles, another on a surface where his record was unimpeachable, with five weeks before the First Test on 5 December.

The Springboks, a young, eager and determined band, had been hearing about Jack for some years. Of all the local cricketers who attended a reception in the tourists' honour held by Victorian Cricket Association president Arnold Seitz at the Windsor Hotel before the game, Jack was the one the visitors most wanted to meet, as their captain Jack Cheetham recalled:

> We had heard a lot about Jack's bowling and, perhaps, had talked a lot about it—the wise men from the stands had told us all there was to know about him, making it sound all so easy—nevertheless, when he demonstrated his grip on an empty glass, there were fifteen very interested spectators.

Nor did Jack disappoint when he took the ball at the MCG the next afternoon. He was on the spot at once, looking to Percy Beames of the *Age* like 'Victoria's most dangerous bowler', and picking up as his first wicket the visitors' accomplished batsman-keeper John Waite. Cheetham recalled:

> Waite had been entertaining us in the dressing room to a
> very apt and demonstrative description of how Iverson
> tricked all batsmen. He had watched 'Wrong-Grip Jake's'
> overs with interest, and was convinced that he could pick
> his off break and play the leg break comfortably. We were
> eager to see the duel, but Jake's second ball moved away—
> it was the leg break—and Johnny played for the other one
> and was bowled.

As South Africa crumbled on a damp pitch for 113, Jack's
figures were a respectable 3–38 from 14 overs; the *Sporting
Globe* decided that he looked 'a certainty' for the First Test. He
should have set off on the Overlander for Adelaide at 8pm on
12 November in good heart. But, it would seem, he did not.

When South Australia won the toss and batted in gloomy
weather, Jack was quickly into the attack, and earning respectful treatment. His final figures of 4–65 included a hard-hit
return catch from Duldig and a waspish wrong 'un to trap Gil
Langley in front. Yet, as he sat with teammates watching the
rain fall at the completion of the home innings, he was patently
unhappy. Doug Ring tried joshing him along: 'C'mon Jack.
Four for 65. They're good figures in anyone's language.'

'They're reading me,' Jack said to no-one in particular.
'They're reading me easily.'

In South Australia's short second innings, as they completed
a seven-wicket win after two Victorian batting collapses, Jack
was even unhappier. He asked Hassett to field at short fine leg
to watch his bowling, and wanted to be taken off after only five
unsuccessful overs for 17. When the train left Adelaide at 7pm
on 18 November, Jack was in a lugubrious frame of mind. The

teammate sharing his compartment, George Thoms, could not extract a word from him. He sat looking out the window into the darkness of the evening.

Later on, he visited Ian Johnson. They opened a couple of beers. 'I'm going out to graze,' said Jack. 'Back to Melbourne fourths.' Johnson asked why. 'I've lost it,' answered Jack. 'They're playing me easily.' Finally, late in the evening, Jack drifted into the dining car where Hassett was talking to Sam Loxton. 'I'd like you to inform the selectors,' Jack said, 'that I'm no longer available.'

Why did Jack's spirits sag so quickly, and so thoroughly? One reason is immediately obvious. Victoria's next match at the MCG in three days' time was against New South Wales: Morris, Miller, Jim Burke, all of whom had played him well in the past, not to mention Sid Barnes, now fighting to rehabilitate himself with the national selectors after his self-imposed internal exile. The visitors, moreover, had apparently laid another ambush for Jack's bowling. George Thoms remembers Barnes saying to him over a drink before the game: 'I see Iverson pulled out. We were going to fix him right up.'

Jack's own remarks after his withdrawal, however, suggest broader and deeper concerns. Indeed, seldom can a cricketer have been so abject and earnest in expressing his lost confidence. He told Jack Dunn of the *Herald* that he was simply being honest about his position: 'I could have hung on until the selectors woke up to me. However, I think what I have done is better.' He told Ben Kerville of the *Sporting Globe*: 'I've lost it, that's all. For some inexplicable reason, I am unable to push the ball through with fizz and control. Rather than make a fool of myself and let the side down I advised the selectors to this effect.' To Percy Beames he mourned: 'Two years is a long time and I can't recapture my old form.'

'Form' is perhaps the most elusive concept in sport. The sensation of its absence is the most debilitating feeling an athlete can know, faith in its presence the most empowering and blessed. As the sociologist John Carroll puts it in his *Ego & Soul*:

> Being out of form is a kind of discord, of inner chaos— literally being at odds with the form. It makes the player frustrated and lonely, not only cut off but feeling some sort of defilement—indeed, teammates have the tendency to respond to one of their number who is out of form as tainted and untouchable, someone to be avoided. Being in form, in contrast, is a state of grace. It is as if some transcendental power has given the player its blessing.

When a slump commences, the search for reasons begins. Perhaps it's a technical flaw. Perhaps it's lapsing concentration. Perhaps it's equipment. Form disappears so capriciously that, even among the best players, responses can seem ungoverned by logic. Around the time Jack Iverson was bowling for Australia, there was a gifted Colombian tennis player, Willy Alvarez, who maintained a constant monologue at his racquet, whispering it blandishments when it hit sweetly, swearing at it bitterly for a mishit. Occasionally he would throw it to the ground and circle it, warning it of the consequences of continued misbehaviour. So completely did he scapegoat it for poor play that, when asked about his form, he would reply: 'I'm playing great; but my racquet's been awful.'

Among the most liberating experiences for a sportsman in a trough of confidence is the discovery of a previously undiagnosed injury. When Dennis Lillee's bowling disintegrated on a tour of the West Indies in 1973, X-rays of his back conducted by radiologist Dr Rudi Webster revealing three fractures in his lumbar vertebrae left him perversely euphoric:

> I will never forget Dennis's reaction when I gave him the bad news and showed him the X-rays. He jumped in the air and said, 'You beauty! I knew there had to be something there. I wasn't imagining it. For a while they had me thinking I was. Perhaps the bastards will believe me now.' The relief on his face was obvious. I had never seen anyone so ecstatic after being told his back was in a mess.

For Jack Iverson, however, there was no inanimate object to curse for his feeling of cosmic disharmony, no injury to which to ascribe his unease. His bowling was so much part of *him*—it was his invention, his creation, his devotion—that the feeling it was fading must have struck like a personal reproach. He had waited his whole career for cricket to reject him, to finger him as an 'impostor'. He had taken precautions against such a predicament, equivocating about total commitment to the game, declining to regard himself as a serious cricketer. Nonetheless, it had arisen.

As Jack was agonising about what might have gone missing in his bowling, one of the best dramatisations of his kind of dilemma had just been published; Bernard Malamud's 1952 novel *The Natural*. For Roy Hobbs and his miraculous bat 'Wonderboy', like Jack Iverson and his extraordinary hand, form proves so evanescent as to border on the supernatural. When Roy falls from the exalted standards he has set and goes to his friend Red Blow for guidance, Malamud captures all the desperation, self-recrimination, hope and hurt that would have been Jack's experience at around the same time:

> 'You haven't knocked up a dame maybe?'
> 'No.'
> 'Any financial worries about money?'
> 'Not right now.'
> 'Are you doing something you don't like to do?...Once we had a guy here whose wife made him empty the garbage pail in the barrel every night and believe it or not it began to depress him. After that he fanned the breeze a whole month until one night he told her to take the damn garbage out herself, and the next day he hit again.'
> 'No nothing like that.'
> Red smiled. 'Thought I'd get a laugh out of you, Roy. A good belly laugh has more than once broke up a slump.'
> 'I would be glad to laugh but I don't feel much like it. I hate to say it but I feel more like crying.'

Jack's announcement of his withdrawal from the Victorian team spelled the end of his hopes—everyone's hopes—that he would play Test cricket again. As Percy Beames told readers of the *Age*: 'This looks like the end of Iverson in big cricket...Even if he bowls sensationally in district cricket, the selectors will be loath to bring him back after this and last year's withdrawals.' In fact, he did not bowl sensationally in district cricket, because he did not bowl at all, standing out of the Melbourne team, and entering Heidelberg Hospital in January 1953 for an operation on varicose veins in one of his legs that precluded another comeback had he even thought of making it. The bowler who eventually took what would have been Jack's place in the Australian team for England was Jack Hill, who had similarly only gained a regular Sheffield Shield berth after the other Jack's withdrawal from the Victorian side.

Whether Jack's absence had a material impact on Australia's defeat in a closely-contested Ashes 1953 series is, of course, imponderable. Many good judges favoured his selection regardless of his appearance in only two first-class matches in 1952–53. Keith Miller believes that Jack 'would have murdered England in 1953', Richie Benaud that 'we would have "walked" the series had he been there'. Jack's Melbourne colleague Jack Daniel recalls saying to Lindsay Hassett: 'Bad luck the big bloke wasn't available.' Hassett replied: 'If he'd come all the matches would've been over in two days.'

To an extent, however, they are talking about two different bowlers. The Jack Iverson of 1950 would almost assuredly have been an irresistible force in English conditions. But the Jack Iverson of 1953 had suffered sufficient setbacks and checks on his confidence to make him less of a known quantity, not least to himself. It is hard to depict his omission from the Australian team of that year as a miscarriage of justice when Jack had grown so expert at inflicting these on himself.

TWENTY-FOUR

While Australia played cricket in England, Jack Iverson played golf in Melbourne. It had been his chief pleasure for the five preceding winters, and he had winnowed his handicap away to six with several titles, including the 1950 President's Cup at Kingston Heath. In 1953, he was undefeated for Kingston Heath in the 'B' pennant season; one of only two players in the competition to win every game.

Jack was a popular player in the competition. Opponents enjoyed playing against—even being beaten by—such a sporting celebrity. The undemanding and enjoyably recreational nature of his golf weekends might also have made him consider an alternative approach to cricket. Because, when he went to see MCC secretary Vernon Ransford ahead of the 1953–54 district cricket season, he tabled a novel proposal.

Jack explained that he would like to play for Melbourne again, but only in the fourth XI, with the idea that he might eventually work his way back into first XI contention. Ransford was taken aback. 'Listen, son,' he said, 'you'll start in the firsts and if you don't find form pretty quickly you'll soon find your way to the fourths.'

Jack evidently pondered this a while; he declared himself unavailable for Melbourne's first few matches, preferring to finish his golf season. But when he did resume on 24 October, playing his first game in nearly a year, his powers were undimmed. He took 5–37 against St Kilda, and followed it with 7–33 on Melbourne Cup Day against Hawthorn-East Melbourne, including three stumpings by the teenage Geoff Longney in a handful of deliveries. Longney recalls:

> I got Cocky Chambers, Mike Fitchett and Dave Kerr, all state players. And I tell you, they weren't stumpings, they were run outs, the batsmen were so far down. The one to get Dave was just a beauty, a leg break, I reckon the best Jack ever bowled. Dave had played state cricket with Jack, but he was three yards down the track when this one beat him as he played for the wrong 'un.

Melbourne now had another talented young slow bowler, nineteen-year-old left-arm wrist-spinner Lindsay Kline, with a career ahead of him that would include thirteen Tests and a hat-trick. Yet he recalls his season as predominantly a waiting game:

> I don't know why they picked me really. I suppose it was because Jack often had auctions and no-one knew exactly when he might turn up. Sometimes, we'd be playing at the

Albert Ground and it'd be about three o'clock and I'd start thinking: 'Clive [Fairbairn] and Jack Daniel have just about had it. I might be due for an over or two here.' Then I'd hear this cheer from some of the older spectators—'good on ya, Jack'—as he arrived. And I'd think: 'Well, that's buggered that. I can forget about getting an over today.'

Statistically, it was Jack's best season for Melbourne; he took 33 wickets in six games for 218 runs. Jack Daniel recalls checking on the averages with Fairbairn at season's end. Each reckoned they'd done the other out of the season's best bowling average, having paid about 17 or 18 runs for each wicket, but it then occurred to them to check the figures for J. B. Iverson as well. 'He had a bowling average of six,' says Daniel. 'Six!'

Each wicket Jack took, too, seems to have had a rejuvenating effect on his self-belief. For, having started the season thinking he'd like to play with Melbourne fourths, Jack Iverson decided to go to India.

Though he wouldn't have known it, Jack owed his chance to join the Commonwealth XI on its 1953–54 tour of India to Bill Johnston's mother-in-law. Former Australian wicket-keeper Ben Barnett, the team's captain, had approached Johnston about making the trip while he was passing through Bombay on the way back from England in September 1953. Johnston had provisionally accepted, gaining the approval of the Australian Board of Control and his employer Dunlop, with the idea that he would replace Sonny Ramadhin midway through the trip when the West Indian had to report for Test duties in the Caribbean, and that he would bring his intended Judy on the journey as a honeymoon. Judy's mother, however, would not hear of any daughter of hers being married in a hurry, so suddenly a new replacement was needed for Ramadhin. Jack Iverson, a spinner, and a mysterious one at that, was the ideal man. On a £250 fee, he left Melbourne by air on Boxing Day 1953.

The Commonwealth XI owed its existence to the reluctance at the time of both England and Australia to depart from a cricket schedule centred around the Ashes: in the two decades since India had become a Test-playing nation, England had visited only twice and Australia not at all. This particular team, styled as the Silver Jubilee Overseas Cricket Team in recognition of the twenty-fifth anniversary of India's board of control, was actually the third of its kind to visit India within five seasons, and composed like its predecessors largely of honest English county sweats sprinkled with top-line Testmen like Ramadhin and Frank Worrell. Its average age was a rather grey thirty-two. It was also the last of its line: India's good results against the team staked its claim to more Test fixtures.

There were a couple of familiar faces when Jack arrived at Calcutta's Great Eastern Hotel on 28 December: his erstwhile Victorian teammates Ken Meuleman and Sam Loxton had been involved in the trip since its inception. A few others took the trouble to welcome him, including the former England wicketkeeper Paul Gibb, who was immediately struck by the Australian's bone-crushing grip: 'He certainly is a hefty chap, very tall and well-proportioned, and when you shake hands with him you wonder what has got hold of you.' Otherwise, the sights and sounds of the Commonwealth's most populous city must have inundated the senses. To think that, not three months before, Jack had aspired to nothing more than Melbourne fourths.

India at the time was *terra incognita* for players from the west, and a landscape that took some getting used to. Riots in Lucknow and vandalism of the pitch had seen the first five-day contest with India abandoned. Long train journeys, hot nights, the press of humanity and the need for constant vigilance about food and water had since tried everyone's patience; Jack learned the last lesson immediately when he spent his first full day of the tour confined to bed with stomach trouble.

Cricket, nonetheless, was a *lingua franca*. Indians were fervent when it came to foreign players. When Sir Donald and Lady Bradman had passed through Calcutta en route to London seven months earlier, they required evacuation in a military vehicle after 1000 local enthusiasts broke through a police cordon. The Commonwealth XI's Indian opponents, too, were taking the tour rather more seriously than some of the visitors had been prepared for; India had routed their guests in what had become the First Unofficial Test at New Delhi, and held them to a draw in the Second at Bombay by the time Jack arrived, thanks to their outstanding spin duo of Subhash Gupte and Ghulam Ahmed. West Indian Roy Marshall recalled: 'Our batting was so bad on that tour that Gupte, a magnificent leg spin bowler, only had to pick up the ball and wickets would start falling.' Vijay Hazare, then in the twilight of his career as India's master batsman, rated the visitors 'easy meat for us'.

Jack's bowling, however, provided an immediate tonic. When the Third Unofficial Test began at Eden Gardens on

New Year's Eve, the unsuspecting Indians found his mysteries impenetrable. On the biggest and most historic ground in India, the site on which the country's first recorded match had been played 150 years earlier, Jack gave a virtuoso performance to rank with anything that had gone before, obtaining 10–125 from 50 overs against local batsmen to whom slow bowling was so facile that they had denied Ramadhin a single wicket in either of the two preceding Unofficial Tests. He dismissed every member of India's top seven bar Polly Umrigar at least once. For someone undertaking his first five-day match in nearly four years, and who had only three days before completed a two-day air journey into entirely alien conditions, it was simply uncanny.

Not surprisingly, the performance took it out of Jack, now in his thirty-ninth year. He pulled a muscle in his right thigh, then could not bowl on the second day of the Fourth Unofficial Test after straining a muscle in his shoulder. Yet otherwise during the next six weeks he proved remarkably durable. Playing at his lowest weight in years of eighty-six kilograms, he shirked no work in bowling 1389 deliveries during six matches for a tour record of 27 wickets at 22. Indians were unprepared for him in more ways than one—when the team stopped in Hyderabad at the State Guesthouses, his bed was found to be too small and another had to fetched—although at the latter end of the trip they showed signs of having assimilated his methods. Cricket correspondent for the *Hindu*, S. K. Gurunathan, commented:

> The bowling of Jack Iverson of Australia played no mean part in the visitors' success at Calcutta. With his peculiar grip, he first bamboozled the Indian batsmen...Iverson met

with fair success in the subsequent engagements also, but he no longer exerted the same fear on the minds of the batsmen who were prepared to strike at him. He succeeded because he kept an immaculate length and flighted the ball cleverly.

The tour itself was what visiting cricketers came to expect of India, a heady mixture of luxury and squalor. Raman Subba Row, the Commonwealth XI's twenty-one-year-old opener from Cambridge, recalled:

> I suppose with hindsight it reflected the country. One moment we were enjoying the grandeur of the Cricket Club of India or the Maharajah of Baroda's palace; the next we were fighting the rats and the cockroaches in some very inferior town hotel. One week you would be fit as a fiddle; the next you might want to crawl away and die.

The mercurial temper of the crowds also left a strong impression on first-time tourists, particularly at Madras. Paul Gibb, a thoughtful and sensitive man who kept an assiduous diary, documented one disturbing sight when local boy Kripal Singh was run out for 90 there:

> As he made his way to the pavilion a youth rushed across the field and tried to reach him with a garland, but was intercepted by khaki-clad police. The youth was then dragged forcibly off, and shortly there was an awful hubbub round the stands. Later I learned from Jack Iverson that the youth received a bit of hammer from the police. Jack heard heavy whacks and thuds and sounds of distress coming from a room in the pavilion and had asked semi-jokingly if someone was being killed. He was told the youth was getting a bit of a lesson.

The team itself cohered as well as could be expected. Barnett proved a dilatory captain, too old at forty-five and too long out of first-class cricket to exert much authority. In his diary, Gibb also gives the impression of tension between the English players and the Australians, whom he regarded as rather crass and insensitive. But Frank Worrell rated George Duckworth as 'the best manager under whom I ever toured'. A stocky, salty and well-travelled soul who had kept wicket for England in twenty-four Tests, 'Sahib' Duckworth had accumulated a store of local knowledge on two previous trips and opened many unexpected doors.

Jack enjoyed it, this late-career bonus of a tour he could hardly have expected to make. In matches where little was at stake, he bowled with tight control and even creativity. In the last game against a Prime Minister's XI at Eden Gardens, a game added to the tour in aid of the National Flood Relief Fund, Sam Loxton recalls him taking a wicket with an underarm:

> I saw this fella miss the first six from Jake, then the second six, and Jake says: 'Mr Umpire, I propose to bowl the ball underarm'. Oh, the umpire's face was a sight to behold. I thought: 'This I gotta see'. Anyway, it floats down and the guy's mesmerised. He pushes forward, straight into my hands, and I caught it and put it in my pocket.

Jack's principal recreation appears to have been shopping, for he accumulated an extraordinary variety of Indian goods for repatriation to Australia in trunks: vases, clothes, an evening purse embroidered with silver for Jean, and no fewer than 200 clay figures of local notables. In his diary entries for Hyderabad, in fact, Gibb commented disapprovingly on the Australians' avidity when it came to local traders:

I went down to the shops with Ken Meuleman and Jack Iverson. The two Aussies went very thoroughly into the inspection of shirts and cloths, and finally decided to have four made up for themselves. They certainly are hot stuff when it comes to saving a penny or two. Fair enough in business I suppose, though as in many things they do appear a little uncouth and aggressive as they pull the merchandise about. Their attitude and search for 'gimmes' come to pure scrounging.

Gibb, however, was also capable of sharing in the general hilarity when Jack's size proved too much of a stretch for local tailors:

He had trousers and a shirt made. The trousers finished literally half way up his calves and his shirt was made for a man half his size. He also had a cricket cap made, quite the funniest one I have ever seen. It was very voluminous, with a big peak and elastic at the back to help hold it in position.

So Jack finished his first-class cricket career as he had begun it, an extraordinary bowler who looked anything but a cricketer.

Throughout the trip, Jean Iverson followed her husband's progress devotedly, cutting and cropping for Jack's scrapbooks, staying up late to listen to commentaries of the Unofficial Tests on short-wave radio. Sherry and Beverley Iverson, now old enough to understand their father's absence, were placated every night at bedtime. Jean had them kiss her on both cheeks, once for her and once for their father, and encouraged them to say: 'Good night Daddy'. 'Now he can hear you,' Jean would say, 'and he's saying good night, too.'

Jack left Bombay aboard the *Strathnaver* on 13 February 1954 with Ken Meuleman for company, arriving in Fremantle a fortnight later to meet Jean. Interestingly, in an example of the pettifogging bureaucracy to which players of the period submitted, Jean had to write to the Australian Board of Control seeking permission to join her husband on the last leg of the ship's journey to Port Melbourne. Yet it was the kind of control which would, for Jack, henceforward be a thing of the past.

On the evidence of Jack's trip to India, he remained even at thirty-eight a bowler of Test class. He had taken 17 wickets at 18 in the three Unofficial Tests against a talented batting line-up—Vijay Hazare, Vijay Manjrekar, Polly Umrigar, Ghulam Ramchand—and lost little by comparison with Gupte, probably then the best leg spinner in the world. Ken Meuleman felt Jack could easily have recommenced his career in Australia, though he never broached the subject with his colleague directly:

> No I didn't. Jake was a very nice type of person to travel with. We got on well on that trip, knocked around a lot together, and travelled home together on the *Strathnaver*. But he was a bit of a loner, not the sort of guy you'd get into a heavy conversation with. And when you're playing cricket you tend not to do that anyway.

In fact, after this last, heady triumph in India, Jack's big cricket career ended without fanfare. We shall never know if he considered one last tilt at the first-class game because, in the event, the decision was made for him. In the course of taking 6–59 for Melbourne in the last round of the district competition against Richmond, he strained his spinning finger and missed the semi-final in which his team was soundly defeated by Prahran at Toorak Park. The finger was still troubling him when Jack joined his Melbourne colleagues Fairbairn and Daniel in their winter drills atop the Commercial Travellers Association in July 1954, and he was dissatisified with his accuracy when he tried his alternate third-finger grip.

Jack consulted four specialists about the injury, but without success. On 28 September, he told his loyal supporter Percy Millard of the *Herald* that Melbourne would have to do without him. It was a muted finale but, one might also think, rather fitting: the mighty middle finger that had uttered the first word on Jack Iverson's amazing career now had the last say.

TWENTY-FIVE

Jack Iverson the bowler was now Jack Iverson the businessman, a full-time member of Melbourne's professional classes. It is easy to imagine father Harry—who turned seventy in January 1955—breathing a sigh of relief that his only son would now be compelled to immerse himself in the concerns of H. W. Iverson.

The business had never been completely reliant on Jack's involvement. Harry had employed an able manager, Beresford Rea, to keep things running during Jack's regular absences. A gruff character who bred wire-haired terriers in his spare time, Rea ran the office at Aldersgate House, 405 Collins Street, with a messiness that was often Jean Iverson's despair. But he had a head for figures and a compendious memory that made him indispensable, and Jack would come to rely on him heavily.

Jack's life as an estate agent was full and busy. His daughter Sherry remembers that, on days when her father worked from home, the telephone seldom stopped ringing. Even on Christmas Day, there might be clients to consult and deals to transact. When Harry let his sub-agent's licence lapse on 1 January 1956, Jack became the sole agent, proprietor and auctioneer for H. W. Iverson at a time when mergers and amalgamations between other firms were making business increasingly competitive for small independent firms like his.

Much had changed, too, in the Iverson family in the decade since the war. Fewer places were being set round the huge dining table that Harry had acquired from Government House; by the mid-1950s, only Jack remained at The Esplanade with his parents. Two daughters were relatively settled: Joy was with Hock Wood in Boronia, having just given birth to her second child, a son, Douglas; Ruth was in Adelaide with Gordon Rinder and their infant son Greg. Marjorie's situation, on the other hand, had become a cause of lingering concern. She had separated from her husband Bill Quintell, and been obliged to fall back on Harry's generosity. She also suffered from an appalling eye condition, in which her eye-balls became engorged with blood, and underwent operations in which her eyelids were partially stitched. As a means of providing her with financial support, Harry had in 1955 invested in a boarding house in Brighton's Kinane Street and underwritten some of her expenses, while Jack became something of a surrogate father to her children Robyn and Ian, including them in family outings to Mount Martha and Dromana, and making sure their birthdays were suitably celebrated.

It wasn't until October 1956 that Jack, Jean, ten-year-old Sherry and eight-year-old Beverley acquired what would become their long-term home in Brighton; a rambling Victorian residence on a 19 by 42-metre block close to Middle Brighton railway station at 44 Black Street. Their existence became the acme of middle-class suburban contentment. Jack had his golf, his reading, joined the fund-raising committee for Brighton Community Hospital and was for a time a popular speaker at functions of the Young Liberals. He followed Melbourne in the VFL football and every year would head for the Barwon River in Geelong to watch his old school compete in the Associated Public Schools Head of the River boat race. Jean had her beloved fox terriers, Polly and Sam, and a wide circle of old friends: especially Mary Rowe and her husband David, a Collins Street dentist; Margaret Sevier and her husband Rex, a company secretary with Willow Kitchenware; Amy Northcombe, formerly Hawthorn, and her new husband Geoff, a public servant. They entertained regularly, often generously. Jack hosted barbecues, enjoyed picking out a tune on his piano accordion, and in his shed behind the house manufactured a massive ping pong table that seemed as heavy as a car. He still loved to spin a ball.

Within the household, the centre of authority was Jean. Jack tended the play the role of benevolent provider, while Jean was tirelessly practical, organised and, if not bossy, certainly knew her own mind. As Mary Rowe says:

> Jean was a lovely person and a marvellous friend to me. I can only speak well of her. But she tended to want control of the other person. She liked getting her way. She was very strong-willed, and she was the strong-willed person in the

house, while Jack was quiet, very easy-going, and tended to, you know, go along with things.

When Jack's undemonstrative demeanour met Jean's strong will, there could be sharp exchanges. Jean could be off-handedly cutting. One evening, when Jack was late returning from work, Black Street's bathroom was being repainted by a painter called 'Johnny'. As Jean sang out asking 'Johnny' if he'd like a cup of tea, Jack came in and said: 'That'd be nice, Pol.'

'Not for you,' Jean said severely. 'Get lost.'

Some outsiders even got the feeling that Jack was at times a little fearful of Jean. Dr Ken Shepard, one of Jack's regular golfing partners, recalls:

> One day he told us this story, in all seriousness, about a game he'd just played at Kingston Heath. He picked up these three old geezers at the first tee and agreed to play three holes with them. They said they usually played for money and, when Jack asked how much, they said 'ten-ten-ten'. He thought they'd meant ten bob and it wasn't until they'd started that he realised they'd meant £10. Jack said: 'I went cold all over. All I could think about was having to go home and tell the wife that I'd lost thirty quid playing golf. But I worked really hard and I actually ended up winning thirty quid.'

One shouldn't, however, think this particularly unusual. Many households of the time conformed to the pattern that, while the father was ostensible head of the household, the mother was quotidian decision-maker. A famous research project by Canadian sociologist Daniel Adler in 1957–58 involving surveys of 1500 children at twenty-five schools described Australia as exemplary of 'the special social phenomenon which we call matriduxy': half of mothers and only two per cent of fathers involved themselves in every aspect of decision-making about discipline, household duties, spending and recreation. The Iverson household also seems to have been, for the daughters, a loving and safe environment in which to grow up. Sherry remembers her father presenting her with the surprise birthday present of a bicycle one year, not only for the gift but for the tender care with which it was presented:

> Dad took me up to Church Street saying he had something to show me, took me into the bike shop and there was this new shiny blue bike. I just thought it was the greatest thing since sliced bread. And I'll never forget this: Dad followed me all the way home in the car driving really slowly with his wheels in the gutter to make sure I didn't get into any trouble.

Church Street was also the place the Iverson family went to watch television after it began in Australia in November 1956. Two doors down from the old post office was an electrical goods store in whose windows these enchanted boxes could be seen; every Wednesday at 7pm, Jack would take his daughters down there for HSV-7's 'Kraft Theatre Playhouse'.

A little later, Beverley remembers, the family's next-door neighbour in Black Street, a Mr J. Lloyd Jones, became the first person the Iversons knew to actually own one of these new-fangled devices. A former executive of the Gas and Fuel Corporation, Mr Lloyd Jones was a kindly old man with a huge train set in his shed and a fruit tree in his backyard, and it was a treat to be invited next door for the latest instalment of 'The Cisco Kid'.

In the records of the Real Estate Registrar, under Mr Lloyd

Jones' hand, are actually two references he wrote for Jack in the period he lived at 46 Black Street. As estimations of Jack in a non-cricket context are rare, they are worth quoting for the light they shed on the quiet, respectable, middle-class world he now inhabited. The first, circa the late 1950s, reads:

> I have known John Brian Iverson for two years. During this time I have been in almost daily contact with him and can testify to his invariably happy, sympathetic and cooperative personality. I have found him conscientious in even the most trivial details and of outstandingly honest and upright character of the highest integrity in his business relations.
>
> His keen interest in community welfare is indicated by his office as an enthusiastic member of the Brighton Hospital committee and of various Brighton social activities whilst his happy domestic life stamps him in every respect as 'a good neighbour'.

Another, signed in October 1962, continued in the same vein:

> I have found him of unimpeachable character, scrupulously honest, temperate and of the strictest moral integrity. His career as an international cricketer proclaims his ready ability to accept without question the vicissitudes of sport and this same ability is amply evidenced throughout his business transactions...The highest tribute I can pay him is to state that, when our dividing fence was recently renewed, it included at my suggestion a party gate (without bolts or locks) so that each of us, as well as members of our families, might have free access to the rear garden of the other.

A wife, two children, his own business, a certain residual fame, and a gate in the fence with his neighbour: for what more could a man hope?

Jack's cricket had, meanwhile, all but played out. Unable to bowl in 1954–55, he played three games for Melbourne's seventh XI unspectacularly, and one game in March 1955 as a batsman for the Real Estate and Stock Institute against the Fire and Accident Underwriters Association at the Fitzroy Ground. He made a fleeting reappearance for three games in Melbourne's first XI the following season, taking 10 wickets at 12 in three games, but these were his last at the club: his Melbourne record was ruled off at 178 wickets, average 10.54. Jack told Harold Shillinglaw, briefly captain-coach of Brighton, that he was thinking of returning to sub-district ranks, but never turned up to practice.

Jack's profile in the game, however, was maintained by his recruitment as a radio commentator by the ABC. He first provided expert comments for local station 3LO in December 1953, just before going to India. His daughters, too young to recall much in detail about their father's bowling, remember his commentating far better. Jean and the girls would head to the Albert Ground with sandwiches, tea and other victuals while Jack performed his duties above, lowering a rope from the commentary box at meal breaks in order to partake of refreshments from the family's supplies.

The idea of Jack the commentator caused a certain wry amusement among former teammates. 'I used to have a bit of a laugh about Jack commentating,' says former Melbourne captain Jack Green. 'Because what Jack knew about cricket was approximately nought.' Nonetheless, he had an excellent, thoughtful and well-modulated radio voice and an engaging manner that gave him a following in often rather unexpected quarters. For several years, Jack was the guest of choice at Pentridge Prison when the prisoners held an awards night for their intramural sporting activities. Jack would often come home with tales about being introduced to some notorious lifer, and laughingly confess his bafflement: 'He's such a nice fella. Can't understand what he's doing in prison.' The Pentridge news-sheet became a regular feature in the family letter box, and Jack always received his share of Christmas cards from prisoners he'd met.

During Melbourne's Olympic Games in November 1956, Jack was even invited to be a judge for the gymnastics at Festival Hall. Beverley, who accompanied him, recalls:

> The scores were rated out of 10 and as the day progressed, Dad became familiar with the judges and settled in well. The next gymnast to come on was a German lass, about 20, tall, slim, blonde, very attractive, and before she started her routine, Dad turned to the judges and suggested they give her 20 out of 10. They all had a laugh over that one.

As television made its mark on sports broadcasting, Jack made the shift. By the early 1960s, when the Iversons bought their own television set, he had a regular spot on *Sports Review*, the weekly round-up program at 7.15pm on Saturdays that separated the news from the *The Donna Reed Show*. Beverley remembers the evening ritual of watching their father, and her mother's long-suffering response to the sight of her husband caked in make-up: 'That collar will be a disgrace by the time he gets home.'

It was quite late in my writing of this book that I made serious contact with Jack Iverson's daughters, Sherry and Beverley. Perhaps, native circumspection was deepened by my early intrusion on Beverley's privacy. I contemplated revisiting the old house at Black Street during the inspections prior to its sale, but to do so would have felt like acting under false pretences. A friend whose opinion I respect said I was being too pusillanimous. But this seemed to cross the line from investigation to invasion.

By the time I finally summoned the courage to contact Sherry, most of my preliminary work was done, my corpus of information quite large, and my *bona fides* at least tentatively demonstrable. In fact, Sherry and her husband Barry Holt could hardly have been more helpful. We sat in their kitchen for most of a day, not so much conducting an interview as exchanging information, my knowledge of the famous Jack, Sherry and Barry's recollections of the non-famous Jack. Later they came to my home, talked some more and I renewed contact with Beverley who had in the interim moved to Tasmania. Their recollections underpin much of this chapter and what follows in this book.

I don't know if they really comprehended my fascination with Jack, one reason being that I'm not sure I was terribly good at explaining it, another that to them he was quite a different figure. As Sherry said a few times: 'People used to ask me what it was like to have a famous father. But as far I was concerned, I didn't have a famous father. To me, he was just Dad.'

Nor, by the time Sherry and Beverley were old enough, *would* many people have recognised Jack Iverson as a famous man. To the casual passer-by, Jack in the mid-1950s would have appeared like any other specimen of the sober, upright, rigid and superficially insensate figures, choked by ties, cocooned by overcoats, who swept in and out of Collins Street before 9am and after 5pm every week day: the human floodtide captured most famously in John Brack's painting *Collins Street, 5pm*.

Interestingly, Brack, then the art master at Melbourne Grammar School, conceived this haunting image just a stone's throw from Aldersgate House in the very first winter Jack was working there full-time. Brack's old army cobber and drinking pal John Stephens worked for stockbrokers Ian Potter & Co., so the artist would regularly find himself waiting outside its headquarters at 360 Collins Street, where he killed time by sketching passers-by. 'It used to strike me as most eerie,' he recalled, 'to be sketching within three feet of so many people, none of whom took the slightest notice.'

The impression was so profound that Brack decided to aggregate the images he'd collected into a painting, using as a backdrop photographs of the local architecture taken by an MGS colleague, Laurence Crouse. As Brack put it: 'There are so many of us whose lives are encompassed by offices in the day and suburbs at night that it seems almost urgent for the painter to say something about it, as clearly as he can.' The painting was first displayed during a solo exhibition in March 1956, and acquired by the National Gallery of Victoria.

On reflection, we might feel it at least piquant that Jack Iverson might have been one of the people Brack studied to create what art critic Sasha Grishin has described as 'arguably the only major existentialist icon to be painted in Australia'. For what was Jack but the embodiment of the ordinary, extra-ordinary man? Behind that tie, under that overcoat, beat the heart of one of the most remarkable autodidacts Australian sport has ever known. Yet, to others, he was simply a father, husband, friend, business acquaintance, boss; a man on a city street.

TWENTY-SIX

Although Jack Iverson had his own hearth and home from the mid-1950s, his father Harry probably remained the chief influence in his life. The estate agency still carried his father's name—and would until the firm became J. B. Iverson Pty Ltd in July 1960—and his father's stamp. Jack did nothing in business without consulting his father, as he had done little in life.

The dynamics of the father-son relationship had been established in early life. It seems always to have been a rather formal one, with Jack keen for paternal approval and conscious of his filial obligations. It was his father to whom Jack had instinctively headed on the day of his Test selection; it was his father who had been his first thought on the day of his greatest Test triumph.

There was, indeed, no disputing Harry's status as family patriarch. Jean's friend Amy Northcombe, picking up on the family's reverence, called him 'The Boss'. He had always been a man of absolutes—recall the speed and completeness with which he detached first from his siblings and later from his business partner Frank Carolan—and became one of decided tastes and established prejudices. The family nickname for him was 'Beansy', apparently bestowed by his son-in-law Bill Quintell, because of a predilection for pork and beans. He savoured cashews, dates and aromatic cigars, but utterly abhorred the 'vicious and poisonous addiction' of cigarettes. He never learned to drive; Ede was always family chauffeur.

His taste in art was conservative; the centrepiece of Moana's dining room was a notably realistic painting of the sun setting behind an old windjammer by Francis Glusing, while H. W. Iverson's office was hung with a rather staid Horace Hooper landscape. Harry also had a fondness for pictures of cows. As far as his health was concerned, he favoured homespun remedies; he professed, for instance, never to have suffered a cold in his adult life, having arrived at the preventative measure of snorting his used shaving water every morning.

Not a boastful man, Harry was nonetheless proud to regard himself as self-made. Here he was, son of an immigrant music teacher whose parents had been dead by the time he was twelve, an established businessman in a handsome home having fathered four grown-up children. Even in retirement, he cut a formidable figure. Perhaps because his upbringing had been so fractured and uncertain, his days with Ede ran to a rigid clockwork pattern, which Jack's daughter Sherry recalls:

They were lovely people but very regimented. You couldn't get there before 10.15am, but no later than 10.30am, and you had to leave before 11.20am. 11.25am they washed their hands for lunch, which was at 12. My grandfather would sit up one end of the sunroom, desk all set up and bedroom off to one side, my grandmother at the other end of the sunroom so she could look out the window across the bay. She'd always have the radio on and, every now and then, she'd go: 'Harry! Listen to this!' So everyone would have to stop talking and listen to what was on the radio.

Harry and Ede were also from the 1950s increasingly inhibited by their arthritis, which meant that they seldom ventured downstairs at Moana, and relied increasingly both on their devoted housekeeper Bloss and on their children. This meant, effectively, Jack; Ruth was far away in Adelaide, Marjorie preoccupied with running the boarding house in Kinane Street and still afflicted by her eye condition, while Joy was also suffering deteriorating health as a result of diabetes. And Jack could hardly look the other way; he had lived under his father's roof until the age of forty-one, and owed much of his standard of living and financial security to Harry's scrupulous stewardship of the family fortune. A question that remains, nonetheless, is how much of that inheritance Jack truly wanted.

The dissolution of Harry's partnership with Frank Carolan in 1932, and Jack's status as the family's sole male heir made it essentially a *fait accompli* that control of H. W. Iverson would eventually pass into Jack's hands. On the face of it, either Harry or Jack might have sold the business to a third party, but Sherry believes this was never in prospect. 'No way,' she says. 'Whilst Beansy was alive, there was just no way it was going to happen, and that's all there was to it.'

How good a fist Jack made of the business once he took it over is difficult to determine. Documentary evidence is slight. The one set of financial figures that survive for the firm in the records of the Real Estate and Stock Institute, from 1960, is incomplete; it shows a rent roll of about twenty properties, but no schedule of auctions. Australian Securities and Investment Commission records only commence in 1973.

From all accounts, Jack made a courteous, conscientious and extremely ethical estate agent. Like his father, he once faced a court action; like his father, he won it. The action, in April 1953, was brought by a wealthy spinster, Miss Beryl Briginshaw of East Malvern, who issued a Supreme Court writ against the firm over a lease she had taken on a Balnarring guest house, alleging that H. W. Iverson and Tulum Lodge's owner Miss Gwendoline Butt had misrepresented its likely takings. The action never went ahead, and the allegations were subsequently and unreservedly withdrawn.

It would seem, however, that Harry left his son a hard row to hoe. From the late 1950s, the growing concentration of ownership and increasing scale of rival businesses made the Melbourne real estate industry increasingly competitive. Commissions were cut more freely, which were difficult for one-man businesses like Jack's to absorb. Jack had the diligent Berry Rea to rely upon, but evidently needed further support, for Jean Iverson took on a sub-agency from 1 February 1957 and often lent her help in the management of the office and on various transactions.

Jack also had his father looking over his shoulder. Harry, naturally enough, given that it was his life's work, retained an abiding interest in the real estate business in general and H. W. Iverson in particular. Perhaps he sometimes made life difficult for his son: Jack's nephew Ian Quintell recalls one day at Moana, for instance, inadvertently intruding on what seemed to be an argument between Harry and Jack, and how the latter had shrunken into a corner like a sulking boy. But whether this was an exceptional or a characteristic incident it is impossible to know.

It is also impossible to ascertain the degree to which Jack wished that things had turned out differently, that he had not inherited responsibility for the estate agency, that he'd had the opportunity to make his own way in life, perhaps on the land. This is the suspicion of his family, but suspicions can never be definitive.

We *do* have some guideposts. The chapters of his life spent at Baringhup East and Tallarook, Jack looked back on with great fondness. On the way to rejoin his unit after leave during World War II, Jack even cut short his time at home to drop in on Landscape; he signed the visitors' book on 4 April 1943 as 'J. B. Iverson (Bdr VX23811), 11 Bty 4 Aust Lt A A Regt'. No-one survives who might recall his arrival, but it smacks of a nostalgic visit, and perhaps a fantasy or two about peacetime life.

One perhaps telling exhibit, too, is Jack's continued close friendship with Alan Meckiff after the war. Alan Meckiff *had* returned to the land after demobilisation, buying a soldier settlement-financed farm called Wedgwood at Darriman near the Victorian country town of Sale in 1947, and the Iversons holidayed there often. Jack also helped build the Meckiffs' holiday home at Loch Sport, and Alan's son Charles learned to refer to his father's friend as 'Uncle Jack'.

Jack was always in high spirits when he drove his family in their little Renault up to Darriman. His daughter Beverley recalls one uproarious journey where her father was finding it difficult, with his long legs, to steer the vehicle round the corners of the winding road. He pulled up, took a saw from the boot, and laughingly cut the bottom off the steering wheel: a neat and spontaneous lateral thought. Once they arrived at Wedgwood, Jack's contentment and pleasure in the atmosphere and routine of rural life were always noticeable. Perhaps, Jack saw Alan's as the life he might have led had circumstances decreed otherwise. Indeed, Alan remembers one occasion when Jack seemed to admit how much he envied the Meckiff family's situation:

> One day, when Jack was down at Sale, we went to a men's club at Yarram, and we got talking to a local doctor. He asked Jack: 'If you'd had the opportunity to do things your own way during your life, what would you have done? If you could exchange your cricket experiences for anything else, what would it have been?'
>
> Jack looked at me and said: 'If I'd had my own way, I'd've been like him.'

Jack was also, undemonstratively but genuinely, sensitive to the dreams of other people. In the early 1960s, for instance, Jack hired to paint 44 Black Street a young Dutch immigrant,

John van Zon. As their friendship developed, Jack learned that van Zon and his wife were saving to buy a house in Brighton. Knowing that it would take years for the newly-arrived van Zons to accumulate the necessary funds, Jack volunteered to lend them the deposit, free of interest. They accepted joyfully and, in due course, repaid every cent. This tender feeling for the van Zons' aspirations may have been an expression, not merely of generosity, but of fellow feeling for one with ambitions beyond reach.

This does not amount, of course, to a life consumed with resentment for opportunities denied. For, while Jack might have seen himself as 'a bit of a rebel', he was surely only a bit of one; his respect, admiration and sense of obligation to his father were too great. If Jack's innermost thoughts were of a different, freer existence unshackled by filial responsibilities, he never asserted them. He was always his father's son.

After the war, too, Jack had responsibilities towards a wife and children, the need to maintain middle-class pieties and to guarantee an expected standard of living. He could not afford to be diverted. Yet reason never triumphs completely over imagination, practicality never wholly subordinates fantasy. As Jack busily did the right thing by others, he could not but have wondered what the right thing was by himself.

The Iverson family suffered a tragic blow in December 1961 when Joy died after a long illness. Jack would have felt the loss especially; of all his sisters, he was closest to her. Joy died, moreover, intestate, which may have prompted others to consider their personal affairs. Harry and Ede drew up and revised a number of wills, while Jack drafted his own with his friend Rex Sevier as executor.

By the early 1960s, the Iverson family was well off. Between them Harry and Jack owned four sizeable properties in Brighton—Moana, Black Street, Kinane Street and a block of Grosvenor Street flats converted from terrace houses—a suburb which was by some measures Melbourne's wealthiest; a February 1963 survey assessing rateable property values in various city locales put Brighton atop the list, at an aggregate £2.25 million.

A fascinating exchange of letters survives from the will-making negotiations between father and son, dated March 1966. Their tone is friendly, but formal, as if between good business acquaintances: a missive headed 'JBI from HWI' is answered by one headed 'HWI from JBI'. Their content is intimate to the family, but this is in no sense an exchange between equals. Harry, now eighty-one, is still the law-giver; Jack, fifty, remains the deferential subordinate.

Much of the correspondence focuses on Marjorie, who had lived and worked at Kinane Street since 1955 with the help of subsidies from Harry and Ede, and who was clearly anxious about her fate should her parents die. Harry reports to Jack an exchange with her the previous week:

> 'Something must be done, Marj, about possession of Kinane Street when we go—You can safely leave this to Jack'. Marj—'But I don't know Jack like I know you and mother'. I said—'You have Jack's sympathy and under-standing and it was he who pressed for your having a long stay at Kinane Street'. Marj—'But I don't know Jack like I know you and Mum'.

Marj is intelligent, has plenty of courage and has had to put up (recently) with bad tenants. One wretch will have cost about £50. She knows what she wants and goes after it and has an eye to her future security. Who could blame her for this?

From the other angle there are others to be considered. It is not fair to them that she has stayed there for 11 years, rent free, all property expenses paid by Ede and myself; Ede with the expensive gifts, which I have partly subscribed to in some cases, and I have paid all additions, outgoings and repairs etc.

Jack's reply was placatory:

Ru, Jan [Joy's daughter], Jean and I all have a good idea for the tremendous backing you have given, and have always been ready to give, to Marj over the years. Those have not been easy years for Marj and we all admire her tremendously for the courage and determination she has shown to overcome the handicap she has had since her eye operations. Since her divorce and those operations she has at times become almost dependent on you both for help financially and otherwise and it is to the undying credit of you both that that help has been given so readily and continuously.

Nonetheless, Jack could also not obscure the hurt Marjorie's comments caused him:

From your talk with Marj it is obvious she does not have the same confidence in me as she has in you and Mum. This is understandable as I do not see that much of her but it is hard to reason out *why* she should have said what she did. Anyone would think from her choice of words that I intended to throw her to the wolves at the first opportunity. Perhaps I am not as demonstrative as Marj would like me to be but in my own quiet way I will see that she is treated fairly and considerately and with the same sincere affection as I have for all other members of the family. All of us want to see Marj adequately protected and even if it means being out of pocket a bit I feel we are all unanimous where her welfare in the future is being considered.

Harry also tells Jack, almost as a postscript, that he has decided to exclude one of his grandchildren from his will for having 'blatantly smoked sigarettes [sic]. I will not reconsider this exclusion.' Jack let it pass unremarked.

The tone and content of the exchanges seem to give us a picture of the protagonists. Harry is not domineering, but certainly authoritative. The reporting of his dialogue with Marjorie would also appear somewhat gratuitous; if not an advertisement of his own virtue, at least a little tactless. Jack is not craven, but assuredly respectful. The first part of his reply is an extremely dignified response to a potentially divisive issue. It is only when Jack addresses the content of Marjorie's comments directly that we sense a certain hurt, for his concern seems disproportionate to what would have been unintended offence; indeed, it smacks of someone who felt misjudged for adherence to his 'own quiet way'. Jack's lack of response to his father's decision about the disinheritance may also be telling. He presumably knew enough of his father's mind to refrain from protest (in fact, Harry later softened his stance). The overall image is of a classic suburban hierarchy: the businesslike but gruffly affectionate elder statesman, striving for fairness but still capable of wilful caprices, his reverent but appreciative offspring, doing his best to honour and obey but whose sensitivity went perhaps unacknowledged.

TWENTY-SEVEN

Jack Iverson had not finished with cricket. Having come so far, he resolved in December 1960 to return to where he'd begun. He applied for a transfer from Melbourne to Brighton with the idea of playing just the odd game with his old club when it was short and he was not denying a youngster a place.

When Jack played his first game against Preston on 21 January 1961, he was evidently rusty, conceding 25 from 11 overs and going wicketless. He ended up playing most of the season in the second XI, for whom he claimed 13 wickets at eight. But all that talk about just playing the odd game was forgotten amid his resurgent enthusiasm the following season, when he harvested 70 wickets at 8.9 for the second XI and helped them nearly win a premiership.

Brighton, which had faded after Dudley Fitzmaurice's

retirement, was suddenly a strong club again under the captaincy of thirty-seven-year-old batsman/leg spinner Lou Carter, an alumnus of Prahran and University who had played five games for Victoria between 1946 and 1954. His presence had attracted a number of accomplished players, including former Australian opening batsman Colin McDonald, Jack's former Victorian colleague Dave Kerr and the Essendon footballer Jack Clarke. Carter's vice-captain, local architect Len Hayball, was also known as probably the fastest bowler in sub-district ranks.

Jack was forty-seven by the time the 1962–63 season began, but there was never any doubt of his involvement. Indeed, his energy and dedication round the club were a byword. As was his custom, he was always among the first to practice, wheeling away at a single stump until someone was game enough to face him. He especially enjoyed bowling to juniors, whom he would utterly bamboozle, but was a match for anyone. 'He loved practising and batting against him in the nets was nearly impossible,' says former teammate Alan Tudor. 'You just couldn't lay a bat on him.' As the ball beat another groping bat, Jack would rise from his follow-through, throw his arms in the air and emit a glorious rumble of laughter.

Carter and Hayball were so impressed with Jack that they insisted on him playing a certain amount of first XI cricket; it was anomalous that a former Test player, however old, should be kicking around in a subsidiary grade. So successfully did they manage this division of his labours that he proved the most successful bowler in both teams, seeing the second XI into the semi-finals of their grade and the first XI to a premiership in theirs.

Jack retained his old limitations as a bowler. He could be amazingly mechanical. Carter recalls various instances when Jack took punishment because he tended to bowl to a virtually unchanging line and length every delivery. 'Jack could land it on a sixpence,' he says. 'But it was always the same sixpence.' Hayball says, too, that unsympathetic pitches tended to find Jack out:

> I had the pleasure of fielding at first slip to him when he played for the firsts and he was quite extraordinary. Even on quite good batting wickets, he was an amazing bowler on most occasions. The only time you saw any weakness was on the odd really hard, flat, dead wicket. He didn't have the temperament or the edge of experience necessary when the conditions were difficult. He'd become a bit of a journeyman.

Alan Tudor recalls the second XI semi-final in March 1963 for the strange sensation that Jack didn't quite know what he was doing. Jack had been expected to round up Camberwell easily, but against left-hander Robin Balfour appeared incapable of bowling other than to the correct line and length for a right-hander. Balfour made 91, Jack took 2–61, and Camberwell made 240; a first innings target of which Brighton fell a dozen runs short.

When Jack was on song, however, there was nothing to hold him. In the second innings of the same game, he claimed 7–23 and with Tudor routed Camberwell for 50. And in the first XI final the following week at Brunswick Oval, his 3–10 polished off Preston for only 69. His figures for the season convey Jack's general irresistibility: 32 wickets at 6.6 for the second XI, 34 wickets at 7.02 for the first XI.

These might have been some of the most contented cricket years of Jack's life. He was bowling against a standard of opposition that gave him a good chance of success, he was a popular and appreciated member of a happy and talented club. As club president Bob Treasure commented in a round-up of the 1962–63 season in Brighton's annual report:

> The enthusiastic Jack Iverson played cricket, practised and bowled as though his life depended on it. We were proud to have such an experienced player to set an example to the younger players and really show them how the game should be played. This psychological influence on them and against opposing players is an asset in itself.

Jack liked his teammates and his teammates liked him. He had great respect for Carter. He invited Tudor to his home, something he rarely did, to play table tennis. His old cobber Col Shipley was still around as vice-president. Jack's name, moreover, still carried a bit of magic in cricket circles. During that 1962–63 season, he and some teammates were invited to bowl in the nets at University Oval by the touring MCC team under Ted Dexter's command. 'They were most intrigued by Jack, of course,' Tudor recalls. 'And he troubled them.'

Off the field, nonetheless, Jack still tended to keep his distance. Carter recalls: 'On match days, Jack never turned up earlier than ten minutes before the game, always dressed in his cricket clothes. Then, when we finished, he'd pack his bag and walk off home again.' He scarcely ever lingered long enough for a drink after a game, and never came back to the club rooms afterwards. Hayball saw him as a shy, rather guarded, personality:

> There was something a little immature about him, something that didn't quite work for him in his relationships with people. I was very fond of him. He had great moments of enthusiasm and a droll, self-deprecating sense of humour. But there was a reserve about him that you couldn't quite get through.

The solitary exception to this rule was consequently notable enough for Hayball to remember:

> The night I recall most with Jack was the one where we won the 62–63 premiership. We were a lot of mostly single guys down at the club and we didn't think anything of staying late after a day's play, fooling round and drinking. That had never been Jack's style and he wasn't usually a part of social life of the club. That night, though, he surprised and delighted us by coming back to the club rooms from Brunswick and being like the life of the party, this big, hearty, gentle giant.

Culmination of the evening was something of a traditional ceremony at Brighton: the celebratory urination on the Brighton Beach Oval pitch. To universal amazement, Jack joined in with relish. Col Shipley recalls Jack coming up to him wreathed in a smile, saying: 'I've just done something I really enjoyed. I've pissed on the wicket.' What pleasure it must have been for Jack, even if only on this night, to slough off inhibition, to forget about being the deferential son and dutiful husband, and behave in the company of his fellows like 'a bit of a rebel'.

Even as Jack Iverson was returning to cricket in the early 1960s, cricket was returning to Jack Iverson, in fulfilment of a prophecy Bill O'Reilly had made in the wake of Jack's great day against England at the SCG a decade before: 'After his great performance in this Test it is certain that there will be many young bowling hopefuls trying to imitate the novel Iverson grip. Their time could be spent less profitably.'

Hopeful imitators had sprung up virtually the instant of Jack's arrival. Having experienced the surge of digital delight at feeling a few come out just right, they then encountered the extraordinary physical difficulties inherent in his style. In Jack's early days at Brighton, he had inspired one of his second XI, Clive Tadgell, to try and become a second Iverson. But he'd gotten nowhere and faded away.

In 1951–52, the sub-district club of Coburg had then unearthed Jimmy Pearse, another bowler in the Iverson vein, who'd purportedly learned to bowl that way from studying newspaper pictures of Jack's action. Several district clubs chased his signature for the following season, and Fitzroy was exultant at obtaining it, but his first training night at the club was a disaster. Wicketkeeper Bill Jacobs recalls the Harvey brothers, Neil in particular, smashing him everywhere. Pearse ended up playing in a premiership side in 1953–54, but as a batsman; he bowled exactly one over in the final.

In May 1954, however, Jack himself took a telephone call at his office from a genuine prodigy. Seventeen-year-old Rex Harry from University High School had, by dint of hard work and determination, just managed with his own version of the

Iverson delivery to claim 70 wickets at six apiece for Ascot Vale Congregational in an Essendon church cricket competition.

Jack was at the time convalescing from the finger injury that had ruled him out of the 1953–54 district final, but he was delighted, and fascinated especially that Harry's stock ball was not the googly but the leg break. He wrote the youth an encouraging letter:

> I was most interested to hear from someone who has managed to bowl a ball with this particular grip of mine. And, what is more, to have success with it as well.
>
> How you manage to make it break from the leg is beyond me. I've been trying to do that for five years and succeed only when it hits some pebble on the pitch or lands on the seam. This gives me to think that our respective grips differ in one way or another.
>
> At the moment I am a bit handicapped by having my spinning finger in plaster. It was injured in the last district game against Richmond and has never since responded to treatment. This rules out comparing secrets until at least the end of June when I hope to have the plaster removed. I would like to hear from you between then and the opening of the cricket season and trust I will be able to help you along the road to further success.

Harry, originally an opening batsman, had begun his experiments with Jack's methods after missing selection in a junior representative side:

> They said I was too slow. And I said: 'Bugger it.' I decided to give batting away and have a go at bowling. Jack Iverson had always been a bit of a hero to me. And I decided to have a go at bowling like him, starting with a tennis ball in

the backyard, and pretty soon I found I had pretty good control.

Harry finally met his idol on the roof of the Commercial Travellers Association on 22 July 1954. Their grips were not after all different—Harry simply found the front-of-the-hand leg break action more natural—and the main distinction was that Jack simply spun the ball much more. Not that this, Harry felt, was necessarily a huge disadvantage for him:

> I wasn't a big spinner, certainly not as big as Jack, because my fingers were quite small, and his were huge: he could almost hide the ball in the palm of his hand. But I was accurate, and there's no point spinning it a foot and missing the bat if you can spin it three inches and get the edge. They kept missing them so I knew I must be doing something right.
>
> People started to say I bowled mystery balls and they were inclined to exaggerate a bit, so batsmen started to wonder about which way they'd spin. A lot of cricket's a mind game. If a batsman thinks you're doing something, even if you're not doing it, then you're halfway there, aren't you?

Harry played one game in North Melbourne's thirds the following summer and, after national service, topped the second XI bowling averages in 1955–56. He remembers in his first XI debut against Collingwood bowling against both Keith Stackpole snr and jnr. Stackpole *pere* spent the whole partnership hissing down the pitch at Stackpole *fils*: 'Watch his fingers! Watch his fingers!'

Then, even as Jack was bowling in Brighton's second XI in February 1962, Harry was called up for a second-string

Victorian side playing Tasmania at Geelong's Kardinia Park. Unfortunately, he was astray in the first innings, conceding 27 in half a dozen wicketless overs, and lacked penetration in the second, taking 1–47 from 18 overs and striking only with the last ball of the match when he had Tasmania's keeper Graeme Hudson caught behind.

> The first night I was very dejected because I didn't do myself justice. In the second innings, though, I bowled all right. The Tasmanians had just come from playing South Australia in Adelaide where they'd played against Sincock, and one of their guys said: 'You were very unlucky today. We reckon you're a better bowler than Sincock.'

It was a high compliment; left-arm wrist spinner David Sincock went on to take 156 first-class wickets and play three Tests. And, though Harry was not selected in first-class cricket again, he took away one other delightful memory of his brief career. Before the match, he'd had measurements taken by the famous Melburnian cobbler Hope Sweeney, the Australian cricketer's shoeman of choice for thirty years. But when Harry visited on match eve, Sweeney confessed he'd not had time to make the boots up and offered some that were ready-made.

'Do these fit you?' Sweeney asked. They did. 'They're Richie Benaud's,' the bootmaker explained. 'He ordered them, but he's never picked them up. You can have them.'

So Rex Harry's three days of first-class cricket were spent filling Richie Benaud's shoes. It would take another bowler, and character, to fill Jack Iverson's.

TWENTY-EIGHT

The bowler who would imitate Jack Iverson most successfully shared more with him than technique. Just as Jack was a 'mystery spinner' for reasons other than the way he spun the ball, so was John Gleeson.

The Gleeson family hailed from the north coast of New South Wales. John Gleeson's father was on the railways, leasing horses to the work gangs as they laid the line through Kyogle, and came into property when he married a girl from the nearby village of Wiangaree who owned land which share-farmers worked. The family's main sporting enthusiasm, incongruously, was lawn bowls; Gleeson's grandfather had cultivated a backyard rink, and young John bowled competitively as a boy at Kyogle. But he and his younger brothers Roy and Ian were also keen cricketers. After school every day, they would adjourn across the road from the family home to a paspalum pitch that they tended with a hand mower. The wicket batsmen protected was a jacaranda tree originally planted as a Great War memorial.

The cream cart that travelled between Kyogle and Wiangaree was the family's link to the wider world: daily, it brought a day-old copy of Sydney's *Daily Mirror* for Gleeson's grandmother; monthly, it brought a precious issue of *Sporting Life* magazine that father and sons pored over. Had it not, John Gleeson might never have played for Australia. As it was, in October 1950, twelve-year-old John was immediately trans-fixed by R. S. Whitington's description of the Iverson method. John Gleeson had naturally strong and supple fingers—'I used to say I got strong fingers from milking cows,' he says, 'but that was bullshit'—and showed a natural flair for the style. Interestingly, like Rex Harry but unlike Jack Iverson, the leg break proved simplest to master; indeed, Gleeson discovered, the more the ball was made to look like an off break, the more it jagged from leg.

As with his inspiration, however, Gleeson's brainchild would need a long gestation. For the moment it was a diversion to vex siblings and confound visitors. As a teenager, he was less inter-ested in projecting spinners than in catching them; attending engineering college in Sydney from January 1956 with the Post-Master General's Department, he joined Western Suburbs third XI as a keeper-batsman. Back in the country a couple of years later as a telephone technician, he confined his spinners to the South Tamworth nets. And his career might have ended here had it not been for a like-minded band of cricket brothers, the Emus.

The Emus owe their origin to a grazier from Muswellbrook

in New South Wales' Hunter Valley, J. S. White OBE, whose love of cricket was so great that he named his cattle-breeding company Broadhalfpenny Down Pty Ltd after the game's first famous ground, home to the Hambledon club in the second half of the eighteenth century. Concerned for country cricket's postwar welfare, White had endowed an annual carnival between teams from all over the state for Edinglassie Shield. The 1959 tournament's purpose was to select a combined side, the Emus, to visit Singapore and Malaysia. Twenty-one-year-old Gleeson made it as a keeper. A couple of years later, he found himself in North America as part of an ambitious world tour, the sixteen-member squad led by future Randwick skipper Johnnie Hayward.

A problem for Gleeson was that the Emus already possessed an accomplished keeper-batsman, Col Elliott. Gleeson missed the first game in San Francisco, and was selected for the second in Vancouver against British Columbia as a batsman. It seemed he mightn't have much to do except chase a few balls, and admire the sylvan setting and mountain backdrop that had inspired Sir Donald Bradman to describe the Brockton Point Ground as 'without question the most beautiful cricket ground in the world'. But just before lunch, Gleeson was stirred from his outfield sightseeing by Hayward's unexpected invitation to bowl an over of his finger-flicked screwballs. He took a wicket, claimed another three after the break, and didn't don his gauntlets for the rest of the trip through Canada, England and Hong Kong, taking 45 wickets at 15.7 and compiling 723 runs at 36.2 for good measure.

Even after his success with the Emus, and a key role in NSW Country's victory in the annual match against Metropolitan at the SCG, Gleeson was unsure if he wished to persist with cricket. Married in Tamworth and settling down, he had few ambitions beyond the odd game of cricket or baseball: 'When I played that game against Metropolitan at the SCG, I'd done just about everything I'd wanted to do in cricket. I'd played in Canada, the US, Asia, England, Hong Kong, the SCG. I'd have been quite happy going along, taking a few wickets in local cricket.'

At the start of the 1965–66 season, however, a New South Wales combination came to Gunnedah under the aegis of Jack Chegwyn, a former state batsman turned selector, and a country cricket evangelist who'd been bringing city teams to off-piste locations in New South Wales for twenty-five years. The hosts invited two Tamworth players to make up their XI: Mark Cornell, a South African expatriate who played locally, and Gleeson.

The visitors' special guest star was former Australian captain Richie Benaud. To Gleeson, 'Benaud was God'. He spent the week before the match premeditating his plan: 'I decided that the first two I'd bowl as orthodox offies, like Ashley Mallett, then the third ball I'd toss in the one that spun from leg and hit his off-stump.'

Word of Gleeson was also sufficiently widespread for Benaud, on match day, to undertake his own reconnaissance:

> We...didn't know what to expect from a wicketkeeper turned 'Iverson'...and I took my binoculars around to a car parked behind the bowler's arm and watched him through the first overs he bowled. In fact, at the fall of a wicket, I

walked out from there to the crease rather than going back to the small pavilion. The ball had been turning quite a bit but that didn't matter too much because I had deduced that he was simply a leg break bowler who looked like an off spinner.

In fact, it was Benaud who was probably better prepared for his brush with Gleeson than vice versa. 'As it turned out,' Gleeson recalls, 'I'd caught and bowled Ray Flockton with the seventh ball of my over, so all my plans were in tatters when Richie came in.' He decided to bowl his special delivery immediately.

Cricketers often surprise you by the vividness of their memories from even quite unimportant matches. This game was, after all, no more than a bit of fun in the country almost thirty-five years ago. But the antagonists remember that first ball graphically. It looked to Benaud for all the world like an off break on leg stump, which he had thoughts of flicking behind square leg, but it evaded his bat and ended up at first slip. Benaud remembers of Gleeson: 'He had the good grace, and common sense, not to smile.' Gleeson remembers Benaud's bottom lip suddenly protruding, as it often did in moments of perplexity, causing Ray Robinson to liken it to 'a tramcar's step'.

Gleeson missed the wicket he wanted that day, but claimed 4–80, sufficient for Benaud to seek him out at stumps and ask whether he had considered playing in Sydney. Gleeson said he hadn't. Benaud responded sagely: 'There'll come a time in your life when you wonder: what would have happened if I'd gone to play in Sydney? And you won't know because you never tried.' Gleeson ruminated and agreed. On Monday, the telephone rang at his office. It was Benaud: 'You're playing for Balmain against North Sydney next Saturday at Drummoyne Oval. Good luck.'

Gleeson's summers would henceforward be dominated by his weekly commute from Tamworth to Sydney and back: 1000 kilometres *in toto*. Balmain paid him the fare for a sleeper train, which Gleeson converted into a deal with a local airline under which he paid full freight to Sydney and returned half-price. He would amply repay the investment.

Coming down from the bush, this slight, jug-eared, crewcut figure with a laconic manner and quizzical air looked anything but a cricketer. But despite missing the first four matches of the season, Gleeson took 43 wickets. His mystery was deepened by the fact that, like a Tamworth Pimpernel, he disappeared spot on stumps for his return flight from Mascot; prompting colleagues to nickname him 'CHO' ('Cricket Hours Only').

Shortly, however, Sydney would see more of him, when he was added to the state squad for the 1966–67 season, entailing an 8am midweek departure from Tamworth for the 5pm session. His first journey entailed a piquant reunion with Benaud. New South Wales maintained a net for some of its old soldiers—including the likes of Tom Brooks, Frank Misson and Bill Watson—and on this particular day Benaud also appeared and invited Gleeson to bowl to him again.

There was about Gleeson already a certain guile—of a kind never harboured by Jack Iverson—and his first ball was not the concealed leggie but an orthodox off break. Benaud shouldered arms. It hit off stump. Gleeson noticed Benaud's bottom lip protrude again. Lobbing the ball back, Australia's former captain muttered: 'I was still in Gunnedah.'

When Gleeson took 5–28 from 25 overs in a second XI match against Victoria in Melbourne a few weeks later, he had another brush with greatness. Jack Iverson himself popped in. Even the unflappable Gleeson was slightly overwhelmed: 'I thought: "You are a bloke I want to meet".'

A famous meeting is recorded on Australia's 1930 Ashes tour between B. J. T. Bosanquet and Clarrie Grimmett—in slow bowling terms equivalent to Stanley meeting Livingstone—at a dinner during the tourists' fixture with Hampshire at Brighton. Bosanquet took one look at Australia's guru of the googly and wondered aloud: 'Am I responsible for you?' Grimmett would relate how he and the googly's progenitor talked all night of their shared enthusiasm, strolling the length of the pier and the beach, and did not part until milkmen could be heard on their dawn round.

One might have expected something similar on this occasion, but the encounter was for Gleeson anti-climactic. Jack, he remembers, got out the first question: 'How do you bowl the leggie?'

When Gleeson explained that the more he held it like an off break, the more it spun from leg, Jack replied: 'That's funny. I could never bowl the leggie. I tried, but it only turned when the pitch was really spinning.' The conversation went nowhere. Gleeson—a serious student of the game—began to talk about the physics of the rotated cricket ball and field placing. Jack had little to contribute.

Gleeson's first-class debut at the age of twenty-eight, against

Western Australia at the WACA Ground on 9 December 1966, was also anti-climactic. He claimed a single wicket for 63 from twenty-three overs, and was made twelfth man for the next game at the Adelaide Oval. But it was here in the picturesque setting of the nets behind its ivy-clad stands, appropriately near what is now the Clarrie Grimmett Entrance, that Gleeson bowled 'the ball that got me into the Australian side'. It was to Sir Donald Bradman, national chairman of selectors, at his invitation, the Don wearing a suit and taking strike without a bat. Gleeson, understanding the moment's significance, gave his first delivery a prodigious squirt. Bradman shaped to let it drift to leg and copped it on the hip when it turned the other way.

The other event of moment in that match was that NSW leg spinner Peter Philpott broke his spinning finger. Gleeson recaptured his place, and his season's haul of 23 wickets at 22 obtained him selection in a second-string Australian team visiting New Zealand at summer's end. Like Jack Iverson on the equivalent 1949–50 trip, he was the tour's leading wicket-taker. And at Christmas 1967 on the Adelaide Oval—fully seventeen years since he'd first spun a ball the Iverson way, if little more than a year since he'd bumped Bradman's hip—John Gleeson demonstrated that cricket history does repeat itself by playing against India the first of twenty-nine Tests.

Comparison of Jack Iverson and John Gleeson presents a paradox. Gleeson was the better cricketer. He could bat effectually, he could field, and he assuredly possessed that elusive faculty of a 'cricket brain'; his hoodwinking of Benaud in the nets at their second encounter tells us all we need know on that score.

At the same time, Gleeson was not quite the bowler Jack had been. Indeed, it could not have been otherwise. Gleeson was a good fifteen centimetres shorter and a dozen kilograms lighter than his precursor, so the extraordinary bounce and near-medium pace that were Jack's greatest weapons were denied him. Gleeson tried bridging the gap by running eight paces and bowling as fast as he could, but physique was always against him. For greatest penetration, Gleeson needed favourable conditions: he was at his most formidable on green wickets with a breeze's aid. Iverson had commanded respect on all but the deadest surfaces.

Nonetheless, Gleeson proved a genuine original, rather than simply a second edition. He was Australia's most effective bowler on its 1968 Ashes tour, claiming 58 wickets at 20.7, delighting the octagenarian Neville Cardus: 'Gleeson need but twiddle a finger and the faces of several English batsmen are sicklied over by the pale cast of thought.' The limitations of Australia's attack during Gleeson's five-year international career condemned him to hard labour, often on surfaces inimical to him, but he accepted the slings and arrows with equanimity, even as he watched Australian teammates spill thirty catches from his bowling in South Africa in January–March 1970.

Nor, as one watched John Gleeson, could one quite overlook his sheer incongruity. That air of the country cricketer in the big smoke never deserted him. Mooching about in the outfield with a detached air and in flannels of decidedly autumn shade, he put Ian Wooldridge of the *Daily Mail* in mind of a man 'looking for his horse'. Indeed, that Gleeson and Jack Iverson will forever be bracketed in cricket history is appropriate: Gleeson, in his own way, was the unlikeliest Australian to don a baggy green cap since the man who inspired him.

TWENTY-NINE

Throughout my research into Jack Iverson's life, the circumstances of his death cast a long and daunting shadow. All but a couple of sources ignore it completely—in some cases, I learned, deliberately. And even where his tragic end was described, there were troubling evasions and omissions.

Something else, too, held me back. I have no trouble admitting it: I liked Jack. Charting the trajectory of his career, collecting stories about his various humours, trying to imagine what was on his mind at various junctures, I felt alternately happy, sad, cheered, sorry, sympathetic and uncomprehending. He had long ceased to be a specimen on a slide. He felt altogether human in every response. Perhaps, I reasoned, this was what I found so beguiling about him; that he was not some remote gladiator out of sporting mythology, but a figure cut from an altogether more familiar cloth. The prospect of sharing in any suffering he experienced later in life was thus somewhat forbidding.

To begin resolving what happened, another trek was necessary to the Public Records Office in the outlying Melbourne suburb of Laverton; a dark, squat building where time feels almost as suspended as the records it encloses. In my case, the quest was for the 1973 coronial index, which proved to be one of those remarkable volumes which the information age will presumably make redundant: a weighty, calf-bound ledger inscribed in the neat hand of some long-forgotten clerk, sterilising in bureaucratese hundreds upon hundreds of untimely ends. Some descriptions were technical ('inhalation of vomitus'), some graphic ('fell and caught beneath slasher'), some peculiar ('trampled by elephant'), some almost comic ('tree fell on him' and, memorably, 'crushed by tombstone'). Intimations of mortality were irresistible and, when three sturdy boxes of material arrived in my cubicle, I opened them with a spasm of guilt. There suddenly seemed something presumptuous about what I was up to. In the face of the hundreds of individual stories in that index, the breadth and complexity of *la comedie humaine*, and the vast continent of the unknowable that exists in every life, were oppressive.

Yet there was nothing for it. Having tried to introduce a little light into Jack's life, I could not hesitate to add the shade of his death. The relationship between a cricketer and his observers is fleeting, like Bede's famous sparrow fluttering momentarily in the banquet hall before exiting into the wintry darkness: 'So tarries for a moment the life of man in our sight, but what is before it, what after it, we know not.' Over a distance of years, it grows more superficial still. The possibility of *finding out what happened* seemed worthwhile, even an obligation.

The files were surprisingly thorough, as if in partial atonement for the scarcity of detail on Jack's life: there were depositions from three doctors, pathology and laboratory reports, even diagrams. The salient document, however, was evidence placed before coroner Harry Pascoe SM in March 1974 from Jean Iverson.

She traced the decline in Jack's health to August 1963, when J. B. Iverson Pty Ltd suffered the unexpected death of its most valued employee, office manager Berry Rea. Replacements did not work out, and Jean Iverson expressed the view that her husband began taking on too much work. By around October 1965, she was seriously concerned about her husband's health:

> He became 'seedy'. Business pressure was building up considerably. He was trying so hard to get established in the business that I believe it started to affect his health…He was a person who worried over small things but, as he went on, these mounted up and he felt he could not cope.

It was, coincidentally, around this time that Jack gave his only lengthy post-retirement interview, his aforementioned talk with the *Herald*'s Alan Trengove. Perhaps its unusually dark tone—'Have you ever wondered what it's like to play Test cricket with an inferiority complex?'—was a reflection of Jack's condition. Jack's remarks certainly read like those of someone who could barely believe he'd once had the gumption to play Test cricket, who saw not glory but irony inscribed in his brief celebrity.

In Christmas week of 1965, Jean took characteristically firm action, insisting that Jack visit Dr Douglas Callister of the New Street Clinic. A mild stroke was diagnosed, three weeks bed rest prescribed, but Jack was still unwell when he returned to work, moody, introverted and apprehensive. Jean said: 'His father felt he should not work alone because of his health, so I assisted my husband working at home and at the office. There were appointments for Jack to attend, but he felt that he could not cope so I had to attend for him.'

There were still days when Jack seemed himself. As his daughter Sherry went on a cruise with her cousin Janis, he pressed an envelope into her hand. It contained £10, and came with a note signed 'from the bloke at 44'. When she then began courting with a young engineer called Barry Holt, Jack was an intent supervisor. 'The first night Barry took me out we went to the pictures in town,' she recalls. 'When we got home about 11pm, there was Dad walking up and down outside Black Street exercising the dogs waiting for this guy to bring his daughter home.'

Jack and Jean laid a dance-floor for Sherry's twenty-first birthday party in July 1967, at which their daughter's engagement to Barry was happily announced. Jack was also well enough to turn out three months later for a game with Brighton's fourth XI at the age of fifty-two, and to claim figures faithful to the entirety of his career of 3–5 and 2–0. His record for Brighton was 312 wickets at an average of nine.

It was, however, his only game of the season, and would prove his last. Early the following year, recurrence of his earlier symptoms caused Dr Callister to refer him to a psychiatrist, Dr Ronald Kingston. They had four inconclusive consultations in which Jack was conspicuously uncommunicative. It was recommended that Jack visit Dr Eric Seal, a neuro-psychiatrist in charge of St Vincent's psychiatric clinic. Dr Seal suspected cerebral arteriosclerosis—a narrowing of the vessels to the brain that, like a chemical imbalance, can cause depression— and recommended a course of monthly electro-convulsive therapy at Moreland's Sacred Heart Hospital.

To our refined modern sensibilities, when we flatter ourselves that we have stripped mental illness of its taboo, ECT seems a barbaric treatment. Yet it was and remains astoundingly effective: even now, for reasons that remain scarcely understood, western clinicians find that four in five of those with suicidal or psychotic depression experience some relief after half a dozen sessions over a couple of months.

The notion that convulsions might ameliorate the condition of the mentally ill first occurred in 1933 to a Hungarian doctor, Ladislaus von Meduna. He observed that epilepsy and schizophrenia rarely occurred in the same patient, and conjectured that the inducing of the former might have a remedial effect on the latter. His original experiments involved the injection of camphor oil, which has convulsive qualities, and were extraordinarily scary. As leading Australian psychiatrist John Cade wrote:

> It was frantically strenuous. The convulsion was appalling

to watch and placed extreme stresses on the cardiovascular and musculoskeletal systems. Initially the therapist wondered if his patient would ever breathe again as respiration was choked off by the fit and he became more and more cyanosed. After what seemed an eternity he relaxed, gave first a deep gasp, then a series of gasps and his colour reverted rapidly from puce to pink…

Perhaps the greatest drawback to its use was that horrible latent period of thirty to forty seconds, terrifying to the patient and repugnant to the doctor, between the injection and the onset of the convulsion and oblivion. Patients suffered the pangs of imminently-anticipated death. One patient who had not uttered a word in eighteen months gasped 'ta ta' as he lapsed into unconsciousness, a brief desperate acknowledgment of his terror.

And yet, the experiments were staggering successful. Patients awoke from catatonic stupors that had lasted for years to speak, eat and move. Even more successful were experiments using electric stocks that induced fits, carried out by an Italian doctor Ugo Cerletti at Rome's Psychiatric University Hospital four years later: electricity eliminated the frightful wait for an injection to take effect, brought on unconsciousness immediately, and even caused a serendipitous amnesia of the treatment.

When ECT was introduced to Australia in the 1950s, it was still a hit and miss affair. It required a nerveless doctor to apply it: patients under treatment would foam at the mouth, even ejaculate, and spinal damage was not uncommon until sedatives and the muscle relaxant scolaline were generally applied. But again, it often worked where nothing else would, liberating countless patients from otherwise intolerable manias and melancholias.

Nonetheless, in the late 1960s, psychiatry remained an infant and inexact discipline. St Vincent's tiny psychiatric ward, named for St Dympna, the thirteenth-century Irish saint considered patroness of the insane, contained even after decades of campaigning by successive heads only thirty beds. Mental illness carried a profound stigma, both for those who suffered it and those who tried to treat it. As Dr Seal's former colleague Dr Ronald Conway, senior sessional psychologist at St Vincent's from 1960 to 1975, recalls:

> Certainly in those days it was considered somewhat demeaning to be in need of psychiatric help. It's like the old saying: 'There are no votes in prisons.' No-one really cares about the mentally ill aside from those who treat them and those related to them. There used to be a saying at St Vincent's: 'When all else fails, try psychiatry.' After ten years of fruitless treatment on a patient, you might get a doctor finally saying: 'Perhaps it's psychosomatic.'

One patient at St Dympna's at the time who experienced both the disorientation and the relief involved in psychiatric care was the humorist Barry Humphries. In his autobiography *More Please*, he writes vividly of his sensations:

> I must have spent many months in the Dymphna [sic] ward of St Vincent's Hospital. John Betjeman wrote me a long and comforting letter containing much information about the life and good works of St Dymphna herself. My father called regularly to see me in my private room, bringing cigarettes and nougat, and Rosalind came a few times without the children. I learned that I was in the psychiatric section of the hospital and a very softly spoken doctor saw me daily for a chat. I was constantly being woken up and

given tablets of various colours and quantities, but they did little to alleviate my self-pity. I spent a lot of times weeping into my pillow and thinking to myself, 'Why should a thing like this happen to a nice person like me?'

Eric Seal was apparently intent on treating Jack as an outpatient. Perhaps he sensed resistance on Jack's part to the idea of hospitalisation. Probably he sympathised with his plight as a healthy sporting man brought frustratingly low by symptoms of a disease whose nature was so elusive. Seal himself had been an outstanding schoolboy athlete and footballer, then an inter-varsity sprint star before the war, in addition to his talents as a classical scholar and linguist. His reputation, too, was as a devoted and empathic healer. His son Peter recalls that the family's Saturday pilgrimages to Windy Hill to watch Essendon play football often ended with his father detouring to visit lonely and isolated patients. In a retirement tribute to Seal, Ronald Conway said: 'The soul of soft-spoken modesty and humorous discretion, and a Christian in the best and truest sense, he is without doubt the most dedicated human being I have ever known.'

Nonetheless, in his treatment of Jack, Dr Seal's powers were circumscribed by the times. The tools of his trade were limited. ECT could relieve symptoms but its effects were temporary, and the available anti-depressants were primitive. Such drugs as the tricyclics imipramine and amitryptyline and the monoamine oxibase inhibitor phenelzine had by now thoroughly permeated American psychotherapy, but these were early days in their application in Australia. Dosages were uncertain, and side-effects often marked, as Jean Iverson noted feelingly in her deposition:

> He was right one day but the next day he would be sick again. There was a period where I noticed he was losing coordination. His speech was slurred and he had trouble sleeping. He would take many anti-depressant tablets…He got upset very easily and on some days he looked shocking. His face and hands were a horrible grey.

The worst and most debilitating aspect of depression is, however, neither the symptoms nor the side-effects of their treatment. It is in its appallingly ungraspable nature. With any other disease, one can isolate the enemy by identifying and sequestrating a physical cause. With mental illness, especially depression, there is nobody to blame but oneself. In the words of John Cade, depression is

> the most painful illness known to man, equalling or exceeding even the most exquisite physical agony. The patient is inconsolably despairing, often guilt-ridden—having committed, he imagines, the unforgivable sin—and completely immersed in his internal world of misery and utter loneliness. There is no pleasure in living, no energy or interest in doing anything except agitatedly bewail or silently brood on his unhappy fate; no hope for the future, abandoned by God and man.

That the patient is denied the honour of a physical scar leads to the expectation—from family, friends, as well as from oneself—that one can soldier on regardless. In June 1968, for instance, Sherry married Barry Holt at St John's Anglican Church in Toorak, where twenty-four years earlier Jack had married Jean. Sherry was shaking, Jack was shaking, Jean had pills and water at the ready, and Sherry recalls the tenacity with which her father made it through the occasion:

> He held my hand all the way to the church saying: 'It's not possible that you're old enough to be getting married.' By hook or by crook, he was going to walk me down that aisle if it was the last thing he ever did. I was shaking, and I can remember standing there at the altar steps and feeling Dad behind me shaking. Mum said afterwards: 'I could just see between you and I thought your bouquet was going to fall apart.'

The dilemma of the depressive can rarely have been more lucidly described than in *Darkness Visible*, a slim autobiographical book written in 1991 by the American novelist William Styron. In it he describes, with the insight only a sufferer can bring, the sort of predicament in which Jack now found himself:

> There is a region in the experience of pain where the certainty of alleviation often permits superhuman endurance...In depression, this faith in deliverance, in ultimate restoration, is absent. The pain is unrelenting, and what makes the condition intolerable is the foreknowledge that no remedy will come—not in a day, an hour, a month or a minute. If there is mild relief, one knows that it is only temporary; more pain will follow. It is hopelessness even more than pain that crushes the soul...This results in a striking experience—one which I have called, borrowing military terminology, the situation of the walking wounded. For in virtually any other serious sickness, a patient who has felt similar devastation would be lying flat in bed,

possibly sedated and hooked up to the tubes and wires of life-support systems, but at the very least in a posture of repose and an isolated setting. His invalidism would be necessary, unquestioned and honourably obtained. However, the sufferer from depression has no option, and therefore finds himself, like a walking casualty of war, thrust into the most intolerable social and family situations. There he must…present a face approximating the one associated with ordinary events and companionship. He must try to utter small talk and be responsive to questions, and knowingly nod, and frown and, God help him, even smile.

THIRTY

Attempting to ascertain the precise cause of Jack Iverson's depression thirty years afterwards would be the ultimate futility and presumption. Single convenient causes for such illnesses do not exist. Melancholia arises imperceptibly, for reasons often impenetrable even to the sufferer. F. Scott Fitzgerald's famous short story 'The Crack-Up' begins:

> Of course all human life is a process of breaking down, but the blows that do the dramatic side of the work—the big sudden blows that come, or seem to come, from outside— the ones you remember and blame things on and, in moments of weakness, tell your friends about, don't show their effect all at once. There is another sort of blow that comes from within—that you don't feel until it's too late to do anything about it, until you realise with finality

that in some regard you will never be as good a man again.

Nor are we dealing with a straightforward personality. Jack was gentle, courageous, forbearing and generous; also unassertive, biddable and easily overshadowed. He spoke of being 'a bit of a rebel' but also of his 'own quiet way'. He spent ten years on the land and at war, but agreed to run a family business in which his interest appears to have been limited rather than challenge his father's wishes. He was an independent thinker who challenged centuries of convention by taking his bowling innovation to cricket's summit. But there were limits to his tolerance of adversity. He took the blows of the game's fortune hard, and required the gratification of constant success to persevere.

We needn't, of course, think these paradoxes so remarkable. The phrase 'complex personality' is bandied about nowadays as though it means something, but contradictions linger in every human experience, and that we don't respond predictably or identically to all eventualities is actually what makes them so rich. At the same time, however, they do impose strains, like divided loyalties or shifting allegiances. And one does detect within Jack a sense of the thwarted, a hint of a character who felt responsibilities keenly but never felt himself quite equal to them. I believe that Jack's bowling was his nearest approach to self-fulfilment, yet even here his advance was checked by frailty in the face of punishment, and awareness that his father felt he 'would be very foolish' to continue playing.

Informed about aspects of Jack Iverson's history, Dr Ronald Conway volunteered some tentative thoughts. Given Jack's close and deferential relationship with his father—his acceptance of his role as heir to H. W. Iverson, and his tenure at Moana until the age of forty-one—he struck Dr Conway as a personality who 'matured slowly in terms of self-reliance and self-esteem, and tended to set his own internal standards, however unrealistic'. He suspected that Jack's ball-spinning habits, whatever they became, may have begun as 'a kind of tension reliever in a buttoned-up personality'. That Harry appears to have known of Jack's illness yet condoned his continuing to run the estate agency might have deepened the depression. 'There is an element of bundle dropping,' Dr Conway says. 'Meticulous and scrupulous personalities who are hard on themselves, often find it particularly wounding when others are hard on them, and despair all too promptly.'

Was the war a contributing factor in Jack's mental decline? There is, after all, anecdotal evidence of some post-traumatic stress. Unfortunately for such a neat solution, Jack experienced no serious psychological impairment until at least two decades after the war. And after that passage of time, the establishment of a direct causation would be problematic in any individual situation, not simply Jack's. Nor can one overlook the influence on Jack's friends and relatives of his tragic final years; the search for a trauma to blame probably nourished speculation, and the accumulation of reinterpretations and myths.

What, too, of Jack's physical malady; the cerebrovascular complaint which Dr Seal identified early in his treatment? In Dr Conway's opinion, however, this probably exacerbated an existing predisposition to depression rather than being a root cause:

> There is a connection and interaction between the pre-morbid and morbid conditions. A stick in the mud, for instance, will become more of a stick in the mud in the

face of depression. People talk about personalities 'changing' in a depression, but they never really completely change. It's more like the differences between an old *Guinness Book of Records* and the new one...An overstructured, reserved and perfectionist temperament would find it far more difficult dealing with a cerebrovascular complaint than someone with an off-the-wall ebullient sort of lifestyle. It was something that I saw in literally dozens and dozens of cases, enough to make it striking. It's as though we must keep our personalities well-oiled and exercised or else they atrophy.

Again, however, this must be read with a *caveat*. We have no access to his innermost thoughts at the time; nor, perhaps, did even Jack. One can only feel for him in the pain he must have borne, and for Jean and their children in their role as uncomprehending and helpless spectators.

Life had to go on for Jack Iverson even in his illness. On 1 July 1969, the daughters threw their parents a party to mark Jack and Jean's twenty-fifth wedding anniversary. It was a happy event, but the last of its kind at Black Street, and on 13 October 1969 Jack's mother Ede died at the age of eighty-two from bronchopneumonia brought on by emphysema.

Dr Callister, who had treated Ede, felt that her final subsidence was related to Jack's own illness; that, feeling helpless to arrest her son's decline, she had 'given up'. In this case, it must have been a doubly grievous blow to one so devoted to his parents, and Jack's condition worsened further. Dr Callister referred him to a Collins Street physician, Dr Luke Murphy, who at a consultation on 8 November found no sign of disease but noticed that he was 'withdrawn, reserved and remote'. At home, Jack continued to vary between the extremely introverted and the relatively calm and lucid, according probably to the recency of his ECT treatments. As Jean remembered:

> My husband was becoming very depressed; he was not working, but spent all of his time at home. He was unable to do anything. He always seemed to be very tired, and spent long periods in bed. There were also times when he would not communicate with myself or my daughter [Beverley]. It was very distressing, but the next day he would be bright as a button, but he could not remember what occurred the day before.

At around this time, a character entered Jack Iverson's life who would loom large in its last few years. Tony Boothroyd was a young estate agent. A personality more antithetical to Jack's could hardly be imagined. Boothroyd came from a family with property in its blood; his father Ron was branch manager for Williams & Co. in Ivanhoe, while Tony was at the time with K. L. Dowling & Co., and would shortly join the international partnership of Richard Ellis, Sallman and Seward as leasing manager. He was in his early twenties, talented, opinionated and determined to make a success of himself in business; the face of bustling entrepreneurship in real estate as surely as Jack embodied the conservative, if fading, ways of the past. But, in a sense, both needed the other to attain their objectives.

While Boothroyd was working at Dowling & Co., he met Jack's niece Robyn Quintell, who was working with a quantity surveyor in the same building. They became a couple and, in April 1970, were married. Boothroyd's personal and commercial aspirations seemed to have conflated; his ambition was to own his own estate agency and in Jack he sensed a willing seller. J. B. Iverson Pty Ltd had suffered from inattention during Jack's illness, and had moved from the front of the second floor at Aldersgate House to smaller premises at the rear of the third floor, but was still a desirable business.

Jack was doing his best to soldier on during the period. Family life was continuing to change. On 31 October 1970, twenty-year-old Beverley was married at St John's Anglican Church in Toorak to twenty-three-year-old John Charles McNamara, a family friend of the Rowes. Though the union produced Jack and Jean's first grandchild, Tracy, it was not destined to be a happy or lasting matrimony. Jack's health, meanwhile, remained at a low ebb. When he visited Dr Luke Murphy in Collins Street again on 11 November, it was recommended that he be hospitalised for treatment of his cerebrovascular condition. Jack refused. Dr Seal then recommended that Jack and Jean take a holiday in Queensland. It was a creative suggestion, and seemed to do the trick, thanks perhaps to the warmer climate enhancing Jack's vascular flows. He played golf, and talked about moving there. But when he returned to the office, Jean recalled: 'He became depressed again...It was too much for him to bear and he was cracking under the strain.'

At around this time, Boothroyd broached the topic of buying J. B. Iverson from Jack. Jack replied that he'd talk it over with Jean. Almost certainly, he also discussed it with his father, now approaching his eighty-seventh birthday, and living at Moana in the company of a housekeeper. In fact, Boothroyd was the ideal purchaser; cashing out to one within the family circle would not incur Harry's displeasure. Jack rang Boothroyd one evening agreeing to sell. He stated a price and agreed in the light of Robyn expecting the Boothroyds' first child to vendor terms of a deposit and monthly instalments for the next six years plus interest. The sale was announced on 7 January 1972.

This is how I found Tony Boothroyd, through the notification of the sale. I got lucky, in fact: there are three A. Boothroyds in the Melbourne telephone book, and he was the first I rang. He may be a different man from the young and thrusting figure of a quarter-century ago, but I found him intelligent, personable and helpful. It struck me as interesting immediately that he expressed no surprise about my finding him. I later learned why.

The business's ownership transition was apparently smooth. Jack signed a letter to clients explaining that they would henceforward be dealing with Boothroyd. Office manager Thelma Harvey was to stay on, and Tony agreed to Jack's suggestion that they might work together on some 'conjunctions'; deals that Jack might bring to the firm and on which they would share commission. They subsequently did two.

The relationship was not, however, altogether easy. Boothroyd was probably a little too ambitious for the Iversons, the Iversons probably a little staid for Boothroyd. The business was also slow to restart, which may have caused tensions, and Jack's health was never good throughout. When Jack's nephew Ian Quintell visited the Iversons in early 1972, preparatory to going overseas, he was shocked by Jack's introversion. All he could elicit from Jack was a smile. It seemed to Ian that, whenever he tried to start a conversation, someone would initiate a distraction. He 'felt robbed'. Visiting from Adelaide, Jack's brother-in-law Gordon Rinder took him to Victoria Golf Club and encouraged him to play a few holes. But he noticed that Jack would say little to well-wishers in the clubhouse, extending merely a limp hand. There is also reason to believe that Jack did not always adhere to his prescribed anti-depressant dosages; it was always a risk with the old slower-acting drugs that patients would become frustrated at the lack of immediate relief and stop taking them. Family friend Mary Rowe recalls visiting Black Street and hearing Jean's voice singing out: 'John, have you taken your tablets?' Jack confided: 'Bloody tablets. I've thrown them out. They're not working.'

Boothroyd dates the deterioration in his relationship with Jack from about November 1972, when he landed his first big sale: a 1550 square-metre office development. He celebrated by buying himself a Ford Fairlane, white with a vinyl roof, much like Jack's—though the older man had a V8 rather than a V6—and feels now that this may have had a bearing on matters. It may be so, though Jack was assuredly not a jealous man, and the likelier cause of strain was the death on 10 November of Harry at the age of eighty-seven after a bout of pneumonia.

Jack had done so little in his life without paternal guidance—for good and, perhaps, ill—that the blow must have been crushing. When Moana was auctioned on 6 December 1972—at the instruction of Perpetual Trustees, coincidentally, by Tony Boothroyd—it must have felt like another link had been severed to past happiness. Jean certainly felt her husband's devastation at the deaths so close together of his mother and father: 'Jack did not recover from these deaths. It hurt and depressed him so much; he was devoted to his parents.' When Jean took him to see Dr Callister in January 1973, the doctor recalled: 'He looked terrible and I asked him to go into hospital. He refused.' Jack did consent to visit Dr Kingston again at his Pasley Street clinic in South Yarra, who recommended another intensive three-week course of ECT at Malvern's Alensen Private Hospital.

While Jack was undergoing this treatment, his second grandchild arrived: Sherry gave birth to Alysa Kaye on 25 February. Momentarily, a sense of normality was restored; the Holts have a photograph of Jack in hospital cradling Alysa with the same infinite gentleness with which he had once held Sherry and Beverley. And when Dr Seal urged Jean to take Jack to Queensland again in June, Jack's spirits seemed to lift a little further. 'The trip went very well, and I watched him progress every day,' Jean said. 'He became relaxed and even played golf.' Jack had 'a bad period on the trip back', which resulted in him receiving a thorough physical examination from St Vincent's neurosurgeon Dr Frank Morgan. But the extensive course of X-rays ascertained, according to Dr Seal, that 'his physical health was reasonably good', and plans began to be laid for a permanent move north.

Over the next few months, as Jack and Jean negotiated to buy a house in Caloundra and to sell Black Street, Jack's condition fluctuated markedly. Mary Rowe recalls a conversation where Jack was alternately pleased and desperate about the prospect of getting away. 'Mary, you'll be our first guest,' Jack said. 'Come up and stay for the New Year.' Then: 'I can't take any more, Mary.' Jean said of the period:

> Some days he would be all right, then he would be no good.
> He got upset very easily, and on some days he looked
> shocking. His face and hands were a horrible grey colour.
> This was caused by the lack of blood getting through to the
> brain. The house sale was nearly completed, and we were
> going to move as soon as the matter was completed. Again
> this worried him and he got upset. Jack was a person who
> went very much within himself. There were many periods
> when he wouldn't communicate with anyone as there were
> periods of blankness.

One day, apparently a good one, he went to visit his old
Melbourne teammate Clive Fairbairn at his sports store in Little
Bourke Street. Fairbairn was out, but his assistant John Scholes,
the Victorian batsman, told him when he returned: 'Big Ivo's
been looking for you. Reckons he's gonna move to the Sunshine
Coast, play a bit of golf, go fishing, do a bit of swimming.'
Fairbairn laughed loudly: 'He's got the job I'm after.'

Another day, probably a bad one, he wrote a note to his
former Australian teammate Ken Archer asking if he might
recommend Jack for membership of the Queensland Cricket
Association. Archer could not help, as it happened; the note,
addressed to the QCA, finally found him in Sydney to which
he had recently relocated. He wrote back apologetically, but
still recalls the original inquiry:

> There were a few lines in it where the tone was a bit 'sorry
> for myself'. Things like: 'I'm only a broken down old crick-
> eter. No-one remembers me now.' All the same, that tone
> of negativity probably wouldn't have registered with me had
> I not heard about what happened a few months later.

THIRTY-ONE

At 2.35pm on Tuesday, 23 October 1973, Victorian Police Constable Esmond John O'Reilly received a call from D24 despatching him to a residential address in Brighton after an apparent shooting fatality. In a ten-by-four-metre shed at the rear of the double-fronted Victorian home, he found the body of a man lying with the muzzle of a rather ancient Remington single-shot rifle still on his chest. The concrete floor was tacky with perhaps a litre of congealing blood. On a bench above the deceased's head was a box of .22 calibre shells, of which two were missing; the expended case of one was in the rifle's breach, the other nowhere to be seen. O'Reilly sketched the attitude of the body and the layout of the shed in a basic stick-figure diagram, then went to take statements from two others in the living room.

One was Jean Iverson, the other Dr Douglas Callister. Dr Callister explained that he had received a call from Mrs Iverson about half an hour earlier at his clinic in New Street, had come directly, and called the police on her behalf. Mrs Iverson identified the victim as her husband John; he had been depressed for some time, she explained, though he had appeared during the morning in quite good spirits, and had spoken optimistically of their imminent move to Queensland. Though evidently still shocked, her speech was collected and lucid.

Constable O'Reilly listened attentively. He was a fresh-faced nineteen-year-old who had graduated only nine months earlier and this was among his first suicide cases, but he had served as a cadet at Brighton Police Station at the age of seventeen and knew the drill. The missing cartridge had probably been used in a test firing to ascertain if the old weapon still worked. As for the advice that the victim had been in good spirits that day, those intending suicide often were; having made up their minds, the theory had it, they often experienced a strange inner calm.

As O'Reilly studied the scene for detail that might prove germane to his investigation, one aspect could not be overlooked. Round the living room in neat array were a host of sporting trophies: mounted cricket balls, cups, shields. He refrained from inquiring about their origin—it did not seem appropriate—but made a mental note to do so. While he waited for a government undertaker to convey the body to the Alfred Hospital, O'Reilly instead made Mrs Iverson a cup of tea; not very well, as it happened, for it was almost undrinkably strong. Alerted to events, Sherry and Barry Holt arrived independently. While Sherry kept her mother company, cradling the infant Alysa, Barry had the terrible task of identifying his father-in-law's body.

When O'Reilly returned some time later, with his more experienced thirty-four-year-old station 'buddy' Constable John Donald, to take a statement from Mrs Iverson, she explained those sporting trophies. Her husband had been a cricketer, a very good one who had played Test matches for Australia, and her pride in his achievements was evident. In fact, O'Reilly found himself warming to Mrs Iverson: 'She was very quiet, unassuming, and seemed to be coming to terms with things. Just one of those lovely ladies you meet in your life, the salt of the earth.'

The trophies and Mrs Iverson's explanation of them also left an impression on Constable Donald. Normally where a suicide without suspicious circumstances was concerned, the police-work would have been relatively straightforward, even perfunctory. For a Test cricketer, they'd better be more thorough. 'Y'know, this isn't your normal Joe Blow,' he counselled. 'This guy's pretty famous. We'd better delve a bit deeper, make sure we do it right.'

Which they did. When Constables O'Reilly and Donald presented their investigation to the coroner, it was, as I discovered, admirably thorough. Nonetheless, O'Reilly went away with a feeling that he still did not quite understand the subject of the investigation in full measure:

> At the end of it, I was still thinking: 'What does this guy want to go and commit suicide for? Yes, he'd been depressed, and it had obviously been hard for him. But he was just about to shift away to Queensland, and things were

really looking up for the bloke.' One thing I learned, though, was that you should never ask too many questions about suicide. Otherwise you just torment yourself. You've got to accept that you'll never really get to the bottom of it.

We'll never know exactly what drove Jack Iverson to his final, desperate act. There was no note, although suicide notes are in any case probably overrated as an aperture on the victim's thoughts. In the period immediately beforehand, Jack's condition had apparently been relatively stable. At Col Shipley's instigation, Brighton was organising a farewell for him, planning to present him with a favourite old bat from the club kit. The day before his death, he had played golf with his daughter Beverley at Sandringham, and kept an appointment with Dr Seal where he seemed 'fit, well and cheerful'.

Two aspects of the coroner's report are probably material to our understanding. One is the report of the Medico-Legal Laboratory, which suggested that Jack had been drinking on 23 October. Post-mortem samples revealed 220 milligrams of alcohol per 100 millilitres of blood. Not incapacitating but quite high. So the influence of alcohol, the sinister depressant, cannot be overlooked.

The other important evidence tendered was Jean Iverson's version of that day's events:

> The day that he passed on, he was feeling all right in the morning. He had slept well and had a good night. Sometime in the afternoon, I had cause to go into the lounge room. Jack was sitting in one of the chairs. His face

and hands were that horrible grey colour, and he was upset and shaking visibly. I told him not to worry and that everything would be all right. I asked him what was wrong and he told me that he had seen an advertisement in the newspaper about some property he had been interested in. They were selling the property without consulting him about the deal. Jack had introduced the buyer of his firm, J. B. Iverson P/L, to the owner of the property. He said that he was deeply hurt and did not know why they did not let him know of the deal.

I did not know why he would say such a thing like that so I asked him to explain. Jack said that the person who bought his business had taken legal advice, and said that he did not have to pay Jack commission on this particular deal. He also told Jack that he did not have to pay Jack commission on two other properties, and said that it would be deducted from the purchase price of the business. Jack believed so much in ethics, and not being told about this transaction was too much for him to take. Well, I thought that I had calmed him down, and he got up and went out the back.

In Jack's absence, Jean began vacuuming, so she did not hear the shot that killed her husband. By the time she visited the back shed, it was too late. She concluded: 'I can't think of any reason why Jack would take his own life, except perhaps the conversation about the property transaction which upset him so much, combined with many other things which caused his state of depression.'

In Tony Boothroyd's living room, I broached the subject of 23 October 1973 with circumspection. He said he'd been expecting it. I asked why. He said that the coroner's report had been in existence for twenty-five years, and it had only been a matter of time before someone had troubled to consult it.

The story he related was subtly different from Jean Iverson's. It dated back to those two 'conjunctions' which Jack had proposed and transacted with Boothroyd, Iverson & Co. Boothroyd had proceeded with them happily until the later stages of the second, a residential property in East Brighton's Talofa Avenue. In the course of a conversation with the vendors about their association with Jack, they told Boothroyd lightly that Jack had introduced them to the property originally, and that on deciding to sell they had simply contacted him again by ringing Black Street. Everyone knew, they explained, that Jack often worked from home.

Boothroyd was annoyed. Strictly speaking, he felt, Jack should have redirected the Talofa Avenue vendors to him. Jack was no longer an estate agent, and Boothroyd owned the goodwill of his old business. He subsequently discovered that the vendors in the earlier 'conjunction' had pursued a similar route. Boothroyd let it slide. 'It did rile me,' he says. 'And I probably should have said something to him about it. But I didn't.'

The call that Jack made to Boothroyd, Iverson & Co. on the morning of 23 October 1973 actually began on a different matter. Jack advised Boothroyd that, as he was moving to Queensland, he wanted the balance of the purchase price on the sale of J. B. Iverson Pty Ltd paid immediately.

Boothroyd demurred. The business was going well, but not that well. To pay out the rest of the money in a lump sum would necessitate borrowing in a period of punitive interest rates; the prime minister Gough Whitlam had just decreed a credit squeeze which would send borrowing costs in Australia soaring. After a debate, Boothroyd finally consented, but he insisted that he would discount it for the half-commissions he had paid Jack on the conjunctions. Jack finished the conversation with: 'I'll think about it.' On Boothroyd's return home, his wife, Jack's niece Robyn, told him that Jack had been found dead, having apparently taken his own life.

I now understood Tony Boothroyd's unsurprised response to my first telephone call. How often since must he have replayed that final conversation with Jack in his own mind, rationalising his own actions, trying to comprehend Jack's. He had surely done no more than play commercial hard ball, like any businessman, in defence of his livelihood and his family's standard of living. Yet perhaps he should have taken cognisance of Jack's troubled state of mind and appeased him; Dr Conway's words recurred to me that 'meticulous and scrupulous personalities who are hard on themselves often find it particularly wounding when others are hard on them'. Boothroyd had paid Jack money to which the older man might not have been entitled, and now was being asked to leverage his finances at the worst possible moment. Yet Jack had not been dishonest or disingenuous; at the very worst construction, he had been only a little naive, in a period otherwise of inordinate distress.

Twenty-five years had elapsed between Boothroyd's conversation with Jack and his conversation with me, and I didn't doubt that some aspects of the story had been unconsciously amended. Yet Boothroyd's recollection seemed sincere and its substance believable. That final dialogue had occurred between two men always destined to be at cross-purposes; Jack could not have understood the position in which he was placing Tony Boothroyd, and Tony Boothroyd could not remotely have imagined the position in which he was placing Jack.

Suicide leaves an appalling legacy. Those who take their own lives make victims not only of themselves but of others. In this case, Jean, Sherry, Beverley, Ruth, even Tony Boothroyd, were left to sorrow, to contemplate, and to try to grasp the ungraspable. The case fits, in a sense, one of suicide's so-called 'classic' causes: a diagnostician would probably have classified it as financial anxiety, rather than matrimonial/romantic breakdown or feared loss of health. Yet, as A. Alvarez wrote in his famous study of suicide, *The Savage God*:

> A suicide's excuses are mostly by the way. At best, they assuage the guilt of survivors, soothe the tidy-minded and encourage the sociologists in their endless search for convincing theories and categories. They are like the trivial border incident which triggers off a major war. The real motives...are elsewhere; they belong to the internal world, devious, contradictory, labyrinthine, and mostly out of sight.

Beyond the coroner's report, a scattering of mementos and scrapbooks, little tangible remains of Jack Iverson today. As he was cremated, there is no gravestone. Most of those who shared his final days of pain most deeply—including Jean, Douglas Callister and Eric Seal—have passed away. So have his sister Marjorie, and his brothers-in-law Hock Wood and Gordon Rinder. The remainder of his relatives are dispersed and, without male heirs, the name in Jack's branch of the family is *sous rature*.

Yet there is one artefact that has thankfully survived the quarter of a century since his death: the table tennis table that Jack constructed in his back shed at Black Street about forty years ago. Having been donated by Jack's daughter Beverley to family friends Cedric and Liz Jansz, it resides in the clubrooms of Bentleigh ANA at King George Reserve, East Bentleigh.

The weighty hardwood table testifies in its painstaking attention to detail to Jack's lifelong fascination with the rotated sphere. It has the considerate feature of legs that can be adjusted to suit players of different height, and is certifiably built to last, fastened tightly together with pin screws and butterfly clips; Cedric Jansz, who was kind enough to admit me to the clubrooms in his lunch hour one Friday, explained that members of the club had recently tried to dismantle the table for winter storage, but could do no more than break it into two.

At Bentleigh ANA, we are in cricket country: the seventy-year-old club was a founding member of the Central Moorabbin Cricket Association and still fields eight teams. There are another twenty clubs within a ten-kilometre radius. Yet it could scarcely be more fitting that Jack's presence is manifested by the pastime that first bewitched him. For me, too, there was a sense of full circle: on the last journey I made for this book, I gazed upon an embodiment of where Jack's story had begun.

THIRTY-TWO

One thing can safely be said half a century after Jack Iverson played cricket: there will never be a player like him again. This is not to say that a cricketer will not appear in club cricket at the age of thirty-one and play for his country four years later. It is not to say that someone will not, by dabbling in some other sport, discover by chance a unique kind of delivery. It is not to say that there won't be a bowler again so outstanding but specialised that their incompetence with the bat and in the field will be overlooked. It is not to say that there won't be cricketers who erupt on the scene in future, then of their own volition vanish off the face of the cricketing earth, and cause barely anyone to wonder why. None of these, while exceptionally unlikely in our global, professionalised, celebrity-smitten and media-saturated game of today, is quite impossible. But no cricketer, surely, will again fulfil all these criteria. I'd sooner bet on another Sir Donald Bradman than on another Jack Iverson.

It is, nonetheless, not altogether surprising that very few people remember Jack today. Fifty Australian seasons ago, he cast a long cricket shadow. Opponents agonised over how to combat him, comrades fantasised of his likely success in England, pundits picked him in imaginary world XIs. Yet anyone starting an interest in cricket even a short time later would have been forgiven ignorance that he had even existed. Rex Harry still calls him 'my hero'. Barry Holt, just a few years younger, confesses that he'd never even heard of Jack until he started courting his daughter.

He is, however, worthy of our regard. He cannot be classed an innovator in the same sense as John Willes and Edgar Willsher, who brought modernity to cricket by causing bowlers to point their hands to heaven rather than earth, or B. J. T. Bosanquet or Ellis Achong, who brought postmodernity to cricket with deliveries that looked like one thing and were the other. No-one replicated Jack's methods with anything like his success; he is one of a kind. But for sheer originality, scarcely anyone in cricket's history comes even close. By curious coincidence, exactly forty years after Jack turned up at Brighton Beach Oval in search of someone to bowl to, another remarkable slow bowler did the same. Yet Shane Warne, astounding as he was and is, had more than a century of slow bowling lore to draw on. Warne speaks the foreign tongue of leg spin fluently. Jack invented his own language.

Had circumstances been only slightly different, moreover, there might have been no Jack Iverson at all. His story involves accidents of genetics: had his fingers been shorter or weaker, or had he been shorter, he'd have been markedly less effective. It has accidents of upbringing: had Jack's family been less well-off, for example, there'd probably have been no table tennis table at Burnett Street, nor a ball to start tinkering with. It has accidents of history: had 11 Battery been sent to Scarlet Beach and not kept in reserve at Moresby, to choose one, Jack might have had neither the opportunity nor the inclination to see his potential future in French cricket.

Even Jack's peculiar innocence where cricket was concerned was, perhaps, a stroke of fortune. All those cricketers who lamented to me the shame that Jack had such a narrow under-standing of the game might have it the wrong way round; only someone from beyond cricket's pale, a Spedegue if you like, could have concocted a technique so thoroughly counter-intuitive. And, as the Bedser twins asked in *Following On*: 'What would a coach, schooled in orthodox theories, have said to Iverson? According to their lights, Iverson did not bowl "properly".' We might think it a pity that Jack lacked a cricket constitution of the hardiness of, say, Allan Border—born, as chance would have it, on Jack's fortieth birthday. But would bustling, bristling, stoical Allan Border have had the imagina-tion to perfect something so against the grain of his learned experience?

Separated as he is by technique and temper from any of the other 380 or so men who've worn Australian colours, Jack Iverson nonetheless shares something with them. Sport is the most precarious of pursuits. In the context of sportsmen's lives, their spells at the very peak will be short. Yet even as we acknowledge how brief and fleeting is our acquaintance, we lean to defining a sportsman with emphasis on the sport to the exclusion of the man, perhaps because we wish chiefly to admire rather than to understand. In Jack Iverson's case, the reductiveness of sporting celebrity is exacerbated by the brevity of his career and the virtual anonymity of his life; for convenience's sake his twenty-three days of Test cricket has time and again been allowed to stand in for the balance of his fifty-eight years. There are actually more photographs in cricket books of his hand clasping the ball than of his face; a striking visual synecdoche, but equivalent to knowing Bradman only for 99.94, or Einstein only for $E = mc^2$.

So here, perhaps, lies a little truth in the life and death of Jack Iverson. More than 2000 men have played cricket for their countries, and what have we *really* known about any of them? Even today, when we study and write about players so exhaustively, the idea that we can obtain a measure of their character seems essentially a journalistic vanity. Those who watched or wrote about Jack Iverson can have had little conception of his frail sporting self-worth. No-one who played with him could have fathomed the depths of his disappointments and fears. By a man's sporting deeds, we can know only the merest fraction of him.

When I started this book, I sensed it would be difficult and problematical to write about Jack Iverson. The man who lived 'in my own quiet way' left little behind; no published works, no journals, no diaries, no boxes of correspondence, only some photos, statistics, reportage of his feats and a scattering of others' recollections. As I traced his fugitive figure, I often learned more than I had expected, but always less than I wanted. The mystery of his life remains preserved as surely as the enigma of his bowling, leaving us mainly with impressions, like those of A. W. Pullin on the death a hundred years ago of Billy Bates, the first Englishman to take a Test hat-trick: 'He had his failings—who has not?—but he also had trials that fall to the lot of few men. He was a great cricketer, and a most kindly soul.'

ACKNOWLEDGMENTS

'Who ever hoped like a cricketer?' wrote R. C. Robertson-Glasgow. The experience of writing the story of Jack Iverson suggests to me that biographers must run them close; it was hope rather than expectation that prompted me to contact many of the people who assisted me, thus hope brought the often surprising rewards. There are, accordingly, a multitude of names to thank.

My interest was aroused by Jack Iverson the cricketer. As I began investigating his sub-district and district careers, many of his former teammates and opponents willingly answered my questions: from Brighton, Colin Shipley, Alan Tudor, Lou Carter, Len Hayball and Geoff McDowell; from Melbourne, Harcourt Dowsley, Jack Green, Clive Fairbairn, Jack Daniel, Geoff Longney, Ian Huntingdon, Lindsay Kline, Colin and Ian McDonald; from Fitzroy, Bill Jacobs, Kevin Kearney, Harold Shillinglaw; from St Kilda, George Murray.

When it came to exploring Iverson's first-class and Test career, I received help and advice from many others: from Victoria, Ken Meuleman, Roy Howard, Bill Johnston, Ian Johnson, Sam Loxton, Neil Harvey, Doug Ring and George Thoms; from Queensland, Bill Brown, Ernie Toovey and Ken Archer; from New South Wales, Keith Miller, Richie Benaud, Arthur Morris, Alan Davidson, Stan Sismey and Barry Rothwell; from England, John Dewes.

Several journalists and historians with an interest in Iverson's career also gave me the benefit of their impressions and observations: my inspirational friend David Frith, John

Woodcock, Percy Beames, Stephen Gibbs, Robert Coleman, Peter Pierce, Jason Steeger, Phil Derriman, Alf Batchelder, Richard Cashman, Warwick Franks, Spiro Zavos and Alan Trengove. Ray Webster, the most generous and energetic of cricket scholars, laid his remarkable accumulation of names and addresses open to me, while Ken Williams provided some wonderfully detailed statistics.

Rex Harry and John Gleeson spoke to me at length of their experiments and experiences with the Iverson method. In assessing my subject's technique, I had helpful advice from Dr Michael Levenda, surgeon Greg Hoy, biomechanist Bruce Elliott and Dr Frank Pyke of the Victorian Institute of Sport. Thanks to the zeal of Rodney Butler at the National Film and Sound Archive, I was blessed with the opportunity to watch Jack Iverson bowl.

I quickly discovered, however, that I was also exploring the life of a most fascinating man. Those I must thank for helping me on my way are chiefly the members of his immediate family: his sister Ruth Rinder, with whom I enjoyed a delightful and fruitful correspondence; his daughters Beverley McNamara and Sherry Holt, who made available priceless recollections, records and images of their father; Jack Iverson's niece Robyn Boothroyd; his nephew Ian Quintell; plus Barry Holt and Tony Boothroyd, who welcomed me into their homes and volunteered much of interest. I was also able to call on friends and acquaintances of Iverson, spanning many years: Alan and Charles Meckiff, Mary Rowe, Amy Northcombe, Margaret Sevier, Cedric Jansz, Ken Shepard and Ivor Carolan.

In trying to piece together Jack Iverson's youth, I had welcome assistance from his old school (and mine) Geelong

College, from Kristin Fry, Deb Carr, Bruce Jamison and Carol Barnard. Many old Collegians took the trouble to write to, see, or offer material to me: especially Jim Carstairs, plus Dr Norman Wettenhall, Herb Tippett, Tom Bleakley, Gordon Eaton, Norman Dennis, Lance Wray, Geoff Hicks, Des Gaunt, Garry Armstrong and Bob Merriman.

Recreating Jack Iverson's period as a jackaroo, I had several strokes of good fortune. On the advice of Aileen Hockley of the Castlemaine Historical Society, I contacted the very marvellous Sam Palmer (a woman with perhaps the funniest answering machine message in the world), who after considerable effort steered me to a former neighbour, Neil Neilson. Jack Long of the Maldon Golf Club filled me in on its history. The daughters of the great industrialist Essington Lewis, Jane Nevile and Mary Munckton, went to enormous trouble on my behalf, showing me round the property on which Iverson had worked for their father in the 1930s. To stand in the same spot as Jack Iverson had, in having his photograph taken more than sixty years before, was an unforgettable experience. Thanks also to the staff of University of Melbourne archives, who steered me to appropriate material in the Lewis papers.

Jack Iverson's war record was researched at the Australian War Memorial in Canberra, whose staff could hardly have been more helpful. I also had the opportunity to speak to several former colleagues, especially Ken Noldt, Bert Davey, Bill Carmody and Max Scott. While in Canberra I was also welcomed by the National Dictionary Centre, responsible for the *Australian Dictionary of Biography*, and offer thanks to both John Ritchie and Anthea Bundock. And I was favoured throughout my stay by the hospitality of Ian and Romula

Templeman, and Kevin and Margaret Hollis, which compelled me, fleetingly but beneficially, to converse about matters unrelated to Jack Iverson; something at the time I was finding rather difficult.

Researching the immediate aftermath of the war, I enjoyed talking to members of the Blind Cricket Association, especially Dick and Jean Wyatt, Doug Sloan, Damien Clemens and Garry Stinchcombe. In looking at Jack Iverson's later years, I had eager and efficient assistance from staff at the Public Records Offices at Laverton and Casselden Place and the Department of Births, Deaths and Marriages. Susan Harcourt of Harcourt Legal Services, a lovely lady, helped with searching property titles. Rosemary Jones of St John's Anglican Church in Toorak, an equally lovely lady, dug out old marriage certificates. Ronald Conway and Peter Seal, the son of Dr Eric Seal, helped me understand a little better the mysteries of the human mind and those who seek to heal it. Leonie Graham of Sandringham Library guided me to source works on the area. Esmond O'Reilly and John Donald, members of the Victorian Police Force who investigated Iverson's death, were an advertisement for the professionalism of the constabulary. Staff at ABC Archives and Australian Archives couldn't help me out much, but Guy Tranter gave it his best.

On a host of occasions, I had the pleasure of working in one of my favourite places in the world, the library of the Melbourne Cricket Club. My thanks to its staff, as always, for their assistance and interest, especially David Studham, Ross Peacock, David Allen and Eric Panther.

Philippa Hawker, a friend and colleague for whom my regard is unstinting, was kind enough to spend a weekend reading the manuscript, and to reassure me that I wasn't off on a folly of my own. A circle of my nearest and dearest also advanced this quest, sometimes by answering requests, driving me somewhere, or simply allowing me to prattle on endlessly about someone they'd never heard of: Caroline Wilson, Richard Sproull, Jim Schembri, James Kirby, Kaz Cooke, Gabrielle Coyne, John Harms, Malcolm Schmidtke, Suzie Freeman-Greene and, as has always been the case, my mother Isabel Haigh. And as so often, I enjoyed the measured and judicious support of my publisher Michael Heyward, Melanie Ostell and Emma Gordon Williams, and the proofreading virtuoso George Thomas. Their faith in this project from inception has been a source of strength.

The dedication for this book is to someone who was and remains someone very special to me. Julie Tootell was a friend of my family's for as long as I can remember. She was also always keenly and sincerely interested in whatever I was working on, and wrote to me whenever I published a book. This is the first time she will not, for, on 5 March 1999, Julie died. Ten days later, I had the honour of delivering the eulogy at her funeral.

Julie was ill when I mentioned to her the first time that I was writing about Jack Iverson. She was, as always, enthusiastic. She mentioned how the gym teacher at her school had told her off for trying to bowl like him. She recommended a title searcher to help me, and wrote on my behalf a letter to Jane Nevile, whom she knew. Even in hospital, Julie was full of questions about what I might have discovered. She dearly wanted to read this book, and I dearly wanted her to, but the last time I saw her when I mentioned that the opportunity might not present itself, she replied: 'Don't worry. Wherever I am, I'll read it.' I hope she enjoys it.

BIBLIOGRAPHY

GENERAL HISTORY

Bate, Weston, *A History of Brighton*, Melbourne University Press, Melbourne, 1963.

Billot, C. P., *A Life of Our Years: A Pictorial Chronology of Geelong*, Lothian Books, Melbourne, 1969.

Blackman, Grant and Larkin, John, *Maldon: Australia's First Notable Town*, Hodder & Stoughton, Sydney, 1978.

Blainey, Geoffrey, *The Rush That Never Ended*, Melbourne University Press, Melbourne, 1963.

Bolton, Geoffrey, *The Oxford History of Australia, Volume 5, 1942–1988*, Oxford University Press, Melbourne, 1988.

Cannon, Michael, *The Land Boomers*, Melbourne University Press, Melbourne, 1966.

Cloos, Patricia and Tamdick, Jurgen, *Greetings from the Land Where Milk and Honey Flows: The German Emigration to New South Wales,1838–1858*, Southern Highlands Publications, Canberra, 1993.

Crowley, Frank, *Modern Australia in Documents 1939–1970*, Wren Publishing, Melbourne, 1973.

Dunstan, David, *Victorian Icon*, The Exhibition Trustees, Melbourne, 1996.

Egan, Bryan, *Ways of a Hospital: St Vincent's, Melbourne*, Allen & Unwin, St Leonards, 1993.

Harmstorf, Ian (ed.), *Insights into South Australian History*, Historical Society of South Australia, Adelaide, 1983.

Harmsdorf, Ian and Cigler, Michael, *Germans in Australia*, AE Press, Blackburn, 1985.

Heathcote, Christopher, *A Quiet Revolution: The Rise of Australian Art 1946–1968*, Text Publishing, Melbourne, 1995.

Johnston, George, *War Diary 1942*, Collins, Melbourne, 1984.

Keith, Bert, *The Geelong College 1861–1961*, The Geelong College Council and Old Geelong Collegians Association, Geelong, 1961.

Lewis, Miles, *Melbourne: The City's History and Development*, City of Melbourne, Melbourne, 1995.

Long, G., *The Final Campaigns*, Australian War Memorial, Canberra, 1963.

McGregor, Craig, *Profile of Australia*, Penguin, Sydney, 1966.

Macintyre, Stuart, *The Oxford History of Australia, Volume 4, 1900–1941*, Oxford University Press, Melbourne, 1988.

McKernan, Michael, *All In: Australia during the Second World War*, Thomas Nelson, Melbourne, 1983.

McKernan, Michael, *The Australian People and the Great War*, Thomas Nelson, Melbourne, 1980.

Massey, J. T., *The YMCA in Australia: A History*, F. W. Cheshire, Melbourne, 1950.

Maughan, B., *Tobruk and El Alamein*, Australian War Memorial, Canberra, 1968,

Moorehead, Alan, *African Trilogy*, Cassell, London, 1997.

Moresby, Emily, *New Guinea: The Sentinel*, Whitcomb & Tombs, Sydney, 1943.

Preston, James, *Brighton Sketchbook*, Rigby, Adelaide, 1974.

Randell, J. O., *McIvor: A History of the Shire and Township of Heathcote*, Shire of McIvor, Heathcote, 1985.

Reid, John (ed.), *When Memory Turns the Key: The History of the Shire of Romsey*, Joval Publishing, Bacchus Marsh, 1992.

Saegenschnitter, Geoffrey, *Greenock and District 1846–1986: A History of Greenock and the Surrounding Districts of Nain, Daveyston, Moppa, Walton and Seppeltsfield*, self-published, Greenock, 1986.

Serle, Geoffrey, *From Deserts the Prophets Come: The Creative Spirit in Australia 1788–1972*, Heinemann, Sydney, 1973.

Voigt, Johannes (ed.), *New Beginnings: Germans in New South Wales and Queensland*, Institute for Foreign Cultural Studies, Stuttgart, 1983.

Vondra, Josef, *German Speaking Settlers in Australia*, Cavalier, Melbourne, 1981.

West, Francis, *From Alamein to Scarlet Beach: The History of the 2/4 Light Anti-Aircraft Regiment*, Deakin University Press, Geelong, 1989.

CRICKET HISTORY & LITERATURE

Barker, Anthony, *The WACA: An Australian Cricket Success Story*, Allen & Unwin, Sydney, 1998.

Batchelor, Denzil, *The Book of Cricket*, Collins, London, 1952.

Benaud, Richie, *Benaud on Reflection*, Collins Willow, London, 1984.

Bose, Mihir, *A History of Indian Cricket*, André Deutsch, London, 1990.

Boxall, Thomas, *Rules and Instructions for Playing at the Game of Cricket, As Practised by the Most Eminent Players*, Harrild & Billing, London, c. 1801.

Brodribb, Gerald, *Next Man In*, Putnam & Co., London, 1952.

Brodribb, Gerald, *The Lost Art*, Boundary Books, Southlands, 1997.

Brodribb, Gerald, *All Round the Wicket*, Sporting Handbooks, London, 1951.

Cashman, Richard and others (eds), *The Oxford Companion to Australian Sport*, Oxford University Press, Melbourne, 1994.

Cashman, Richard and others (eds), *The Oxford Companion to Australian Cricket*, Oxford University Press, Melbourne, 1996.

Christen, Richard, *Some Grounds for Appeal: Australian Venues for First-Class Cricket*, self-published, Parramatta, 1994.

Coleman, Robert, *Seasons in the Sun: The Story of the Victorian Cricket Association*, Hargreen Publishing, Melbourne, 1993.

Dunstan, Keith, *The Paddock That Grew*, Cassell Australia, Melbourne, 1975.

Ford, John, *Cricket 1700–1815*, David & Charles, London, 1972.

Frith, David, *The Fast Men*, Corgi, London, 1981.

Frith, David, *The Slow Men*, Corgi, London, 1984.

Frith, David, *By His Own Hand*, Stanley Paul, London, 1990.

Haigh, Gideon, *The Summer Game*, Text Publishing, Melbourne, 1997.

Harte, Chris, *A History of Australian Cricket*, André Deutsch, London, 1993.

Lucas, E. V., *English Leaves*, Methuen, London, 1933.

McGilvray, Alan and Tasker, Norm, *The Game Is Not the Same*, ABC Books, Sydney, 1985.

Moyes, Johnnie, *Australian Bowlers*, Angus & Robertson, Sydney, 1953.

Murphy, Patrick, *The Spinner's Turn*, J. M. Dent, London, 1982.

Pollard, Jack, *Australian Cricket: The Game and the Players*, Angus & Robertson, Sydney, 1988.

Pollard, Jack, *From Bradman to Border, Australian Cricket 1948 to 1989*, Angus & Robertson, Sydney, 1989.

Pollard, Jack, *Bumpers, Boseys and Brickbats*, Murray, Sydney, 1971.

Robinson, Ray, *On Top Down Under*, Collins, Sydney, 1975.

Robinson, Ray, *From the Boundary*, Collins, London, 1951.

Stewart, Bob, 'The Commercial and Cultural Development of Australian First-Class Cricket 1946–1985', PhD thesis, Faculty of Arts, La Trobe University, Melbourne, 1995.

Treasure, R. W. and Tudor, A. T., *Cricket at Brighton Since 1842: 150 Years of the Brighton Cricket Club*, Brighton Cricket Club, Melbourne, 1993.

Whimpress, Bernard and Hart, Nigel, *Australian Eleven: Test Cricket Snapshots*, limited edition of 100 self-published, Adelaide, 1997.

Wilkins, Brian, *Cricket: The Bowler's Art*, Kangaroo Press, Sydney, 1997.

TOUR BOOKS

Beecher, Eric (ed.), *Cricketer Annual 1976*, Newspress, Melbourne, 1976.

Berry, Scyld, *Cricket Wallah*, Hodder & Stoughton, London, 1982.

Cheetham, Jack, *Caught by the Springboks*, Hodder & Stoughton, London, 1953.

Fingleton, Jack, *Brown & Company*, Collins, London, 1951.

Fingleton, Jack, *The Ashes Crown the Year*, Collins, Sydney, 1954.

Green, Michael, *Sporting Campaigner*, Stanley Paul, London, 1956.

Gurunathan, S. K. (ed.), *Indian Cricket 1953–54*, Kasturi & Sons, Madras, 1954.

Harris, Bruce, *In Quest of the Ashes*, Hutchinson, London, 1951.

Kay, John, *Ashes to Hassett*, Altrincham Sherratt, London, 1951.

Miller, Keith and Whitington, R. S., *Catch!*, Latimer House, London, 1951.

Miller, Keith and Whitington, R. S., *Straight Hit!*, Latimer House, London, 1952.

Miller, Keith and Whitington, R. S., *Cricket Typhoon*, MacDonald & Co., London, 1955.

Moyes, Johnnie, *The Fight for the Ashes 1950–51*, Harrap, London, 1951.

Moyes, Johnnie, *With the West Indies in Australia 1951–52: A Critical Story of the Tour*, Angus & Robertson, Sydney, 1952.

O'Reilly, Bill, *Cricket Task Force*, Werner Laurie, London, 1951.

Robertson-Glasgow, R. C., *The Story of the Test Matches: The MCC Tour in Australia and New Zealand*, The Times, London, 1951.

Swanton, E. W., *Elusive Victory: With F. R. Brown's MCC Team 1950–51*, Hodder & Stoughton, London, 1951.

Warner, Rex and Blair, Lyle, *Ashes to Ashes: A Post-Mortem on the 1950–51 Tests*, MacGibbon & Kee, London, 1951.

Wellings, E. M., *No Ashes for England*, Evans Bros, London, 1951.

BIOGRAPHIES & AUTOBIOGRAPHIES

Bedser, Alec and Bedser, Eric, *Following On*, Stanley Paul, London, 1954.

Benaud, Richie, *Anything But…An Autobiography*, Hodder & Stoughton, London, 1998.

Blainey, Geoffrey, *The Steelmaster*, Melbourne University Press, Melbourne, 1970.

Bose, Mihir, *Keith Miller*, Allen & Unwin, Sydney, 1979.

Brown, Freddie, *Cricket Musketeer*, Nicholas Kaye, London, 1954.

Caffyn, William, *Seventy-One Not Out*, William Blackwood, London, 1899.

Compton, Denis, *In Sun and Shadow*, Stanley Paul, London, 1952.

Cowen, Frederic, *My Art and My Friends*, Edward Arnold, London, 1913.

Daft, Richard, *Kings of Cricket*, Simkin Marshall, London, 1893.

Darling, Sir James, *Richly Rewarding*, Hill of Content, Melbourne, 1978.

Davidson, Alan, *Fifteen Paces*, Souvenir, London, 1963.

Eytle, Ernest, *Frank Worrell: The Career of a Great Cricketer*, Hodder & Stoughton, London, 1963.

French, Sean, *Patrick Hamilton: A Life*, Faber & Faber, London, 1993.

Grishin, Sasha, *The Art of John Brack*, Oxford University Press, Melbourne, 1990.

Grout, Wally, *My Country's Keeper*, Pelham, London, 1965.

Harvey, Neil, *My World of Cricket*, Hodder & Stoughton, London, 1963.

Hazare, V. J., *A Long Innings*, Rupa & Co., Calcutta, 1981.

Hawke, Lord, *Recollections and Reminiscences*, Norgate, London, 1924.

Holmes, Richard, *Footsteps: Adventures of a Romantic Biographer*, Hodder, London, 1985.

Hordern, Herbert, *Googlies*, Angus & Robertson, Sydney, 1932.

Humphries, Barry, *More Please*, Penguin, Melbourne, 1993.

Howat, Gerald, *Len Hutton: The Biography*, Mandarin, London, 1990.

Johnson, Ian, *Cricket at the Crossroads*, Cassell, London, 1957.

Jones, Nigel, *Through a Glass Darkly: The Life of Patrick Hamilton*, Scribners, London, 1991.

Lindwall, Ray, *Flying Stumps*, Arrow Books, London, 1957.

McCool, Colin, *Cricket Is a Game*, Stanley Paul, London, 1961.

McGregor, Adrian, *Greg Chappell*, William Collins, Sydney, 1985.

McHarg, Jack, *Lindsay Hassett: One of a Kind*, Simon & Schuster, Sydney, 1998.

McInnes, Graham, *The Road to Gundagai*, Hamish Hamilton, London, 1965.

McInnes, Graham, *Humping My Bluey*, Hamish Hamilton, London, 1966.

Mackay, Ken, *Slasher Opens Up*, Pelham, London, 1964.

Mallett, Ashley, *Clarrie Grimmett: The Bradman of Spin*, University of Queensland Press, St Lucia, 1993.

Marr, David, *Patrick White: A Life*, Jonathan Cape, London, 1991.

Miller, Keith, *Cricket Crossfire*, Oldbourne, London, 1957.

Oldfield, Bert, *The Rattle of the Stumps*, George Newnes, London, 1954.

Rae, Simon, *W. G. Grace: A Life*, Faber & Faber, London, 1998.

Reid, John, *A Million Miles of Cricket*, A. H. & A. W. Reed, Wellington, 1966.

Ringwood, John, *Ray Lindwall: Cricketing Legend*, Kangaroo Press, Sydney, 1995.

Root, Fred, *A Cricket Pro's Lot*, Edward Arnold, London, 1937.

Rosenwater, Irving, *Sir Donald Bradman: A Biography*, Batsford, London, 1978.

Sheppard, David, *Parson's Pitch*, Hodder & Stoughton, London, 1966.

Styron, William, *Darkness Visible*, Jonathan Cape, London, 1991.

Swanton, E. W., *Swanton in Australia*, William Collins, Glasgow, 1975.

Taylor, Leslie, *So Passed My Year*, Winn & Co., Sydney, 1944.

Warner, Pelham, *Long Innings*, Harrap, London, 1951.

Whitington, R. S., *Keith Miller: The Golden Nugget*, Rigby, Sydney, 1981.

Whitington, R. S., *The Quiet Australian: The Lindsay Hassett Story*, Heinemann, Melbourne, 1969.

FICTION

Bebbington, W. G. (ed.), *Fancy Free: A Selection of Short Stories*, Allen & Unwin, London, 1949 (includes 'How Jembu Played for Oxford' by Lord Dunsany).

Beresford, J. D., *The Hampdenshire Wonder*, Martin Secker, London, 1926.

di Lampedusa, Giuseppe, *The Leopard*, Fontana, London, 1963.

Conan Doyle, Sir Arthur, *The Maracot Deep and Other Stories*, Murray, London, 1929 (includes 'The Tale of Spedegue's Dropper').

Fitzgerald, F. Scott, *The Crack-Up*, Penguin, Harmondsworth, 1950.

Hamilton, Bruce, *Pro: An English Tragedy*, Cresset Press, London, 1946.

Household, Geoffrey, *Fellow Passenger*, Michael Joseph, London, 1955.

Lardner, Ring, *The Best Short Stories of Ring Lardner*, Chatto & Windus, London, 1974.

MacDonnell, A. G., *How Like an Angel*, Macmillan, London, 1934.

Malamud, Bernard, *The Natural*, Eyre & Spottiswoode, London, 1963.

MISCELLANEOUS

Alvarez, A., *The Savage God: A Study of Suicide*, Weidenfeld, London, 1971.

Cade, John, *Mending the Mind: A Short History of 20th Century Psychiatry*, Sun Books, Melbourne, 1979.

Carroll, John, *Ego & Soul: The Modern West in Search of Meaning*, HarperCollins, Sydney, 1998.

Davies, A. F., and Encel, S. (eds), *Australian Society*, F. W. Cheshire, Melbourne, 1965 (includes 'Matriduxy in the Australian Family' by D. Adler).

Davies, Brian, *An Introduction to Clinical Psychiatry*, Melbourne University Press, Melbourne, 1981.

Douglas, Keith, *Alamein to Zem-Zem*, Editions Poetry, London, 1946.

Eddowes, Nigel, *The Language of Cricket*, Carcanet, London, 1997.

Garton, Stephen, *The Cost of War*, Oxford University Press, Melbourne, 1996.

Gregory, L., *Fundamentals of Psychiatry*, W. B. Saunders, Philadelphia, 1968.

Iverson, Gerald, *The Iverson Story: The Family History of Ludwig Iversen and His Wife Mary Anne Elizabeth Carpenter de Pomeroy*, self-published, Wentworthville, 1995.

Marriott, Charles, *The Complete Leg-Break Bowler*, Stanley Paul, London, 1968.

Muirhead, J. H. (ed.), *Bernard Bosanquet and His Friends: Letters Illustrating the Sources and the Development of His Philosophical Opinions*, Allen & Unwin, London, 1935.

Mullins, Pat and Derriman, Phil, *Bat and Pad: Writings on Australian Cricket 1804–1984*, Oxford University Press, Melbourne, 1984.

Ross, Alan, *The Penguin Cricketers' Companion*, Penguin, London, 1981.

Webster, Rudi, *Winning Ways*, William Collins, Sydney, 1984.

Williams, Marcus (ed.), *The Way to Lord's: Cricketing Letters to* The Times, Fontana, London, 1984.

Williams, Mark, *Cry of Pain: Understanding Suicide and Self Harm*, Penguin, London, 1997.

Williams, Stewart, *The Test of Time: The History of the Kingston Heath Golf Club*, Macmillan, Sydney, 1981.

Winter, Graham, *The Psychology of Cricket*, Pan Macmillan, Sydney, 1992.

NEWSPAPERS & PERIODICALS

Age, Albury Daily News and Wodonga Chronicle, Argus, Australian Cricket, Brighton News, Courier-Mail, Cricket: A Weekly Record of the Game, Cricket Quarterly, Cricketer (Australia), *Cricketer* (UK), *Daily Mirror, Daily News, Daily Telegraph* (Australia), *Daily Telegraph* (UK), *Dominion, Herald, Hindu, Illustrated, Leader, Real Estate and Stock Institute Diary, Romsey Examiner, Sandringham News, Southern Cross, Sporting Globe, Sporting Life, Sports Novels, Sun, Sydney Morning Herald, Sydney Sun and Guardian, Tarrengower Times, West Australian, Wisden Cricket Monthly, Wisden Cricketers' Almanack.*

INDEX